# Conversations
# With The Goddess

by
## Mark Amaru Pinkham

D1453009

**Adventures Unlimited Press**
Kempton, ILLINOIS

# Conversations with the Goddess

# Conversations With The Goddess

Cover art by Cheryl Adams
Cover photo by James Kumle

Picture of Sanat Kumara Copyright 1985
Reprinted with permission, Church Universal and Triumphant,
P.O. Box 5000, Corwin Springs, Montana 59030
Tel: 406-848-9200 Email: tslinfo@tsl.org Website: http://www.tsl.org

ISBN 0-932813-81-X

Printed in the United States of America

Published by
Adventures Unlimited Press
One Adventure Place
Kempton, Illinois 60946 USA
auphq@frontiernet.net

# THIS BOOK IS DEDICATED TO

## THE

# GODDESS

## IN ALL HER MYRIAD FORMS

# Table of Contents

The Goddess talks to me; "Stop persecuting My Son;" The Flaming Goddess and Her Twin Sons; "Lucifer, My First Son;" The Light Bearer; Lucifer, the King of the World; Lucifer is in us all.

Lemuria; Lucifer, the Essence of all Mystery Schools; The Goddess Spiritual Tradition; The purpose of the Great White Brotherhood; The consciousness of a Kumara;The Seven Rays of the Goddess; The Kumaras in the Holy Bible; Aghartha and Shamballa.

Venus, the Celestial Goddess and Guru; The Atlantean Venus Culture; The Venus Culture in Egypt; The Worldwide Bull Cult; The Hebrew Venus Culture; The Venus Culture of India; The Peruvian Venus Culture; The Greek Venus Culture; The Venus Culture in Britain; The Mesopotamian Venus Culture;

Atlantis; The Birth of Patriarchy; The Spread of Patriarchy.

Hitler leads the Patriarchy; The United Forces of the Matriarchy: The Gnostics; The Ishmaili and Knights Templars; The Witches; The Illuminati; The New World Order; The Avatar.

# Acknowledgements

I want to give a special thanks to Cheryl Adams for all the time and energy she put into creating the cover for this book. Her husband, Irv Lefburg, was also very helpful.

James Kumle gets a big hug for taking the radical photo which eventually transformed into the cover.

My wife, Andrea-Abhaya, deserves honorable mention and a kiss for her support in writing this book.

And to my teachers, Ammachi and Muktananda, who helped to open me up spiritually so I could receive the information in this book. Jai Ma!

# *Introduction*

The new era of the Goddess has dawned! The female principle is now fully re-emerging into the world, as well as within our hearts and minds. For ages, the Goddess has been dominated by the traditions of the God and the disparaging advocates of patriarchal ideology. It is now time for the Goddess to re-ascend Her throne, and for Goddess spirituality to be given equal recognition with the fundamentalist religions of the Patriarchy.

The re-emergence of the Goddess officially began on August 16, 1987 and then moved into high gear on August 11, 1999. On that pivotal summer's day, a large group of us gathered on Glastonbury Tor, England, to witness a special solar eclipse officially marking the rebirth of the female principle. This eclipse occurred as part of a cosmic Grand Cross, wherein seven of the nine astrological "planets," the Sun, Moon, Mars, Saturn, Jupiter, Uranus, and Neptune were united in the heavens. Their rare cosmic link-up had the effect of uniting the four fixed signs of the Zodiac—Taurus, Scorpio, Leo and Aquarius—as well as the "animals" associated with these signs—the bull, the eagle, the lion, and the human. The union of these four "animals" created a celestial Sphinx, an ancient manifestation of the Goddess. The Goddess was, therefore, put back together and resurrected.

When the time of the eclipse arrived at 11:11 AM, GMT, those of us on Glastonbury Tor experienced time suddenly stop, and the Dream Time or Fourth Dimension engulf us like a thick fog. As we interfaced with the next dimension, some of us had visions of the Goddess or other etheric deities, while others of us felt our spirits soar and witnessed our lives pass in front of our eyes. Collectively, we all felt that the end had, indeed, arrived.

When the Moon finally separated from the Sun, we were thrown back into time. But something was different. Many of us on the Tor intuitively sensed that the Goddess era had officially begun, and in our joy we spontaneously began beating drums and chanting the ancient songs of the Matriarchy. A lively pagan festival ensued upon the Tor's summit as we lovingly welcomed the Goddess home.

## About this book

The book you are about to read is a compilation of conversations which spontaneously occurred between myself and the Goddess during 1998-99. The Goddess first entered my consciousness as a separate voice during a backpacking trip in the mountains of Washington State, and has periodically dialogued with me ever since.

Why the Goddess originally chose me as Her scribe, I can only guess. Perhaps it is because I have been an active devotee of Her's for sometime, or perhaps it is because I have an obsessive interest in esoteric history (my first book, *The Return of the Serpents of Wisdom*, is full of esoteric history). As you will find in this book, the Goddess has an abundance of both historical and prophetic information to share with you. This includes specific details concerning the conflict between the matriarchal and patriarchal traditions which has raged for thousands of years on Earth, as well as its pre-destined resolution preceding the coming Fifth World of Venus. The Fifth World is due to officially commence on December 21, 2012.

Please read on with an open heart and mind. The Goddess is waiting for you. She ensures me that you will not only learn about Her ancient tradition through this book, but also experience Her divine presence as you read it. Come meet your Mother—again.

**Note**: As the Goddess was elaborating about world history during our conversations, She often alluded to specific events and organizations connected with Her matriarchal tradition which are obscure or even dubious. I have, therefore, added an **Appendix** section at the end of the book in hopes of giving them added clarity and crediblilty.

My blessings to you,

Mark Amaru Pinkham

Sanat Kumara
The First Son of the Goddess

## THE TRIDENT, SYMBOL OF SANAT KUMARA

ne trident represents the three powers of the Goddess which are wielded by Sanat
Kumara: the powers to create, preserve and destroy. These three powers are
represented in Hinduism as the gods Brahma, Vishnu and Shiva; and within the
igion of Christianity they have become the Trinity of Father, Son and Holy Ghost.

# MEETING THE GODDESS

Gasping and exhausted, I trudged up the final length of trail to the mountain lake. I had not been prepared for such a steep trail and for most of this warm summer's day had been feeling thoroughly outmatched by it. Although strikingly beautiful, with patches of dense green forest alternating with stretches of wild flowers and thick green grass, the trail had many rigorous inclines and sections of dry, loose dirt which frequently caused me to loose my footing and stumble backwards. But I persevered, even though my rebellious body urged me otherwise. "You have fasted for two days, you should never have even considered taking this trail," it continuously screamed. Well...it was probably right. Fortunately, the ration of overripe bananas I had had the sense to bring with me was just enough sustenance to provide the necessary lift when I needed it most.

I had anticipated this day with great excitement, but also with a good measure of skepticism and fear. For today I was going to find Lucifer, that notorious entity who is sometimes referred to as Satan, the Adversary, as well as the Devil, the King of Evil. For some reason I had lately felt an overpowering urge to know this ancient enemy of the human race, to meet him face to face.

1

I wanted to see him for what he truly was, not for what Christian dogma told me he was. And like the intrepid Faustian characters throughout history, I was going to find him alone and on his terms. Of course, I hadn't tried very hard to find an accomplice. Anyone I had confided in about my plans had either playfully chuckled at the idea of meeting Lucifer or else stared blankly at me in wide-eyed disbelief. I attributed their unsupportive reactions to fear-based Judeo-Christian programming, and certainly not to first hand experience. So in the end I decided it was best to go it alone and let my experience speak for itself.

In preparation for my meeting with Lucifer I had done an extensive "back ground" check on him. I had researched many of the libraries within Washington State and gathered numerous versions of his famous legend. Ultimately, I discovered that, contrary to popular belief, Lucifer was *not* the evil Christian Devil, in fact he had pre-dated him by thousands of years. And while the Devil appears to be the obvious product of a myth, Lucifer may have been an actual player in history. The standard texts on the subject claim that he was the original fallen angel, the first angel to descend into physicality, thereby paving the way for other angels to follow. Initially he was a worker for God, an employee of the Almighty, who later acquired the evil nature we now commonly associate him with. The name Lucifer, I found, translates as "Bringer of the Light" or "Light Bearer," which is obviously not a malicious moniker. The epithet refers to the Morning Star, Venus, that glistening beacon which illumines the sky each morning and heralds the arrival of the beneficent Sun. There was obviously much that was good and beneficent about Lucifer. Hopefully, that was the nature of the Lucifer I would meet.

So ultimately, my research confirmed my belief that there was more to Lucifer than Christianity was letting on, or perhaps even knew. Therefore, with building confidence, I progressed to the next stage of my mission, that of receiving some supernatural guidance as to where and when to meet Lucifer. In pursuit of this goal I sat daily in meditation while awaiting some intuitive flash to shoot through my consciousness. When the guidance did finally arrive, it took the form of an overpowering urge to climb to a secluded lake in the heart of the Olympic Mountain range. This cosmic directive was accompanied by a surge of energy along my spine, as well as a profound euphoria. It was as though Spirit was saying "Yes, this is your answer, and peace be with you." While enveloped in such a timeless peace, how could I doubt the guidance?

I was suddenly jolted out of my reverie as I inadvertently slipped again on the trail, this time on a moist, exposed tree root. Regaining my balance, I looked ahead of me and noticed that I had almost reached my destination. Not more than two hundred feet away was a paradisiacal scene composed of a small azure lake nestled within a glen of lush, green grass and vibrant wild flowers. Bleached white glaciers, which covered precipitous slopes surrounding the lake, rapidly melted under the transforming influence of the warm, summer sun to form a network of crystal clear streams which fed the tranquil lake and its surrounding vegetation. The entire scene so reminded me of a paradisiacal place I had often escaped to in my mind when I was a child that it took me awhile to convince myself I wasn't dreaming. And, amazingly, just as it had been in my juvenile fantasy there was even a beautiful little island in the center of the lake which beckoned for me to visit. So, with both excitement and deep gratitude, I set off towards the narrow isthmus which connected the island to the lake's shore. It appeared as though Spirit had led me to the ideal place for a ritual.

I had already planned in detail how I was going to summon Lucifer. First, as instructed by my higher guidance, I was going to imbibe a sacrament (a substance consumed for spiritual communion and consciousness expansion) similar to the ergot (a fungus) once used by the Renaissance prophet Michel de Nostradamus to increase his clairvoyant abilities. Since I had taken a sacrament of hallucinogenic fungus in the past and been transported into a dimension populated by unfriendly demons, I decided to proceed very cautiously with my present rite by invoking the protective influence of my primary deity, the Great Goddess. Hopefully She would guide and protect me on my journey into the unknown. In order to summon Her benevolent presence, I decided to chant a special Sanskrit hymn of 108 "names" which honor Her attributes. I resolved to repeat the chant out loud seven times; seven is a sacred number of the Goddess.

As I ingested my sacrament, I gave thanks to the Goddess for Her guidance and protection. I felt confident about Her guidance and the efficacy of my sacramental rite because sacraments have, for ages, been an important adjunct of the Goddess's spiritual tradition. They are recognized by the devotees of the Goddess to be special gifts given by Her for the purpose of communing with Her. They also serve as guaranteed "windows of opportunity" for adventurers like myself seeking to enter alternate dimensions. If Lucifer was near, a sacrament would give me the surest opportunity of meeting him.

With one-pointed devotional fervor I commenced my rhythmic chant to the Goddess and then continued it for the following two hours. As the Goddess's attributes floated from one end of the magical lake to the other, I felt at peace; everything seemed to be going perfectly. But then, all of a sudden, a thick, ominous fog suddenly appeared and slowly proceeded to engulf both the lake and my tiny island paradise in darkness. For awhile all I could see and hear was my little chanting book and the reverberations of Sanscrit mantras echoing against the cool, opaque mist. It was initially very exciting and mystical, but the fascination quickly wore off when I began to shiver convulsively from the penetrating cold. At that point I made the pragmatic decision to leave the azure lake and begin my descent back down the mountain trail.

Not knowing whether the sacrament had taken any effect yet, I cautiously arose from my grassy seat, gathered up my belongings, and slowly put one foot in front of the other until I had re-discovered the trail. As I sliced through the thick, damp mist I began to hear distorted voices coming rapidly towards me. In my present state of mind I could not tell if they were near or far, or even if they were from this world or another. A sick feeling arose within my stomach and my heart began to race as I nervously conceded to myself that "Maybe Lucifer really is the Devil?!" Then, just as I thought I would vomit out of fear, first the head and then the body of a teenaged boy scout emerged out of the mist, followed by the rest of his troupe. As the small band of scouts smiled and hiked enthusiastically by me, I let go a weary sigh of relief, feeling sure that I had been spared a horrible encounter. But I also felt a deep sadness and frustration born out of feeling that I had played right into my old fear-based programming. If Lucifer had appeared, I probably would have died on the spot from a coronary and ended up a statistic in the next day's local newspaper. Obviously, if I was going to be successful in meeting Lucifer I needed to change my mindset and begin cultivating an attitude of faith and confidence in the Goddess. Otherwise, I was courting impending disaster.

I left the misty lake behind me and was soon back enjoying the trail and the soothing forms of nature surrounding it. My mood soared as my frigid body was rapidly warmed by my forward movement and the shafts of brilliant sunshine which occasionally broke through the tall trees and flooded the trail with a joyful effulgence. The thought of Lucifer and his myriad dark associations were soon replaced by numerous engrossing etheric colors and shapes which appeared to shimmer and dance all around me. The sacrament was definitely working now, and I was moving into a new world. Both my intuition and clairvoyance were becoming sensitized to an astral universe which co-existed with my physical environment, and I fully expected to encounter Lucifer at any moment. But the fear was gone. I was ready.

What did happen next, however, was 'off the chart' in terms of predictability. While I was searching for signs of Lucifer, a voice suddenly began talking loudly within my head. At first I decided it was my imagination playing tricks on me, but then the voice became forceful, asking questions and demanding answers. I decided to listen attentively and respond as though I was communicating with another entity. Then the voice aggressively asked something about Lucifer...

4

Unseen Voice: *"Are you inquiring about my beloved Son, Lucifer? Are you seeking to persecute my Son as he has been so many times in the past?"*

"I have no intention of persecuting Lucifer or anyone else," I responded in relative shock. "I am only interested in knowing more about him. And who are you anyway?"

Voice: *"I am the Mother of All. I am Lucifer's mother and I am yours. I am the one who answers your prayers. I always watch over you. You are My son."*

## "STOP PERSECUTING MY SON!"

With great delight and anticipation I realized that I was conversing with my beloved Goddess. She was actually talking to me! A thousand questions quickly flooded my consciousness, all demanding to be asked first. But just as I began to prioritize them in order of importance, my divine mentor began what was to become a very in-depth lesson on Her Son Lucifer.

The Goddess: *"My Son has been maligned throughout much of recorded history. He and I have been denigrated by the Patriarchy, even though originally we were devoutly worshipped by all."*

"Yes," I said sympathetically. "Most of what I know of Lucifer has come from the patriarchal religions and not much of it is favorable."

The Goddess: *"The Patriarchy has tried to understand My Son through the intellect. It has perceived Lucifer as unbridled, wild passion, and in the extreme, raucous anarchy. The prejudicial intellect judges such tendencies to be destructive, and therefore evil."*

"Was Lucifer originally associated with extreme behavior, or was this solely the work of the Patriarchy?"

The Goddess: *"Lucifer has always been associated with destruction. He was originally an esteemed deity of My matriarchal tradition and worshipped as one of My dual powers of creation and destruction. Only later did Lucifer become an evil demon of the Patriarchy because his destructive nature threatened to disturb their status quo. One pre-eminent goal of the Patriarchy has traditionally been to control the environment at all costs, and anything*

5

*which interferes with this control, such as the forces of destruction and transformation, is considered evil."*

"I'm sure You are right about that. We humans have a tendency to associate destruction with evil spirits and demonic gods."

The Goddess: *"Yes, you do. This is because destruction threatens your security. Destruction has become evil to you, and this is even reflected in your English language wherein evil is the reverse of live. 'Live' denotes creation and continued survival, while 'evil' denotes death and destruction."*

"I guess I have not thought of it that way..."

The Goddess: *"It was because of this link between destruction and evil that my entire tradition eventually became perceived as evil. The uncontrolled nature of My rites was thought by the Patriarchy to provoke reckless, aberrant behavior, as well as anarchy. The conservative social systems of the Patriarchy were threatened by such behavior, so those in the higher ranks of the movement did the logical thing which was to label and attack My Son and I as evil co-conspirators of the established order. For this reason, My Son eventually acquired the title of 'Devil' and 'Minister of Evil."*

"It's sad that the Patriarchy has so harshly judged Your tradition, especially since it has not a clue about what Your devotees are experiencing. They judge Your followers according to outer appearances, and because they fear for their own preservation."

The Goddess: *"Yes. That is human nature, to live in fear and seek security."*

"I assume that people did not hold so tenaciously to security before the advent of Patriarchy?"

The Goddess: *"Their security was in knowing that My power of destruction would eventually lead to a new cycle of creation and abundance. They knew that without My power of destruction there could not be any new life on Earth. You cannot have the Spring without the Autumn or the Summer without the Winter."*

6

"Or day without night."

**The Goddess:** *"Exactly. And since the flip side of destruction is transformation, there cold be no evolution of the soul either."*

"That still seems to be the attitude in the East where the gods of destruction, such as 'Shiva,' are also worshipped as the lords of transformation."

**The Goddess:** *"Right. Those in the East recognize that My power of destruction is a necessary part of the cycle of life. To them it is not evil. Can God, the ultimate controller of all powers of nature, be evil?"*

"Not from my understanding. God is the pure consciousness which transcends the duality of good and evil. It is the intellect of man which judges something to be beneficent or evil. Therefore, if one comes from a spiritual, non-dual approach, Lucifer can not be either good or bad. But aren't there some characteristics of Lucifer which are less than praiseworthy?"

**The Goddess:** *"Actually, yes. Lucifer's tendency to control and dominate, which are actually aspects of his destructive power. Through control and denial of freedom, the soul is destroyed and withers away. Ironically, this destructive tendency is precisely the one the status quo-minded Patriarchy has inadvertently cultivated. Through Luciferian control of the masses, the leaders of the Patriarchy have inhibited and destroyed the soul growth within many."*

The Goddess's words certainly rang true. From the little I knew of it, the Patriarchy has always been associated with control and dominance. Meanwhile, the Matriarchy has been distinguished by the softer qualities of love and allowance.

"Will there ever be a reconciliation between the Matriarchy and Patriarchy?"

**The Goddess:** *"Yes. When my two Sons reunite."*

"What two Sons? Do you mean Lucifer and a brother of his?"

## THE FLAMING GODDESS AND HER TWIN SONS

The Goddess: *"My two Sons are the polar opposite halves of Me. Lucifer is My power of destruction and his twin brother is My power of creation. These dueling brothers are manifest as the myriad pairs of opposites throughout the universe, such as light and dark, day and night, proton and electron, as well as the male and female genders, hot and cold, as well as the ultimate polarity, Spirit and matter. They are represented in the sky as the Morning and Evening Stars and traditionally worshipped within my spiritual tradition as two eternally young boys."*

"If Your two halves are the Morning and Evening Stars, You must be the planet Venus..."

The Goddess: *"I am the entire universe, but Venus is a special manifestation of Mine because it reflects My androgenous nature and dual powers. It also symbolizes My polar opposite Sons."*

The mythological and androgenous images of Venus as the bearded goddess Aphrodite and the Sumerian Inanna, goddess of love and war, emerged into my mind. Obviously the ancients recognized the Goddess's dual nature and emphasized it in their esteemed images of Her.

The Goddess: *"You will find My androgenous nature not only reflected in the classical images of Venus, but also in her myth. Remember that Goddess Venus was born from the union of Heaven and Earth?"*

"Are You referring to the Greek myth of Venus's birth from the sexual organ of Uranus?"

The Goddess: *"Yes. Venus was conceived from the sperm contained within Uranus's organ which fell to Earth. The sperm of the 'male' Uranus, or Heaven, fecundated the 'female' sea covering the Earth, and Venus arose as the androgenous union of the male and female principles."*

"Was the Middle Eastern myth which recounts Venus's origin as a flaming meteorite arriving from Heaven and falling into the Mediterranean Sea, an evolution of the sperm myth?"

The Goddess: "*Yes. The meteorite is a nuance of the sperm theme. Its fiery nature as it enters the Earth's atmosphere mimics Uranus's hot sperm. But the flaming meteorite motif had additional implications to My devotees in the Middle East. They worshipped it as Me because it reflects the power of Spirit. Like a molten mass which crystallizes out of the sky, I am the fiery power of God which condenses out of infinite Spirit. I am what you call the serpentine Kundalini, God's power of creation and destruction.*"

"Okay, I understand how a falling meteorite reflects Your fiery nature. But how about the planet Venus itself? It reflects Your androgenous nature, but does it also reveal Your fire?"

The Goddess: "*Well, as you know, being as close as it is to the Sun, the planet Venus is naturally fiery hot. But it is also 'fiery' in its movement. If you watch closely, you can occasionally find that the planet leaves a fiery tail in its wake which gives the appearance of a celestial fire serpent. For this reason and others, the ancients worshipped Venus as a fiery, celestial dragon.*"

"There is speculation that Venus began as comet.[1] Could this also be why the ancients associated it with a fire dragon?"

The Goddess: "*Venus was never a comet, although it has been known to give the appearance of one on occasion. But Venus was recognized as a fire dragon by the ancients not just because of its fiery tail, but also because it creates a pentagram during its eight year cycle.[2] The pentagram is intimately associated with the Golden Proportion and the geometrical spiral, which is the shape of the fire dragon or serpent.*"

"I have heard of the pentagram being associated with the Goddess, but also with Lucifer or the Devil. Whose symbol is it really?"

The Goddess: "*We share the symbol of the pentagram because we are both intimately associated with the fire serpent or Kundalini and what it condenses into, the four elements of nature. Remember that I am called 'Mother Nature?' And as for Lucifer...do you remember his manifestation as the Horned God? The Horned God is also an embodiment of nature.[3] In this form you might call Lucifer 'Father Nature.'*
"*But if you want to be immaculately precise about it, since I have two*"

9

*Sons, the normal, up-right version of the pentagram is the symbol of my creative Son, while the reversed or upside down pentagram is the symbol of My destructive Son, Lucifer."*

"Okay, please help me to understand something. If Lucifer is the Horned God and nature, why is he simply associated with Your power of destruction. Isn't the power of creation also inherent in nature?"

*Inanna, Goddess of Love and War, with the weapons of war strapped to her back and horns attached to her head. The circle next to her is her planet, Venus. The eight rays which emanate from it refer to the planet's cycle of eight years. From a Sumerian Cylinder Seal, circa 2300 BC.*

The Goddess: "*Yes. Originally the Horned God was worshipped by My devotees as the embodiment of both powers of nature and the synthesis of My Twin Sons. But for the sake of clarity, some of My devotees affiliated the creative forces of nature with the Horned God and nature's destructive forces with the underworld serpent.*"

### Lucifer, "My First Son"

"So let me get this straight. Lucifer was both the Twins united, as well as one of them?"

The Goddess: "*Yes. He was 'Father' of the Twins, as well as the destructive Twin. He was the serpentine life force which manifests in nature as the dual powers of creation and destruction. But he was also the Lord of Destruction.*

"*So, you ask, how can Lucifer be both father to the Twins and one of them simultaneously? It is because of the dualistic nature of the life force, which is also known as Kundalini and Cosmic Fire. The life force or Cosmic Fire is both creative and destructive, but leans more on the side of destruction. This is because Cosmic Fire is the first and purist form of matter, and the seeds of time and destruction dwell within matter as its inherent tendency to decay and die.*

"*Lucifer's numerous manifestations, such as the Horned God, reflect his androgenous nature as the Twins united. This is especially true of his first manifestation at the beginning of time when he emerged from Me as a spark of Cosmic Fire. He then took the form of My androgenous First Son and the greatest of the Angels.*"

"Lucifer was Your First Son and the greatest Angel?"

The Goddess: "*Yes. He and the other Angels began as parts of Me—fiery particles of Cosmic Fire which arose out of the cosmic darkness at the beginning of time. But Lucifer, the First Angel, was special because he embodied the qualities and powers of all the rest. He was a perfect reflection of Me. And he was androgenous.*"

"Apparently You and he had a lot in common..."

The Goddess: "*Yes. Know that Lucifer and I were essentially synonymous. We were both the serpentine Cosmic Fire or the Kundalini life force, and the male*

11

*and female principles united.*

"*As the life force, we were also both Spirit embedded in matter. The serpentine life force is created through the union of the Twins in their manifestation as Spirit and matter. The inner essence of 'androgenous' Cosmic Fire is, Spirit, My creative Twin, and its substance or matrix is My destructive Twin. This should help you to further understand the androgenous nature of Lucifer and Myself.*"

"I have heard Lucifer referred to as the first spirit to enter a material form. Does this relate to his being androgenous Cosmic Fire?"

The Goddess: "*Yes, this is a reference to his incipient form of Cosmic Fire. But it also alludes to him being the first incarnated angelic spirit on Earth. Lucifer, as Cosmic Fire, arrived on Earth when the planet was still steaming. He was the first angel to take a body at that time.*"

"Lucifer existed within a physical body millions of years ago when the Earth was still extremely hot?"

The Goddess: "*His body was not physical at first, but etheric, so it was not scorched by the Earth's heat. Later his body became more dense.*"

"Does the portrayal we have of Lucifer living in a world of fire reflect his arrival on Earth when the planet was still fiery hot?"

The Goddess: "*Yes. Lucifer walked among the developing life forms as their lord when the Earth was still a burning cauldron. But Lucifer is principally associated with fire and the fiery netherworlds because he was Cosmic Fire, the Kundalini.*"

"I think the fire most of us associate with Lucifer is the fire of unbridled desire and heated passions. Isn't that what eventually lead to his 'fall?"

The Goddess: "*It's true that in time Lucifer was compelled to control others in order to satisfy his own limited desires, and that ultimately led to a downfall. But initially he was a pure, angelic entity.*"

"I suppose Lucifer must have become progressively more egocentric and self-serving the denser he became..."

The Goddess: "*Yes. Initially he was one of the greatest teachers of light the Earth has ever known, and wielded wonderful supernatural powers and unfathomable divine wisdom. But eventually, as the forms on Earth acquired greater degrees of crystallization, he became synonymous with density, passion and the self-serving ego.*"

"Is the later, dense version of Lucifer the Lucifer we today commonly associate with evil dragons and serpents?"

The Goddess: "*To some degree. But Lucifer and I have always been associated with dragons and serpents. We were both the serpentine Cosmic Fire or Kundalini, which travels as a great dragon or serpent.*"

"I do recall the ancient cosmologists maintaining that the first form of Spirit was Cosmic Fire which took the form of a great dragon. They called it the Kundalini, as well as the Serpent Goddess and the First Son."[5]

The Goddess: "*Right. And ever since, My Son has always been associated with the serpentine life force. You may recall from your research that the serpent is a definitive symbol of My First Son in almost every tradition he has manifested within. The serpent is, for example, one of the forms of My First Son as Dionysus (Greece), Tammuz (Mesopotamia), and Murrugan (India).[6] These divergent versions of My First Son were worshipped as embodiments of the serpentine life force or Kundalini, and each of their legends allegorized the cycle of nature. Like the life force, they were said to be born annually, mature quickly, mate with Me and then die with the falling leaves of Autumn.*"

"Were these First Sons versions of Lucifer?"

The Goddess: "*Yes, of course. All versions of My First Son describe the same entity. Each represents the first spirit to 'fall' into my womb, the womb of matter.*"

"And this is why they were all accorded virgin births?"

The Goddess: "*Yes. They originated from 'virgin births' because their 'father' was pure Spirit and their 'mother' was matter. They were Spirit enveloped in the cloak of matter."*

"I wonder if anyone has made a connection between these First Sons and Lucifer?"

The Goddess: *"My children, the Yezidhi,[7] have. They have revealed a conclusive link between Lucifer and the Hindu First Son, Murrugan."*

"The Yezidhi? Do You mean the infamous Devil worshippers of Asia who worship Lucifer in the form Melek Tau?"

The Goddess: *"Right. Remember that Melek Tau or Lucifer is depicted as a forever young boy with peacock feathers growing out of his hind end? This is an almost exact replica of the image of Murrugan worshipped in India.[8] Melek Tau and Murrugan are the same entity, and both are worshipped as the Peacock Angel, the first and greatest of the Angels."*

"Obviously there is a definitive link between Lucifer and Murrugan..."

The Goddess: *"If you need further evidence of their connection, study the respective legends of Murrugan and Lucifer and you will find that their origins are similar. Murrugan was born after Shiva, the Spirit, deposited his burning seed within a lake. Similarly, Lucifer came to Earth as fire from Heaven. His origin is allegorized in the legend of the Roman Vulcan who was cast out of Heaven and thrown down to Earth to work within the bowels of the Earth as the smith or fire god."*

"Murrugan's and Lucifer's origins are strangely reminiscent of Your own."

The Goddess: *"Yes. My First Son and I were born from Cosmic Fire which fell from Heaven."*

"If Lucifer is Vulcan, the underworld smith god, perhaps that is why when Lucifer became the Devil he was given a fiery underworld to rule."

The Goddess: *"Yes. And why the Devil was given a reddish, dragon-like appearance with horns attached to his head and hoofs for feet. These are all symbols of the Cosmic Fire he embodied."*

"If the Devil is an evolution of Lucifer and Cosmic Fire, shouldn't he have androgenous features?"

The Goddess: *"He does. For example, the bull features he inherited from the Horned God are symbolic of androgyny."*

"Are You implying that the bull is androgenous?"

The Goddess: *"Yes, in that it represents the life force or Cosmic Fire, and therefore the union of the polarity. The massive body of the bull was recognized by many of the ancient priests to be the symbol of an intense concentration of life or life force. Remember that the Egyptian priests worshipped the sacred bull Apis as a manifestation of the life force? He had androgenous black and white coloring, and legends claimed he had been born from the union of the Sun and the Moon, the celestial polarity."*

"Yes, I remember that he was androgenous. Come to think of it, the glyph for the sign Taurus, the Zodiacal bull, unites the Astrological symbols for the Sun and Moon, thus making it androgenous."

*Taurus's glyph*

The Goddess: *"Right. And Tau, the root of Taurus, is the name for a version of the cross, the archetypal symbol of androgyny. Taurus's androgyny makes possible the next sign of the Zodiac, Gemini. In Gemini the androgenous Bull divides to become the Twins—i.e., the androgenous Horned God or Lucifer becomes the Twins."*

"You also had bull associations, didn't You? I remember seeing statues of Isis wearing horns..."

The Goddess: *"Yes. Since both My Son and I are the life force and the union of the Twins, we are both represented by the bull or the bull's horns."*

"It follows that if both You and Your First Son are the first form taken by Spirit, Cosmic Fire, then the bull must somehow symbolize that primeval

15

form of Yours..."

The Goddess: "*It does. The bull's meaty body represents the huge primeval matrix of life force which bursts apart and then condenses into all the concrete forms of the physical universe.*"

"Why does the bull rather than the serpent represent the life force in the Zodiac? The serpent is a more common symbol of the life force worldwide."

The Goddess: "*In ancient times they alternated as the symbol of the life force. And for this reason, today you will find them existing together in the Zodiacal sign of Taurus. In the body of Taurus the bull is the celestial serpent, the Pleiades, the Serpent Goddess of your galaxy.*"[9]

"Their intimate Zodiacal union seems to imply an intimate relationship between the bull and serpent."

The Goddess: "*Yes. The ancients knew that the bull and serpent are both the life force, and give rise to each other.*"

"Perhaps this is why the ancient Cretans used to chant: 'The Bull is the father of the Serpent and the Serpent is the father of the Bull.'[10] I have always loved that paradoxical riddle and have often contemplated its meaning."

The Goddess: "*Yes. The bull and serpent are both symbols of the life force, and are therefore father and son to each other. The creative power of the life force, the bull, eventually gives rise to the destructive power of the life force, the serpent, and vice versa. It is because of their common association with the life force that both bull and serpent have been adopted by My devotees as powerful fertility symbols.*"

"Could this be why they became evil among the Patriarchy, because the Bull and serpent are associated with sex?"

The Goddess: "*This is one reason. But they also became 'evil' because they represent the life force and what it crystallizes into, dense matter. According to patriarchal philosophy, matter is devoid of Spirit and therefore evil.*"

"But matriarchal thinking has always maintained that Spirit resides within matter..."

The Goddess: "*Yes. Spirit is My essence. I cannot exist without it.*"

"It does appear as though the Patriarchy has a tendency to depict the mythical serpent or dragon as Spirit-less..."

The Goddess: "*Right. In patriarchal cultures the lowly serpent is often portrayed in battle with a male solar hero representing Spirit.[11] The Patriarchy divides Me into My Twins and then pits them against each other. In truth, matter cannot exist without its essence, Spirit, but the discriminating mind of the Patriarchy always tries to categorize by separating.*"

## Lucifer, The Light Bearer

"Well I must admit that I am beginning to see Lucifer in a new light. I have suspected that he was not the evil demon many Christian Fundamentalists have portrayed him as being. If he was, how could he be called Lucifer, a name which means 'Light Bearer?' His name seems to suggest a beneficent bearer of light or wisdom."

The Goddess: "*The name Lucifer, the Light Bearer, does indeed refer to My First Son's spiritual light and wisdom. It refers to Lucifer's light as the First and brightest light of all the Angels. But it also refers to Lucifer's destructive, transformative power which bestows 'light' by destroying ignorance. And thirdly, the name alludes to the light of wisdom Lucifer brought to Earth as a light bearing emissary of Mine and the founder of My matriarchal spiritual tradition on the planet.*"

"So Lucifer really did bring light to our planet..."

The Goddess: "*Yes. His arrival is remembered in the ubiquitous legend of the Twins, which maintains that My Twin Sons first brought to Earth the rudiments of civilization. This includes My spiritual tradition.*"

I was on familiar ground here, having become well acquainted with the Twins' legend while writing my first book. As amazing as it seems, almost every major culture has its unique version of the mythological Twin boys who came

17

to Earth as culture bearers.[12]

"There have certainly been numerous references to Your Twins around the world. Are there any descriptions of Your Twins which are more authoritative than the others?"

The Goddess: *"Well, the name of the Twins which best reveals them is Kumara, the Hindu name of the Twins. Kumara unites the seed syllables for the universal male and female principles, ma and ra, with Ku, a syllable which denotes their union. My Sons are the union of Spirit and matter, God and Goddess."*

I was aware of the Twins in their manifestation as the Kumara Twins from having lived in India and studied yoga there. The Kumaras were portrayed in that country as either two, four or seven eternally young boys who had arrived on Earth ages ago and brought the wisdom of yoga.

"Yes. I have heard a lot about the Kumaras..."

The Goddess: *"Remember what you heard from your teacher Sister Thedra[12] about them? She rightfully called them Sanat and Sananda Kumara. These name were given her through direct communication with the Twins. She also learned first hand that Sanat is a name for Lucifer and Jesus Christ is Sananda."*

"I know that Sister Thedra talked to Sananda Kumara in person. She told me that she was on her death bed when Jesus Christ spontaneously materialized in front of her and healed her of terminal cancer. At that time he told her his true name was Sananda Kumara."

The Goddess: *"Yes. And she also eventually met Sananda's brother, Sanat, and then became the prophetess for both Twins. Sananda and Sanat informed her that they were the two halves of Me."*

"Yes, I remember the conversation she had with Sananda during which she was told that they were two halves of a whole. She published it in one of the monthly lessons she offered through her organization, *The Association of Sananda and Sanat Kumara*."

*The above reproduction is from a photograph taken on June 1, 1961, when Sananda (Jesus) appeared physically at Chichen Itza in Mexico and allowed this photo to be taken. At that time he gave permission for Sister Thedra to use it in association with the work she was to do in spreading his words. Copies of the photograph and transcripts of his words are available by writing to:*

**The Association of Sananda and Sanat Kumara**
**P.O. Box 197, Mt. Shasta, CA 96067**

The Goddess: "*The Twins, Sanat and Sananda Kumara, also told Thedra that they originally came to Earth as culture bearers from my planet, Venus, many thousands of years ago. They came to share My wisdom with evolving humankind.*"

"Why haven't I heard more about Sanat and Sananda? Why are they not in the history books?"

The Goddess: "*You know why. Mainstream history is not ready for them. They would turn history upside down. Anyway, there is not enough hard evidence to support their existence yet.*

"*As you know, there are some books which maintain that the Kumaras existed on the Pacific land mass of Mu or Lemuria. When Lemuria sank to the bottom of the Pacific Ocean students of the Kumaras took its records and teachings to different parts of the world, such as Asia and South America. Your Sister Thedra gained access to some of those records in South America when Sananda sent her to the Monastery of the Seven Rays.*"[14]

"Was Aramu Muru, the founder of the Monastery, a student of the Kumaras?"

The Goddess: "*Yes. As you know, one of the magnificent artifacts he brought with him to Peru was the great Solar Disc. This disc had anciently been imported from Venus by the Kumaras and hung in an important temple on Lemuria for thousands of years. Aramu Muru built a vault around it in the Monastery for its safekeeping.*"

"And it eventually hung in the Coricancha, the main temple of the Incas in Cuzco, right?"

The Goddess: "*Yes. You have seen the place it once hung. Now, the records and artifacts of Mu can also be found in the underground crypts of Tibet and India and within the mystical traditions of those countries. James Churchward found some of those records in India.*[15] *Madame Blavatsky also accessed some of these records and passed them on to the current members of the Great White Brotherhood.*"[17]

"By current members of the GWB are you referring to Elizabeth Clare

Prophet and her organization, the Church Universal and Triumphant?"[17]

The Goddess: *"This is one branch of the GWB. The members of this branch are distinguished by calling themselves 'Keepers of the Flame.' This title affiliates them with Sanat Kumara, who was the first 'Keeper of the Flame."*

"Is Sanat Kumara associated with a flame because he was Lucifer and therefore wielded the fire or power of God?"

The Goddess: *"Yes. Sanat was Cosmic Fire incarnate and wielded both the wisdom and power of God. As the will of "*

"So, what You are essentially telling me is that when Lucifer took physical incarnation he was Sanat Kumara from Venus?"

The Goddess: *"Right. Sanat Kumara was Lucifer, the first angel on Earth to wield the wisdom and three powers of God. Sanat's powers are represented by Lucifer's trident."*

"And Sanat came as Your envoy?"

The Goddess: *"Yes. He carried the trident, the symbol of My authority and My three powers. The three prongs of the trident create the shape of the female vagina and womb, so it is a symbol of the Goddess."*

## Lucifer, The King of the World

"If Lucifer ruled the world with the trident as his staff, this must be why in the Judeo/Christian tradition Lucifer-Satan has at times been designated the 'King of the World."

The Goddess: *"Not only did he rule the world in ages past, but he continues to rule even now. Lucifer or Sanat is the will and power of the Earth. He is the Earth's monarch, the consciousness which guides all activity on the planet, as well as its Kundalini. He is the subtle power which oversees the transformation and evolution of Earth."*

"Lucifer really the King of the World now?! Perhaps as a result of my

21

outdated Judeo-Christian programming, I have to admit that I shudder a bit at the thought."

The Goddess: *"Lucifer or Sanat Kumara is not an evil ruler as he is often portrayed. You have known him before."*

The Goddess's words jogged my memory and I was able to recall an experience I had had some years previously. The image of a secluded fern grove deep within a forest in Washington surfaced in my mind, along with the memory of how I had spontaneously 'awakened' there to a part of me which had been asleep or dormant for thousands of years. The personality of a Lemurian priest king suddenly emerged within me, along with the vivid memories of my lifetime on Mu. Soon I was dancing around the forest like a man possessed while loudly proclaiming 'I'm back, I'm back.' I knew with an uncommon certainty that I was a Lemurian king who had returned to Earth. As the memories of my former existence gradually filtered into my awareness, so did my place in the Lemurian theocracy. Apparently, even though I had been a powerful king on Lemuria, I had still been a vassal to a much greater monarch. This grand ruler had been Sanat Kumara, the King of the World.

"Yes, I remember. Sanat Kumara was an impeccably righteous ruler..."

The Goddess: *"Kings ruled under Sanat, as you did. And they continue to even today. Sanat established a lineage of kings throughout the world and the symbols of his authority, the trident and the ank, were passed down within these lineages for countless generations. Those monarchs who served under Sanat were all Dragons; they were manifestations of My Kundalini power and representatives of My First Son."*

"I have heard that Neptune's trident symbol was supposedly inherited by each succeeding Atlantean king as a symbol of his authority. And the ank...well apparently it was a common prop carried by the ruling pharaohs of Egypt."

The Goddess: *"Yes. Sanat played an important role in establishing lineages in both Atlantis and Egypt."*

"I don't imagine too many rulers of the Earth today are aware of the king they are serving."

The Goddess: *"Only those who are very spiritually evolved. And among those, most do not know Sanat by name, they just know they serve a higher will.*

*"Most commonly Sanat, who is the will of Spirit and the primary will on the planet, works secretly to inform the individual wills of all monarchs and presidents. These are the primary 'movers and shakers' of the world's countries."*

"But most rulers seem to govern in accordance with the desires of their egos. They do not appear to rule in alignment with a higher will."

The Goddess: *"That is true. They govern from their lower will or ego. But remember that the lower will is also Sanat Kumara's will. Sanat rules the will on Earth in a general sense, which includes the lower will of the ego.*

*"The creation of the lower will is the result of what many of you call Lucifer's 'fall.' When Lucifer, the will, first took his seat in evolving humans he was pure. Humans at that time were like Adam and Eve in the early stages of the Garden of Eden; they implicitly obeyed a Higher Will. But eventually the human will became individualized and self-serving and the ego or 'lower will' was born. Human's then became like Adam and Eve in the later part of the Eden myth, when they disobeyed God's will and ate of the forbidden fruit.*

*"Since Lucifer or Sanat's fall, the lower aspect of Sanat's will, the ego, is now what most people know of as 'Lucifer.' But technically, the lower will is Sanat-Lucifer, while the Higher Will is Sanat-Sananda. They are both aspects of Sanat Kumara. Sanat or Lucifer is both a Twin and father of the Twins.*

*"Throughout time the ego or lower will has continuously rebelled against the directives of the higher will. Lucifer has consistently rebelled against Sananda. This is why Lucifer has come to be known as My 'Rebellious Son."*

## Lucifer is in Us All

By this time the day had quieted and the afternoon shadows were bathing much of the trail in twilight. I had almost hiked back to the lower lake and knew I had to make a crucial decision. Should I stay at the lake for the night or return home? If I remained at the lake I risked forgetting some of the information the Goddess had blessed me with, but if I left I took the chance of

23

doing permanent damage to my already weary body. After some thoughtful deliberation, I finally resolved to leave the lake and pray to the Goddess to support me in my return trip home.

Upon returning to my campsite, I quickly set about packing my belongings and taking down my tent. If I worked diligently, I decided, I could be down the trail in no time. And the brisk walk could potentially move the sacrament out of my blood system so I that I would be able to drive home. It didn't take long, however, before it became clear that my agenda was unrealistic and my expectations unattainable. Every so often, while rolling up my sleeping bag and tent, I found my attention drifting. I would often slip into a deep trance and additional information from the Goddess would flood into my consciousness.

As I was coming out of one of these periodic trances, an irrepressible urge caught hold of me, and before I knew what was happening I found myself walking with great determination towards the lake. With each step a sort of reckless abandon became more pronounced within me, and I soon felt compelled to rapidly undress myself. I proceeded to toss each piece of encumbering clothing aside until I was standing completely naked in front of the lake.

I was now fully revealed for the entire world to see. And even though there were other people at the lake who were probably watching me, I felt wonderfully liberated and excited. With a new-found sense of freedom, I began to survey my surroundings as though I were its king. If I caught anyone watching me, I merely waved to them. This liberated attitude was certainly a radical departure from my normal modest demeanor. I usually go out of my way to remain anonymous around people.

As my desire for outlandish behavior became stronger, I soon became convinced that I was not myself. Something or some being was taking control of me. This notion was corroborated by a ferocious roar which slowly gathered within my stomach before powerfully exiting through my mouth. The sound of the roar was so forceful and loud that the mountains surrounding the lake echoed with it for a full five seconds. Apparently this other consciousness was now in such perfect control of my body that it could even growl through me. Then, to add to my confusion, my body began to rapidly change. With both fascination and anxiety I watched as multicolored threads of red, orange, green and blue formed on my fingers, along my arms, and eventually covered my entire body. I was glowing with a shimmering iridescence. Meanwhile, something unusual was happening to the shape of my hands and the texture of my skin. My fingers were rapidly transforming into sharp, pointed claws and my multi-colored skin was becoming rough and scaly. In amazement I realized that I was turning into a human reptile! But as repulsive as the notion was, I found myself reveling in it. Why? Because I knew this reptile intimately, in fact it was a long lost part of me. It was Lucifer. I was becoming Lucifer!

With budding excitement, I decided to fully own and enjoy my new Lucifer persona and body, at least for awhile. I exulted in the cosmic energy which surged through me as an adjunct to my new persona, and rejoiced in its implicit power. I felt that, if I so desired, I could use it to create and destroy universes. I could have anything I wanted, when I wanted it, without restriction. I boasted out loud that my rightful role was King of the World, and the world should be at my feet. No person, law or governing body would dare suggest otherwise. I sneered and laughed spitefully at the thought of anyone at the mountain lake even attempting to tell me what to do. I dared them to stop me from running naked through their camp sites and indulging in lewd sexual acts with everyone watching me. The world was my private playground and I was going to do exactly as I wished. "Yes," I concluded, "Lucifer is indeed the Rebellious Son."

But there was also another side to Lucifer I was also experiencing. As him, I possessed an endless fount of spiritual knowledge. I knew the esoteric wisdom of the ages because I was its author. My homes were underground crypts and dark, moonlit glens wherein the secret esoteric teachings were transmitted during clandestine initiations. And I was ever present unseen power dwelling within those places.

But even with all my new wisdom and power, something was missing. As Lucifer I still felt limited. But something within told me I could permanently transcend this limitation and achieve complete power was to become one with my mother, the Goddess. So with all the strength I could muster, I loudly cried out towards the sky: "Give me Your power Mother, make me one with You." Again and again I called, until I had worked myself into an impassioned frenzy and my cries were horse screams heard by everyone at the lake. Nothing but complete union with my mother could satisfy me.

As I called out to the Goddess, I realized that Lucifer did indeed have a heart and soul, even if it was well buried. His cries betrayed an intense love for his mother and revealed an underlying desire to completely loose himself in Her love. I felt that if Lucifer succeeded in uniting with his mother, this complicated entity would be the Goddess's best representative on Earth. From that point onwards he would consciously strive to spread Her wisdom and power throughout the planet.

When the majority of Lucifer's pleas issuing from my sore throat had softened to those of a penitent and deserving Son, the Goddess finally acquiesced to the desire of Her progeny. Soon I could feel and see Her energy move into my claw-like fingers and course through my multi-colored body. Her power continued to accumulate within me until I was shaking violently, but I still continued to call out. I knew that only through the Goddess's transformative power could I become one with Her, and this was my opportunity to completely satisfy my longing. Finally, when it felt like I was on the verge of death and ready to blow apart like an over inflated balloon, I let out one last pain-filled scream and then sank to my knees and onto my back. I lost consciousness at that point, and for some time lay sprawled naked on the beach. For how long, I don't know.

When I finally opened my eyes, I was my old self again. Lucifer was gone. With great effort, I slowly struggled to a sitting position and then began a detailed review of my amazing communion with Lucifer. Soon a satisfied "aha" loudly emerged within me as I realized that I finally understood Lucifer because I had been him. Or he had been me. I wasn't sure. At any rate, I knew that Lucifer was a part of me. The entity I sought had always been right inside me. He had been that part of me I refer to as my inner, rebellious child which continually seeks uninhibited freedom. He had also been my inner dictator who clamors for total control and power from my environment in order to satisfy my egocentric needs. But he was also the part of me which is the teacher and servant of the Goddess, as well as the lover of the Goddess. I certainly found Lucifer's love for Her to be unparalleled. And why not? Even with all his faults, She loved him unconditionally. But was Lucifer truly ready to loose himself in union with the Goddess? That was the question I was left with to ponder.

In conclusion, I decided that the characteristics of Lucifer could be found in both the Matriarchy and Patriarchy. His wild, frenzied, and exuberant behavior was definitely matriarchal and reminiscent of the raucous tendencies of the Goddess's devotees. By contrast, the desire to gain power and control others in order to satisfy his own selfish desires was certainly patriarchal. But even though Lucifer's "destructive" nature was inherent in both traditions, there was a significant difference in how it manifested. I felt that through his intense, exuberant behavior I could break through limitations and become greater than myself. I had no such feeling as I contemplated the power to control others. That desire was an end in itself, and certainly did not promise union with the Goddess or with a power greater than itself. So, just as the Goddess had previously maintained, control was not a rung in the ladder of evolutionary success. Perhaps it truly was the worst kind of destruction.

With newfound wisdom about myself and Lucifer, I slowly gathered up my clothes and headed back to my campsite.

# CHAPTER II
# LEMURIA, BIRTHPLACE OF THE MATRIARCHY

    While walking back to my campsite it wasn't long before another supernatural influence began to erupt within my body. My clairvoyant abilities suddenly increased exponentially, and the "flood gates" of communication between myself and the Goddess were thrown wide open. I subtly sensed that I had arrived on the threshold of an ancient etheric mystery school wherein all the wisdom of the universe was stored. So, with renewed enthusiasm, I flung my pile of clothes back onto the ground and returned to the lake shore for more lessons from the Goddess.

    Once I was back combing the lake shore, the Goddess began showering me with a radically new overview of the human drama. Her discourse commenced with this drama's underlying theme, which according to Her has been the ongoing battle between her Twin Sons, Sanat and Sananda or Lucifer and Christ. Throughout history, this perpetual conflict has outpictured as the acrimonious battle between Patriarchy and Matriarchy, control and allowance. The masculine qualities of control and dominance have consistently characterized the Patriarchy, thus making Sanat-Lucifer, the lower will, its patron deity. In the meantime, the feminine qualities of love and acceptance have been the guiding motives of the Matriarchy, thus bringing it under the patronage of Sanat-Sananda, the Higher Will. While matriarchal civilizations worldwide have consistently strived to accept each other and love the Mother Earth, the patriarchal civilizations have exalted the intellect and implemented ongoing technological programs designed to divide, control and conquer the world.

The Goddess revealed to me how the Twins' battle has been repeatedly allegorized within certain mythological traditions worldwide. The conflict between Lucifer and Sananda can, for example, be found in the famous Gnostic version of the Garden of Eden legend wherein Lucifer is Ialdaboath, the cruel god of the world, and Christ is his nemesis, the infamous Serpent on the Tree. At the outset of this Eden scenario, Ialdaboath was commissioned by his mother, the Goddess Sophia, to oversee Her creation (the universe), but rebelliously overthrew Her authority soon afterwards and crowned himself as king over it. He then proceeded to implement a harsh program of oppressive laws which were designed to control humans and keep them in darkness in regards to their divine origins. Sensing the pain of humanity's oppression under Ildaboath, the Goddess sent to Earth Her other Son, the Serpent of the Tree, which the Gnostics recognized as Sananda or Christ. The Serpent instructed Adam and Eve on a path leading to inner spiritual freedom, or Gnosticism, which they in turn passed on to their descendants.

I was particularly enthralled by the Gnostic's version of the battle between the Twins. The Goddess's retelling of the Garden of Eden legend according to the Gnostic perspective had shed much needed light on what I had always considered was a distorted myth. I had never subscribed to the notion that God or Spirit was the harsh deity depicted in the Bible. My own deliberations had told me that only a demi-god could have the severe qualities ascribed to Jehovah because Spirit is a neutral observer of all human actions. A god with qualities may represent Spirit, but it is nevertheless a rung or two below the Infinite. It made sense to me that Jehovah or Ildaboath was one of the Goddess's Twin Sons, but not pure Spirit. As I contemplated this new possibility, I strutted back and forth with excitement along the lake shore. Then the Goddess abruptly cut into my thoughts again:

**The Goddess:**"*Yes, the Gnostics were right from their perspective. But there are many levels of interpretation inherent within the archetypal Eden myth, and each is valid in its own right. The Gnostic perspective is given to you now because it reveals the origins of the conflict My Twins became embroiled in.*"

"But doesn't certain versions of the Twins' legend worldwide maintain that they were not always in conflict? If I remember correctly, according to some myths they started out as friends..."

The Goddess: *"This is true. As polar opposites, My Twins are complimentary principles, and they have on occasion worked harmoniously together. It was not until the 'fall' and development of the ego that Lucifer acquired the characteristics of oppressive control and waged an ongoing battle against the Christ."*

"So, when in history did the Twins live in co-operation with each other?"

The Goddess: *"It was a very distant period. I will show it to you..."*

My clairvoyant abilities heightened even more than they had been, and I instantly plugged into what I guessed was the Akashic Records. A vivid "movie" began to play behind my closed eyes, commencing with a beautiful deep-blue ocean, in the middle of which was an island covered with rolling hills and newly blossomed flowers of strikingly vivid colors. Over one of these hills I saw a huge, oval light hovering. This light proceeded to land on a soft grassy knoll and immediately a series of smaller, egg-shaped lights emerged from it. These lights quickly congealed into the tangible forms of young boys and I knew intuitively that I was witnessing the arrival of the Kumaras.

"Is this Lemuria I am seeing?"

The Goddess: *"Yes. You should recognize it, having been there yourself. What you are witnessing is the initial arrival of the Kumaras at the beginning of the current cycle which is now coming to completion."*

"I assume You are referring to the 104,000 year cycle which ends 2012?"[1]

The Goddess: *"Yes. Even though the Kumaras had come to Earth many times before, they had always returned to Venus. During the visit you are witnessing they established a permanent headquarters on what you know as the 'White Island.'"*

29

My thoughts quickly turned to what I had heard and read about the legendary "White Island." Theosophists contend it existed millions of years ago in the center of a great inland sea which covered most of what is now the Gobi Desert. According to their records, after landing on the island—perhaps by lightship—the Kumaras proceeded to erect a radiant, jewel encrusted palace and then encircled it with a ring of protecting serpents. It was here that Sanat Kumara, the King of the World began his reign. The area where the island once existed has since become known by occultists as Shamballa.

"The lightship of the Kumaras is intriguing. Are there any references in existing legends about them arriving in lightships?"

The Goddess: "*You know of one. In the Book of Ezekiel of the Bible there is a vivid description of a lightship which served as the vehicle for the 'Ancient of Days.' Remember that it arrived in a cloud of fire and had wheels within wheels?*"

"Are You implying that the Ancient of Days is Sanat Kumara?"

The Goddess: "*Yes. In the Bible Sanat Kumara is called the Ancient of Days. He is also referred to as the 'Father,' because he was both a Twin as well as the 'Father' of the Twins. When My Twin Jesus-Sananda said 'I come to do the will of my Father,' he was in part referring to Sanat Kumara.*"

"Traditional Christian doctrine contends that the Father resides in Heaven. Are You implying that Shamballa, Sanat's headquarters, is Heaven?"

The Goddess: "*Sananda-Jesus said 'The Kingdom of Heaven resides within.' The Kingdom of Heaven is within your heart. The polarity unites within your heart as the androgenous Father of the Twins. Therefore, if you are immersed in your heart, you are communing with the Father in Heaven no matter where you are.*"

"I find it very interesting that, according to legend, Sanat Kumara lives in a palace within Shamballa's capital city which was laid out in the form of a heart. So, apparently, the 'Father' resides within a heart on the continent of Asia."

**The Goddess:** *"This is true. But his primary seat is in your heart where he exists as the androgenous Spirit and the Cosmic Fire or Kundalini which emerges from Him. The heart is a seat of Cosmic Fire within the body."*

"You said that Lucifer arrived on Earth as Cosmic Fire. So, at least initially he must not have needed to travel in a lightship."

**The Goddess:** *"Right. He first arrived millions of years ago as Cosmic Fire. Through your study of Reiki you have heard of a time when Sonten, the Reiki name for Sanat, arrived on Earth as the life force, right?"*

"Yes. The Reiki tradition[2] maintains that Sonten or Sanat arrived as the life force on Mount Kurama in Japan millions of years ago."

**The Goddess:** *"Yes. And as you might recall, part of the legend maintains that when Sonten-Sanat landed he divided himself up into three parts. These three parts are references to the three powers of Spirit and the three prongs of Sanat's trident."*

"If Dr. Usui[3] founded Reiki on Mt. Kurama, I guess we can conclude that he learned the art of moving the life force from the spirit of the life force itself, Sanat Kumara."

**The Goddess:** *"Yes. Reiki, which means universal life energy, is actually a name for Sonten-Sanat. He is its founder and patron."*

"Well, one thing appears quite obvious to me. If you transpose a couple of letters of Kurama, you get Kumara."

**The Goddess:** *"They have the same meaning. They both denote the coming together of the polarity as the Father. Kurama denotes 'Home of the Father,' 'Home of Spirit' or 'Home of Sanat.'"*

"Was Mount Kurama once part of Lemuria?"

**The Goddess:** *"Yes. It was also a sacred place where the art of Reiki was taught and practiced during the time of Mu. Dr. Usui was an adept Lemurian Master who reincarnated on Japan to revive the ancient art of energy*

31

*movement and activation."*

"I would guess that the ancient Lemurians were well acquainted with the life force, especially since their king, Sanat Kumara, was the life force incarnate."

The Goddess: *"Yes. The early Lemurians were very psychically sensitive. They lived primarily out of their fourth dimensional energy bodies, and this allowed them to both feel and see the life force as it moved within each other and along the surface of the Earth. They were able to followed the planetary dragon lines' back and forth to their destinations in the same way you travel modern streets and highways."*

"Or perhaps in the same way birds and other animals follow the Earth's electromagnetic lines when they migrate?"

The Goddess: *"Yes. Like the birds, the Lemurians were attuned to the higher frequencies of the electromagnetic spectrum. Because of their keen 'sixth sense,' they were also able to formulate the designs of their homes and temples simply from observing the movements of the spiralling life force. Did you know that a subtle pyramid of pure life force naturally forms over a vortex? This was the origin of the physical pyramid."*

"Well I know that vortex means 'spiralling' or 'whirling,' so I guess You are telling me that the spiral ascends at the same angle as a pyramid..."

The Goddess: *"Exactly. The first pyramid builders simply filled in physically the etheric models they found existing upon Earth's fourth dimensional landscape."*

"Did acupuncture begin similarly? I mean did it also begin with the human energy system perceived psychically and then manipulated physically?"

The Goddess: *"Yes. However acupuncture did not begin as a physical art. Originally thought projection and subtle laser beam applications were used to influence the human vortexes or 'acupuncture points.' And it was not so much physical health but consciousness which was effected by the procedure."*

"Then what some Taoists contend, that acupuncture was first used by the monks for their own spiritual transformation, has some basis in truth?"

**The Goddess:** *"Yes, it is true. Originally all medicine effected consciousness. Only by altering a person's consciousness in some way can a complete healing take place. Medicine was initially more holistic than it is today."*

For a few moments I reflected on the world of subtle energy inhabited by the Kumaras and the Lemurians. In my mind's eye I watched as the Kumara brothers traveled along ley lines until they arrived at a natural standing wave pattern of energy. This became the shell of some magnificent temple. Then the Goddess's voice interrupted my vision...

**The Goddess:** *"Many subtle wave patterns on Lemuria were the result of the natural geo-centric movements of the life force, but others were produced directly by the projected thought forms of the Kumaras. Their thought forms would crystallize into etheric templates within which the life force would condense and eventually become solidified matter. Because their will was one with the Creator, whatever the Kumaras willed was instantly manifested. They were the early angels and nature spirits of legend."*

"Did the Kumaras just construct temples and other habitable structures, or were they also responsible for creating certain flowers, minerals, animals etc.?"

**The Goddess:** *"They assisted in the birth of both sentient and insentient life forms. A list of their creations can be found within their various legends worldwide."*

"Where did the Kumaras get the ideas or blueprints for their creations?"

**The Goddess:** *"My Sons received them in waking dreams. Since they were directly linked to the Divine Mind of God, an archetypal pattern would simply appear in their minds and then they would manifest it physically. The Aborigines of Australia refer to the dream realm they existed within as the 'Dream Time."*

"Were their creations devoid of any intellectual process?"

The Goddess: *"There was a modicum. But the intellect had not been fully developed on Lemuria, so the Kumaras did not intellectualize the whys and hows of their creations. They manifested them spontaneously, without any pre-meditated agendas."*

"That sounds like an easier approach than we follow these days. The mind can certainly get in the way of manifesting."

The Goddess: *"Yes. Many of My children sabotage their manifestations by incessantly worrying about the hows and whys. If their mind tells them something cannot be done, they believe it. But remember what Jesus-Sananda said 'If you had faith, you could move mountains."*

"Obviously the Kumaras had a lot of faith..."

The Goddess: *"Yes, because they knew it wasn't them doing the creating, but Me working through them. They also did not create with a selfish motive and therefore had no investment in the outcome. That gave them the freedom to act without hesitation on their inspired guidance."*

"Everything about the Kumaras seems entirely feminine to me. Their faith, their dreaminess, their faith in a higher power, and their desire to harmonize with the Earth—these are all female characteristics."

The Goddess: *"In truth they were androgenous, but their feminine traits of love and allowance superseded their masculine tendencies of aggressive control. And for this reason the culture they created on Lemuria was based upon loving feminine principles. It became My incipient matriarchal culture on Earth, and a model for all future Goddess cultures."*

"It must have been the purist of all matriarchal cultures to ever exist, especially if you consider that the Kumaras' prime objective was to serve You only."

The Goddess: *"Yes. My Sons were on Earth to serve Me alone. They were able to establish My kingdom in its absolute purity because self-serving egoistical tendencies did not exist among them. And because the forces of Patriarchy had not yet emerged on the planet, Matriarchy could flourish unopposed."*

34

"But what about the humans the Kumaras encountered on Earth? They were not as evolved as the Kumaras, were they? How were they assimilated into the Kumaras' civilization on Lemurian?"

The Goddess: *"Before the arrival of the Kumaras, man was generally instinctual and possessed very primitive tendencies. Many humans resembled lower animals in the way they fed and sheltered themselves. In order to evolve primitive Earth humanity and instill within it love and obedience to a higher will, the Kumaras founded the Solar or Great White Brotherhood. This organization was established to teach humanity all My arts, both spiritual and mundane."*

"Are you saying that humanity did in fact evolve from lower life forms as the science of evolution insists?"

The Goddess: *"Yes. But at critical junctures in Earth's history human evolution has had the intervention of extraterrestrial emissaries like the Kumaras. Such ETs have arrived from different parts of the universe in order to accelerate the evolution of humanity by interbreeding with the human species."*

"But according to the Puranas, the Hindu legends, the Kumaras refused to procreate and instead led humans on the path of renunciation."

The Goddess: *"This legend is only partially correct. Some Kumaras did in fact mate with the human species on Earth, while others came primarily to teach the yogic path of renunciation."*

"The progeny of those Kumaras who did mate must have been very advanced."

The Goddess: *"Yes. In the Bible, the Kumara Twin boys are referred to as the 'Sons of God' who mated with the 'Daughters of Men.' Their union did indeed produce perfected human beings. But the reason the Kumaras interbred was not to create just a few perfected progeny, but rather to implant the fire of transmutation into the human gene pool so that all humans could eventually experience their divinity. Their transmitted evolutionary fire is referred to in the legend of the Twins as the twin boys' 'gift of fire' to the human race.*

"*Unfortunately, there has been a tendency among certain mythologists to interpret the Kumara's fire as the common heat producing element, but it was not. The fire they brought was the Cosmic Fire or Kundalini, the fire of creation and destruction or transmutation. This is the true nature of the fire they wielded. Those Kumaras who mated with the 'Daughters of Men' transmitted this evolutionary power through their sperm. Others transmitted the fire into humans through the mediums of thought and touch.*"

"I always thought the 'fire' brought by the Twins was the fire of wisdom..."

The Goddess: "*It is. The Kundalini is the fire of wisdom. The Kundalini is both the power and wisdom of God. Etherically, the Kundalini bestows wisdom on the human species by accelerating the development of the human nervous system and brain. When the Kundalini condenses, it becomes seminal fluid which feeds the cells of the brain and nervous system.*"

"When the brain evolved on Lemuria via the Kundalini, wasn't there a corresponding evolution of the intellect? It seems as though the descendants of the Kumaras should have been intellectual giants."

The Goddess: "*The descendants of the Kumaras were brilliant, but it took many generations for their genius to filter into the common gene pool. The progeny of the Kumaras were stepping stones in the evolution of the human brain, which would eventually split into two halves and give rise to the faculties of intellection and discrimination. But this evolution was destined to occur over the course of thousands of years, and come to its fruition on the motherland of Atlantis.*

"*Since Sanat Kumara wielded an abundance of Kundalini, he was especially involved in the awakening of the intellect within the human species. In fact, Sanat or Lucifer is sometimes referred to as the 'Spirit of Intellectual Awareness' because he was responsible for bringing the discriminative faculty to Earth.*"

"Isn't this function of Lucifer especially associated with his manifestation as the Serpent on the Tree in the Garden of Eden?"

The Goddess: "*Yes. According to the yogic interpretation of the myth, the Tree is a representation of the human spine and the Serpent which coils around it is the Kundalini which rises to the head and evolves the brain. The Serpent is Sanat, the Cosmic Fire, which evolves the brain and awakens the intellect."*

"I believe the Jewish Kabbalics also subscribe to this interpretation of the Eden myth. They call the Serpent on the Tree Samael, the 'Spirit of Destruction.' Apparently they must know that the Serpent is the destructive Kundalini."

**The Goddess:** *"Yes. Samael is Sanat, the Kundalini which destroys ignorance with its transformative fire."*

## THE GODDESS SPIRITUAL TRADITION

"Is the awakening of the Kundalini what distinguishes your matriarchal path from the patriarchal spiritual Path?"

**The Goddess:** *"Yes. Simply stated, My path involves using Me as power or Kundalini to unite with My essence, the Infinite Spirit. My power dwells fully within the enlightened adepts of My tradition, as well as the tools of My path, which includes mantras, certain alchemical substances, and mind-expanding sacraments."*

"If I am correct, doesn't the patriarchal path try to circumvent your power and unite with Spirit directly through meditation and contemplation?"

**The Goddess:** *"Yes. Just as you would expect, the patriarchal path is predominately intellectual. It seeks to find God through intellect contemplation and it is strongly opposed to using My power in any form. The spiritual seekers of the patriarchal path regard My power as evil—a force which needs to be reckoned with, otherwise it can be harmful to spiritual progress. For this reason, the patriarchal path is often very austere, with continued vows of renunciation. Some of its members completely isolate themselves from the world so they will not be at the mercy of My corrupting influence."*

"But your path is the opposite. It's about finding joy in the world not abandoning it, right?"

**The Goddess:** *"Yes, the social qualities of the feminine gender are inherent in*

*My path. My devotees are normally sociable and some are even very sensual. They move the power within their bodies rather than inhibit it, and it is their Kundalini power which assists them in experiencing the joyous ecstasy of life. In order to move and awaken the inner life force, they dance uninhibitedly while joyously singing the mantric praises of God, and they observe Yogic disciplines and imbibe sacred sacraments. They do not traditionally abandon the world, although some advanced seekers find it necessary to live in solitude for awhile in order to completely lose themselves in My essence, the transcendent Spirit."*

"Your path certainly contrasts with the patriarchal path, which espouses more disciplined and intellectual pursuits..."

The Goddess: *"Yes, the patriarchal path exhibits the masculine tendencies of independence, reclusiveness, while espousing the intellectual contemplation of the scriptures and philosophical treatises. The patriarchal path has been the dominant one on the planet for the past two thousand years, which is why scriptures have become the final spiritual authority in many traditions, and why so many secluded monasteries have sprung up."*

"But your path was the dominant one in ancient times, was it not?"

The Goddess: *"My path was dominant during those eras when humans strove to live in balance with the Earth, such as the time of Lemuria and the Neolithic Age. The people of those periods worshipped images of Me, the patroness of the Earth, and performed rites which would assist Me in My work of growing vegetation and rotating the seasons. It was during those ages that the legend of My Son spread around the globe, and a Horned Bull Cult flourished in its wake."*

"The rites of the Bull Cult were ecstatic and there was the consumption of numerous sacraments, right?"

The Goddess: *"Yes. The agriculture rites, especially those of the harvest, included the consumption of wine, meat, and various herbal beverages. Wine and meat were consumed sacramentally with the awareness that they were the flesh and blood of the holy bull, which was considered by the ancients to be a manifestation of both Me and My First Son. This was the origin of Holy*

*Communion. My agricultural rites and those of My Bull Cult contributed to the rites of the later Tantric (of India) and Witchcraft movements."*

"It appears to me that the goal of both the matriarchal and patriarchal paths is essentially the same, that of uniting with the essence of creation, the Spirit. The only difference is the approach."

The Goddess: *"This is true. All paths lead to the same place. My children are drawn to a specific path according to their temperaments. The matriarchal and patriarchal paths have been specially designed for certain people, cultures and ages. But almost no path or culture is purely patriarchal or matriarchal in its approach to enlightenment. The majority of spiritual traditions have elements of both because My children have both male and female characteristics and need to nurture both parts of their nature. If they were to follow a purely matriarchal or patriarchal path they would be unbalanced in some way because they would not be walking a 'middle path."*

"Right. All people have both emotions and intellect. To some degree, everyone is both social as well as reclusive. It's just that one part of everyone's nature is more pronounced. I for one love to chant, but I also enjoy reading scriptures and philosophizing about the nature of god."

The Goddess: *"As your teachers have told you, understanding and experience are both necessary on the spiritual path. Without the experience of joy provided by My path, spiritual life is very dry. But without the understanding provided by the patriarchal path, a seeker cannot discern what is good or harmful for spiritual progress. Without discernment, a person is likely to succumb to blind belief and/or harmful addictions, and then their spiritual progress stagnates."*

"It seems to me that at some point in history Your rites were toned down or reformed to become more disciplined, and therefore patriarchal. Perhaps there was a need to make Your path more balanced at those times?"

The Goddess: *"You are perhaps referring to the rites of My Son Dionysus which were reformed by the Orphics? Or maybe you allude to the rites of the Hindu Tantrics which were reformed by the patriarchal Vedantists? Either way, You are right, there was indeed a need for more discipline among My devotees. You see, there are elements of My rites, such as the consumption of mind-expanding sacraments, which provide only a temporary spiritual high or communion with Me. In order to become permanently established in My essence, a seeker needs to give up the attachment to such outer tools and focus on experiencing Me without them, otherwise addiction sets in. At such a time a disciplined program of meditation, chanting, and service are invaluable, as is time spent in solitude."*

"Its interesting that it is the other way around in Your Shakta Path of India. Within that path, the disciplined patriarchal practices precede Your wild, ecstatic rites."

The Goddess: *"You are right, within the Shakta Kaula Tradition[4] it is prescribed that a student first follow the orthodox rites of the patriarchal or 'Right Hand Path' in order to develop the disciplined and discerning temperament necessary for observing the rites of the matriarchal or 'Left Hand Path.' These latter rites include the consumption of wine and meat, and sexual intercourse. An undisciplined seeker could easily get addicted to any of these matriarchal practices, especially the consumption of wine and sexual intercourse. While sexual intercourse may be an excellent way to unite the polarity and awaken the Kundalini, it can definitely bring about a downfall."*

"I often wonder about some of the rites of the Left Hand Path, such as the eating of one's own excretion and performing rituals on top of human corpses. I find them completely nauseating and fail to see how such practices can promote an attitude of love and joy."

The Goddess: *"If you just look on the surface of such rites, you won't be able to. In truth, these unusual rites are performed so one can eventually experience continual love for all things. If My devotee can become equally as content eating dung or sleeping among corpses in a graveyard as he or she is living within a palace, then equal vision will have been attained, and he or she can then begin to love all things equally. For such a person, all material forms become just different manifestations of Me. Furthermore, by living extremely austerely and in morbid environments, My devotees are forced to look within and find an inner joy and beauty which their outer world is devoid of. Eventually their inner search leads them to unlimited joy."*

"Okay, I'll try to begin seeing love and allowance in these practices."

The Goddess: *"Please do. Love and allowance has always been the ultimate goal of My rites. Certainly there have been black magicians who experimented with My rites to control others, but they are not My true devotees. My true devotees are only interested in serving Me and the Higher Will .*

*"Now, there is one additional reason why My rites come after the patriarchal rites. They are much older, and they endow one with the secret wisdom and power of the ancient Sons of God."*

"They align one with the Lemurians?"

The Goddess: *"Yes. By contrast, the patriarchal rites arose within the Atlantean culture and generally align a seeker with the masters from that continent and time period."*

"Are there any references in scripture to when Your rites first arrived on Earth."

The Goddess: *"I have told you, they arrived with My Sons, the Kumaras. But their is also an allusion to their arrival in the Jewish 'Book of Enoch."*

"Are You referring to the story of Azzazel and the Fallen Angels at the beginning of the *Book of Enoch*?"

The Goddess: *"Yes. Azzazel is a name for Sanat Kumara, and the term 'Fallen Angels' refer to the Venusian Kumaras, the 'Sons of God,' who accompanied Sanat to Earth. After Azzazel and the Fallen Angels mated with the 'Daughters of Men,' they proceeded to share with their women certain occult mysteries, such as the secret art of alchemy, herbology, astrology, geology and divination. These became the foundation stones of My matriarchal tradition."*

"Why were Azzazel and the Fallen Angels considered evil?"

The Goddess: *"In the original version of the Books of Enoch they were not evil, but heroes. It was only later, during patriarchal times, that they became judged as demonic because of their sensual natures. In truth, they were the saviors of humanity and My envoys.*

41

"*Azzazel and the Sons of God revealed to evolving humans how to harmonize with the Earth and use its abundant resources for spiritual evolution. They taught My children that all was vibration and how different frequencies influence each other; they revealed how certain crystals and herbs effect the human energy system and how these tools can alter consciousness; and they also taught how to harmonize with the astrological energies arriving from other planets and star systems. In this way, Azzazel-Lucifer and his entourage taught how to change and adapt one's energy field to harmonize with the environment, as opposed to changing one's environment to harmonize with one's electromagnetic field.*"

"So the mission of the Fallen Angels was to reveal how to vibrationally harmonize with both the Earth and the cosmos?"

The Goddess: "*Yes, as well as how to alchemically evolve. Azzazel, their leader, was both the teacher of alchemy⁵ as well as the embodiment of the alchemical mead which makes humans divine. He was Sanat Kumara, the Kundalini incarnate, and his name means 'Power of God.*"

## THE PURPOSE OF THE GREAT WHITE BROTHERHOOD

"I assume that the wisdom brought by Azzazel was taught within the schools of the Kumaras."

The Goddess: "*Yes. In order to have a school within which to teach the wisdom of Azzazel-Sanat and the Fallen Angels, an academy of esoteric wisdom consisting of 13 levels, My sacred number, was founded on Lemuria. This school marked the establishment on Earth of a inter-stellar organization which had existed throughout the cosmos for billions of years. You know of it as the Great White Brotherhood, although it was originally known on Earth as the Solar Brotherhood.*"

"So the secret societies began way back then?"

The Goddess: "*Originally the Solar Brotherhood was not a secret society, but an organization open to anyone who was ready to dedicate their life to serving Me. On Mu, the priest king, Sanat Kumara, was its titular head, and any of his worthy subjects could become an initiated member. The organization mirrored My matriarchal tradition on later Crete, which was also presided over*

42

*by the priest king and open to everyone."*

"Why was the organization established by the Kumaras initially called the Solar Brotherhood? Doesn't the symbol of the Sun affiliate it with the Patriarchy?"

The Goddess: *"My children on Mu did not worship the physical Sun. Instead, they worshipped the Sun behind the Sun, i.e., the Infinite Spirit which is the essence of the physical Sun. The goal of the Solar Brotherhood was union with the androgenous transcendental Spirit. The term 'brotherhood' originally denoted both male and female membership. The word is a bad translation of an earlier term which was inclusive of both genders."*

"Did the Solar Disc which the Kumaras brought from Venus become a symbol of the Solar Brotherhood?"

The Goddess: *"Yes. It once hung in one of the important temples of the brotherhood on Mu, the Temple of Divine Light. The temple was very large, about the size of your Vatican, and its walls were made of clear, transparent quartz crystal. When the rays of the Sun struck the Solar Disc, they became amplified and the crystal temple simultaneously vibrated at a very high frequency. The influence of the Disc and Temple were then felt throughout the land of Mu."*

"Were Sanat and the Kumaras the exclusive founders of the Solar or Great White Brotherhood?"

The Goddess: *"They played a critical role in its founding, but they did not act alone. The were assisted by missionaries from other parts of the cosmos, such as Sirius, the galactic headquarters of the GWB. They also came from other planets in your Solar System."*

"I have heard of pyramids on Mars and Venus and the possibility of physical life having once occurred on those planets in the past, but I have not heard that in regards to the other planets."

The Goddess: *"Like the Kumaras, the extraterrestrial missionaries did not initially arrive in physical embodiments. Generally they came from planets*

43

*which did not have physical but etheric civilizations. Remember that your teacher Muktananda mentioned having traveled astrally to the etheric dimension of Jupiter?"*

"Yes. He claimed that the planet Jupiter was populated with enlightened masters living in their subtle bodies."

The Goddess: *"Yes. Many of the early masters who came from Venus or Jupiter did not need physical bodies. Only after their arrival on Earth did they lower their vibrations enough to necessitate them."*

"Did they all come at once? I mean, was the Earth swarming with extraterrestrials at one time?"

The Goddess: *"No. I called them to come at different periods. They arrived when their own unique approach to polarity union and Kundalini awakening could benefit the planet. And the races they worked with were generally those they had a special karma with."*

"Are you saying that all the extraterrestrials who came to Earth brought the wisdom of Kundalini?"

The Goddess: *"Yes. Either directly or indirectly. You see, the entire drama of Earth emerged out of a galactic need to create a planetary crucible for the union of the polarity. Those souls which intensely desired to undergo this evolution and return to their primeval origins as androgenous Spirit elected to incarnate on Earth. And those extraterrestrials who had special karma with them and could teach the path of polarity union and Kundalini arousal through love, yoga, service, etc., volunteered to come as their guides and teachers."*

"What do You mean by 'special karma?'"

The Goddess: *"On their way to Earth, souls often pass through certain star gates and interdimensional portals, such as the Pleiades and Sirius, where they lower their frequencies in preparation for coming to Earth. In these places they create karmic alliances with the souls residing there."*

"And later our soul 'mates' from these places come and assist us our evolution on Earth?"

The Goddess: *"Yes. They come and assist you in uniting the polarity and awakening the Kundalini. For this purpose, they have come as both your teachers and as your lovers."*

"They have come as our lovers?"

The Goddess: *"Yes. The art of making love is a natural way to awaken the Kundalini. When the genders attract and unite, there is a natural release and activation of the Kundalini."*

"But there does not seem to be many of us finding peace or enlightenment through our relationships."

The Goddess: *"This is because the Kundalini energy you release as a couple is both destructive and transformative. It can either evolve a union to greater degrees of intimacy, or it can tear it apart.*

*"Anyway, the ultimate plan was never for you to find perfect peace in an outer relationship. You were meant to find it within. When, after many ages of failing to find complete satisfaction from a mate, you are destined to look inside yourself for that completeness. There you discover your own inner polarity waiting to be united, and the Kundalini serpent ready to rise and take you into your heart. Finally, having merged your consciousness into the heart, you unite with the androgenous Spirit and the drama is over."*

"Did we know what was involved when we made the commitment to come to Earth? Did we know we would never find that completeness with another?"

The Goddess: *"You had an idea. But you were incomplete and needed the physical plane experience to understand it fully. Anyway, it's a moot point now. For many of you, graduation day is just around the corner."*

"Do You mean that the polarity has either united or is about to within many of us now?"

The Goddess: *"Yes. The polarity is uniting now in many of My children on*

45

*Earth. For others, the female principle must be revived and developed before it can unite with the male principle. The current movement to access the inner female and inner child is assisting this process, as is travel to feminine vortexes like those in Peru."*

"Do you mean Lake Titicaca, the primary female vortex on the planet?"

The Goddess: *"Yes, and Mount Shasta in California. These places will precipitate the re-awakening of the intuition and the feminine qualities of love and acceptance."*

"Does the revival of the feminine principle have anything to do with peoples' current interest in direct spiritual experience we are now witnessing on the planet?"

The Goddess: *"Yes. Direct spiritual experience is an emotional need which is intimately linked to the awakening of the female principle. The intense desire some people are now experiencing for profound experience also comes from having participated in certain patriarchal religions which advocate analytical contemplation of scripture to know God. Many of these traditions also traditionally espouse the need of priestly intermediaries to talk to God, thereby effectively precluding individual communion with Spirit."*

"But direct spiritual experience has always been a component of Your path, right?"

The Goddess: *"Yes. The chanting of sacred names, yoga, meditation, sacraments—they are all practices of My tradition and each can give spontaneous and direct experience of God."*

"Most of the practices of Your path culminate in Kundalini awakening. Is it possible to awaken the Kundalini without having the polarity united?"

The Goddess: *"No. The male and female principles need to unite physically for the awakening to occur. The female principle, which exists in the lower extremities as sexual fluids, must be ignited and 'set on fire' by the male principle before it can be transmuted into Kundalini and rise up the spine."*

46

"And how do you suggest heating up the lower extremities?"

The Goddess: *"There are many methods. Sexual Tantra, or ritual sex performed with a spiritual intent, is one way. Sexual love unites the polarity by joining the opposing genders together, and the passion it produces will heat up the lower extremities. Meditation, yoga, mantra repetition, the consumption of sacraments, controlled breathing techniques—all these practices will heat up the body and produce the desired transmutation."*

"Were the secrets of Sexual Tantra also brought to Earth by the Kumaras?"

The Goddess: *"Yes. Sexual Tantra was first taught by Azzazel-Sanat to the 'Daughters of Men' and has since been passed down through the branches of the Great White Brotherhood. As you may have learned in your studies, Azzazel's home planet, Venus, is intimately associated with sex and sexual fluid. In the Hindu tradition, Venus and Azzazel are both referred to as Shukra, a name for sexual fluid, which is the physical crystallization of the Kundalini. When the fiery Kundalini becomes awakened during Sexual Tantra, this fluid transmutes back into the Kundalini."*

"Are the sexual fluids transformed if the Kundalini is awakened through the transmission of spiritual energy from a Guru?"

The Goddess: *"Of course. The transmission of the Guru's fiery Kundalini will initiate a process within the disciple whereby the female fluids are continually being transmuted by fire and raised up as Kundalini."*

"If the wisdom regarding Kundalini has been on Earth for thousands of years, why has it not been known about by very many people?"

The Goddess: *"It was known about by many during the time of Mu, but later it became necessary for this wisdom to become more circumspect. There were certain persons on Atlantis who began awakening their Kundalini for the purpose of empowering their egos, but not for spiritual evolution.*

*"Anyway, the secrets of Kundalini have their own time table. They were not destined to become popular on a large scale until now. Not enough of the population has been ready to receive them."*

47

"Did the Kumaras know it would take so long before the world would again be ready to receive them?"

**The Goddess:** "*Yes. This was one reason they founded the Solar or Great White Brotherhood on Earth—to keep the teachings alive even during the darkest times on the planet. The title 'Keepers of the Flame,' which some members of the Great White Brotherhood have adopted, also denotes 'Keepers of the Flame of Spirituality.' The Great White Brotherhood has kept the flame of wisdom alive for thousands of years and now it can reach much of the world.*"

"I guess you could say that we have the Kumaras to thank for the coming New Age. They brought the wisdom which will now make it possible."

**The Goddess:** "*Yes. The Kumaras were instrumental in the creation of the New Age through sharing the wisdom of Yoga and how to love and be loved. They came from the planet of love with the mission to teach love.*"

"If love is the theme of the New Age, will it be a new Lemuria?"

**The Goddess:** "*In some ways, yes. However, by continuously returning to Earth during the current cycle, those souls which incarnated on Lemuria have accumulated a vast amount of experience, as well as an intellect and ego. So the New Age or Fifth World could not possibly be a carbon copy of ancient Lemuria.*"

"But perhaps in the expression of divine love? Could this be how Lemuria will return?"

**The Goddess:** "*Yes. When My children become established in their hearts, they will live and breath divine love. Divine love will cover the Earth in the Fifth World as it did on the continent of Lemuria.*

*"And similar to Lemuria, the New Age will also be about achieving Gnosticism, the intuitive knowledge of one's divinity. When the heart is awakened, the gnostic revelation which resides within the heart of I AM GOD, or I AM SPIRIT, or I AM THAT, also awakens.*"

48

# THE CONSCIOUSNESS OF A KUMARA, A SON OF GOD

"This gnostic wisdom of the heart You speak of—is this the consciousness of a Kumara?"

**The Goddess:** *"Yes. A Kumara experiences himself as both Spirit as well as a child of Spirit, as both Father and Son. In this regard, a Kumara possesses the consciousness of My First Son, Sanat Kumara. You were given an experience of this awareness on Mt. Shasta, were you not?"*

Once again my mind journeyed back to a pivotal experience in my life. This time I found myself on Mt. Shasta and the year was 1997. I had come to the sacred mountain with my friend James in order to expand my consciousness and access some specific esoteric information. I felt inspired to discover what I called the "mystery of the Kumaras," although I did not know exactly what that meant. From previous experiences on Shasta I was aware that a "Kumara Consciousness" pervaded the mountain. My wife had tapped into it years before and left Shasta as a channel for the Kumaras. Perhaps it was my turn now.

On the morning of our third day on the mountain, James and I hiked laterally along the mountain to a place called 'Squaw Meadows' in hopes that we would find a power spot there suitable for connecting with the Kumaras. I suggested we hike in a lateral direction rather than upwards because four days of fasting had greatly weakened me.

When we finally arrived at our destination, we were greeted by a magical mountain glen which was markedly different from the dry, sparse terrain which covered most of the rest of the mountain. The area was thickly covered with tall green grass interspersed with mountain flowers and fed by a stream of transparent, crystal clear water which moved in a circuit around the idyllic setting. Every twenty feet or so the stream would descend abruptly to a lower plateau, thereby creating a sparkling little waterfall and a shimmering pool of water below it.

I immediately sat down next to one of the waterfalls and its accompanying pool, and then slowly consumed a special sacrament I had been guided to bring with me. Then, while I waited for the sacrament to enter my blood stream and circulate to my brain, I chanted a Sanskrit hymn of 108 verses called the "Guru Gita" in honor of the Goddess and my other spiritual guides of the past and present. This "sloka mantra" was designed to protect me while my body assimilated the sacrament, and especially after it took full effect.

After about one half hour of chanting, I had reached the one-hundredth verse of the chant when an unexpected surge of Kundalini energy bolted up my spine to my neck and apparently became stuck. In order to free it up, my body automatically assumed a yoga position, and soon the energy was ascending even higher. By the last verse of the prayer I could feel the Kundalini moving within both my head and heart. It was then that I decided to stand up and experience its full impact on my consciousness.

As I rose to my feet, a tremendous flood of cosmic energy began to spiral out of my heart. It was so powerful and forceful that I told myself it must be the same raw power which has created and sustains the universe. At that point I felt compelled to close my eyes, and as I did so my consciousness spontaneously descended into my heart. The personality of Mark was simultaneously transcended, and I merged into something much greater than my normal, limited self. I became one with the unlimited consciousness within my heart, that which some call Spirit, and others refer to as God, the Father. I was the center of the entire cosmos and its eternal witness, but I was also its creator. I watched with wonder as the power which had created and sustains the universe emerged from out of my own infinite beingness, and then spiralled to parts unknown with a pre-destined assignment. This seemingly independent power of mine had always existed, and so had I. And as far as I knew, the universe was also eternal. In my transcendent world there was no time, no beginning or end, only one eternally blissful moment.

After a short time I opened my eyes to find my friend James standing inquisitively in front of me. In the short time I had had my eyes closed, James had transformed into my son, my creation, and I felt an incredible love for him. His welfare and protection were my sworn duty. As I looked around Squaw Meadow, I realized that I felt that same unconditional love for every part of nature I could see. Everything within my visual perception had become my immediate family.

After a short time the personality of Mark suddenly re-emerged, and for awhile I had an anchor in two worlds. I was still the Creator of the Universe, but now I was also that which had been created. I was experiencing the dichotomy of being both Father and Son simultaneously. I was finite and infinite at the same time. My true Self or essence was my Father, the Creator, and my personality was his Son, Mark. But, surprisingly enough, even this paradoxical experience felt supremely natural to me.

I remained in two dimensions for many hours while fully savoring the union of Spirit and ego, intellect and intuition it engendered. Ultimately I realized that my prayer had been answered and that I was being given a glimpse of the consciousness of a Kumara, a Son of God. This was the "mystery" of the

Kumara I had come to Shasta for—to be both Father and Son simultaneously.

As I finished my flashback I took a deep breath. I was then greeted once again by the soothing presence of the Goddess.

**The Goddess:** *"You were guided to Shasta because there it is possible to awaken the consciousness within the heart and discover therein the awareness of the Kumaras. Mount Shasta is the heart chakra of Earth. It is actually two mountains united as one, thus reflecting the polarity which unites within the human heart. It is difficult to be within its aura very long without having some kind of heart awakening occur, as you found out.*

*" An interdimensional doorway links Shasta, the Earth's heart chakra, with Venus, the dual star and heart chakra of the Solar System. Shasta is also linked etherically to Sirius, a dual star and heart chakra of the galaxy. These cosmic corridors allow the transmission of heart centered consciousness to flow from the heavens to the Earth."*

"Can the Kumaras be contacted via the corridor between Venus and Shasta?"

**The Goddess:** *"Yes, some Kumaras still travel interdimensionally between Shasta and Venus. But keep in mind one thing: the Kumara is the consciousness of the heart, it is not an ego or a personality. If you want to commune with the Kumaras, go within your heart. There you will find the entire brotherhood waiting for you. When Andrea contacted the Kumaras, she did so through her heart."*

I was again transported back in time as I reviewed my wife Andrea's unique experience on Mount Shasta in June of '94. On that day, we drove to the 9000 foot level of the mountain and then trudged together through knee deep snow until we reached a clearing suitable for meditation. Once she was seated, Andrea instantly fell into a deep trance, and soon tears were flowing freely down her cheeks. She had spontaneously descended into her heart and contacted the loving vibration of the Kumaras. Soon a deep and commanding voice began to issue from her mouth. "I am that which is known as Kumara" it announced. Then, for the following twenty minutes, I sat spellbound as Andrea allowed herself to bring forth the authoritative voice of the Kumara consciousness. As she rattled off profound spiritual truths and answered some of my most intimate questions, I decided I had met a special friend on the snowy white slopes of Mount Shasta.

When the voice finally departed, I felt joy for what I had received, but sadness in loosing a new friend and mentor. After Andrea returned to normal consciousness and slowly opened her eyes, we sat silently together for some time while soaking up the stillness of Mount Shasta. When she was finally able to speak, Andrea got teary eyed as she recounted the loving presence which had just filled her being. She could not remember the dialogue very clearly, only the feeling of unconditional love which had moved within her.

When we left the mountain that day Andrea's Kumara presence came with us, and she has been channeling its wisdom ever since. The voice has never been as strong or imposing as it was that day on Mt. Shasta, however. When I inquire why this is so, it tells me that before the Kumara presence can become as forceful as it was again within Andrea she must become fully and permanently merged with her inner Kumara. What she experienced on Shasta was an initiation, of sorts, and a glimpse into future possibilities.

"I think it is clear to me now that the true nature of the Kumara is love," I said as I resumed my conversation with the Goddess.

**The Goddess:** *"Yes. A Kumara lives within the heart and is constantly united with the consciousness of love which resides there. My Sons Sanat and Sananda Kumara came to teach others how to find that love and become permanently established in it. As you know, Sananda returned recently as Jesus Christ to reveal the mystery once again to his brothers and sisters on Earth.*

*"Everything about Kumara is love, even the name itself. Kumara is the vibration of love. If one repeats this name/mantra long enough with faith, the inner polarity will naturally unite and the heart chakra will awaken."*

"So by infusing the body with the vibration and name of Kumara, one becomes a Kumara?"

**The Goddess:** *"Yes, that is the mystery and science of mantra. By repeating a mantra, a person becomes whatever that mantra signifies. By repeating Kumara one becomes My First Son and an embodiment of love. Similarly, by repeating the mantra of MA, My name, one also becomes established in love. I exist as the power, wisdom and love which resides within your heart."*

"Both You and Your First Son reside in the heart?"

The Goddess: "*This is correct. My First Son and I are One. We are both the androgenous vibration of love which exists within the heart.*

"*As proof that the heart is My home, I have placed there My androgenous symbol, the Star of David, and My androgenous color, green. The Star of David, which is composed of two interlocking triangles, represents the union of My Twin Sons. Green is the union of Blue and Yellow, the colors of My Twin Sons.*"

## THE SEVEN RAYS OF THE GODDESS

"What exactly do you mean by the 'colors' of your Sons."

The Goddess: "*Once again I am referring to vibration. Blue, the color of Sanat Kumara is the vibration of Spirit and the Will. Yellow-gold is the color of Christ or Sananda and the vibration of both love and wisdom.*"

"Are you referring to what are commonly known as the Rays?"

The Goddess: "*Yes. Colors are sometimes referred to as Rays. They are vibratory frequencies which travel as rays.*"

"If color is vibration, and You are the Om, the synthesis of all vibratory frequencies, then all colors must be shades of You."

The Goddess: "*Yes. All color Rays are collectively Me. I emanate out of unmanifest Spirit as the seven primary color Rays, each of which rules a power or characteristic of Mine. My primary colors of blue, yellow and red are the vibration of My three powers of creation, preservation, and destruction. My four secondary colors are the vibrations of the four elements of creation which My three powers engender.*"

"Do the three primary colors also represent the three prongs of Sanat Kumara's trident?"

The Goddess: "*Yes. While grounding the higher will of Father Spirit on Earth Sanat Kumara wields My three powers as his trident.*"

"But even though he is associated with all colors, Sanat is especially associated with the color blue because he is the Will of Spirit on Earth, right?"

**The Goddess:** *"Yes. The Blue Ray of Will is his principal Ray. However his wisdom and power are intrinsic to the second and third Rays of yellow-gold and red. These are the other two prongs of his trident."*

"But as Spirit doesn't he encompass all the Seven Rays?"

**The Goddess:** *"Yes. Actually the fourth through the seventh are all nuances of the Third Ray of Action, so Sanat, like Me, rules them all. Sanat delegates the lordship of these other six Rays to his six brothers."*

"Are you saying that there are seven Kumaras ruling the Rays?"

**The Goddess:** *"Yes. The Seven Kumara brothers rule the Seven Rays. The Twin Kumaras are personifications of My split into halves, and the Seven Kumaras are manifestations of My division into seven principles or Rays.*

*"By ruling a Ray, each Kumara governs one seventh of My creation. As the Blue Ray of Will, Sanat rules everything governed by a will, including all My children on Earth. But Sanat's influence is felt the strongest among those rulers whose will becomes law. As the Yellow-gold Ray of Wisdom and Love, Sananda oversees all institutions of true wisdom on Earth, such as the Brotherhoods and Mystery Schools, as well as the more mundane colleges and universities. Another of My Sons is the lord of the ruby Red Ray, the Ray of Power. He rules over all creative activity. Under his supervision are those who set things in motion in the world, such as the money makers and financiers. My Son of the Fourth Ray is lord of the vibration inherent within the orange and white colors. White is his color because as the lord of the Fourth Ray, the Ray of Balance, all the other Rays merge into him. He has rulership over artists and those on the path of spiritual ascension, the process of completely merging into the white light. Orange is also his color because this Son rules the emotion of joy, and he has some influence over the release of the creative aspects of the Kundalini. My Fifth Ray Son is green, the color of healing. Healers and diplomats fall under his compassionate supervision. My Sixth Ray Son is indigo and rules over priests, monks, and diplomats. Finally, My Seventh Ray Son is purple/violet and rules over alchemy and ascension. This is the last of the seven colors and it sits on the threshold of the next, higher octave. Through its portal a shift can be made to a higher dimension. The Violet Ray is ascendent on the Earth now."*

"If the Seven Rays are ruled by your Sons, the guiding masters of the GWB, does that mean that everyone who falls under the guidance of a Ray is part of the Great White Brotherhood?"

The Goddess: "*No. Everyone on Earth is ruled by a Ray in the same way they are ruled by a planet, but not everyone is a member of the Brotherhood. What distinguishes one who is, is that he or she has firmly merged his or her lower will with the Higher Will of the Father Spirit and lives within the heart. In all their actions they serve the Father, not their egos.*

"*Father Spirit is the union of Will, Love and Wisdom, or the Blue and Yellow-gold Rays united. He is My First Son, Sanat Kumara, who exists as the Twins, Sanat and Sananda, the rulers of the Great White Brotherhood.*"

"How can I know if I am part of the Great White Brotherhood?"

The Goddess: "*Ask yourself whether you are serving God or your own ego.*"

## THE KUMARAS IN THE BIBLE

A gentle breeze licked my exposed body as I meditated on the Great White Brotherhood and my place within it. I had always felt aligned with the organization, but I would be far from truthful if I claimed that all my actions were inspired by a higher will. So rather than belabor the point, I decided to change the topic and move in a fresh direction.

"Can one find references to Lemuria and the Kumaras in the Bible?"

The Goddess: "*Yes. But most references to them have become veiled or distorted.*"

"What then, if anything, is left?"

The Goddess: "*Actually the first reference to My Sons can be found at the beginning of Genesis. Remember the passage which states 'and the Elohim[6] moved upon the face of the waters'? The Elohim are My Seven Sons, the seven parts of Me which created the physical universe and rule over it. They are the Seven Rays or Seven Kumaras I have been telling you about.*

"*My Seven Sons were once known collectively as the Seven-Faceted Serpent Goddess.[7] As one mammoth Serpent they moved together upon the*

55

*face of the cosmic waters at the very beginning of time. The creation myth in the Popul Vuh of the Quiche Mayas, which explicitly states that a primeval serpent initially moved 'upon the waters,' is how Genesis originally commenced before being altered by patriarchal theologians."*

"Do the Kumaras only appear in the Bible as the 'Serpent on the Waters?"

The Goddess: *"No. They also appear as the Serpent on the Tree in the Garden of Eden. Together they cling to the famous tree's branches as Me, the Primal Serpent."*

"But I thought the Serpent on the Tree was Sanat Kumara?"

The Goddess: *"You are right, Sanat is the sum total of My seven Sons. The Gnostics knew this, which is why they referred to the Serpent on the Tree as a manifestation of both Me, Sophia, and My First Son, Sanat."*

"Wasn't the Sumerian serpent, the seven-headed Enki, the ancestor of the Biblical serpent? Was Enki both You and Your First Son?"

The Goddess: *"Yes. Both My First Son and I were Enki. Enki was also depicted with seven heads[8] which were representations of the Seven Kumaras or seven principles of creation. And like myself and My Son, Enki was also the life force. The syllable ki of Enki is the universal seed syllable of the life force. A further link between Enki and Sanat is revealed by their common epithets, 'Lord of the Earth."*

"This brings up an interesting question. Did Satan, the patriarchal name for the Serpent, derive from Sanat? The names are very close..."

The Goddess: *"Yes, within the patriarchal Hebrew culture Sanat was distorted to Satan, which means adversary or obstacle.[9] Satan refers to Sanat's fiery power of destruction which opposes life. It is a name for Sanat-Lucifer who opposes his creative brother, Sanat-Sananda."*

"There is a Jewish legend which maintains that Eve copulated with the Satan or Samael, the Serpent on the Tree, in Adam's absence. And the fruit of their union was the evil Cain. How would you interpret this myth?"

The Goddess: *"Satan and Samael are both names of the fiery Kundalini.[10] The Jewish myth is an allegorical account of the Kundalini power which was passed down through a lineage of masters beginning with Satan or Sanat. Sanat transmitted his fire to the next master of his lineage, Cain, whose name means 'Smith,' and he in turn transmitted it to his spiritual son, Enoch. Both Cain and Enoch are names for the Kundalini masters of the Thoth-Hermes lineage who once presided over the Atlantean and Egyptian mystery academies."*

"You have maintained that the Biblical Tree is representative of the human spine and the Serpent is the Kundalini which spirals upon it. But why were there two trees depicted in the Garden, one of Good and Evil and One of Eternal Life? We humans have only one spine."

The Goddess: *"Originally the two trees were united as one, as they still are in some Kabbalic mysteries. At some point the Biblical authors had them separated, but their meaning as one unified tree, or spine, still persists among occultists. The Tree of Good and Evil depicts the downward descent of the Serpent to the base of the spine where it became dormant, and the Tree of Eternal Life represents its eventual return ascent up the spine following Kundalini awakening. The cherub which guards the tree's base with his fiery sword is a manifestation of Enki, the Kundalini, which guards the base of the spinal cord. When the Serpent Kundalini eventually ascends up the Sushumna, the subtle channel within the spinal cord, the seeker achieves eternal life."*

## OUR VENUSIAN ANCESTORS

My dialogue with the Goddess regarding humanities' roots and the Garden of Eden brought up a slew of intriguing questions. With excitement I paced back and forth along the lake shore trying to decide which to ask first.

"If the Kumaras were our ancestors, shouldn't we resemble them in some way?"

The Goddess: *"Remember that within your human ancestry you have traces of both Earth man and Extraterrestrial man. The Kumara influence often manifests as pale skin, blond hair, and blue eyes. But the influence of the Kumaras was not so much to contribute to the human gene pool as much as it was to evolve and perfect the genes it already possessed."*

"There are legends of our ancestors having been reptilian. Were the Kumaras initially serpentine featured?"

**The Goddess:** *"In part. Initially the Kumaras and other extraterrestrial Sons of God existed in etheric bodies comprised of spiralling standing wave patterns which gave the appearance of serpents or reptiles. But there have also been physical reptilian aliens who have contributed to the human DNA pool in the past."*

"What about the Gnostic legend which states that Adam and Eve were shocked and horrified when they saw that their 'Reptilian Creators'? Does this legend harken back to the time of the etheric Kumaras or the physical reptilian aliens?"

**The Goddess:** *"The legend alludes to both your Kumaras and reptilian ancestors, including the dinosaurs. They helped 'create' you by serving as your ancestors.*

*"As you know, the Kumaras did not remain permanently etheric and reptilian. Eventually they assumed physical, human-like shapes. Many acquired what you commonly refer to as Nordic features: white skin with yellow or golden hair and blue eyes. Such features reflect the pinnacle of human evolution. White is in some regards the most evolved color because all colors merge into and out of it; gold is the color of wisdom; and blue is the color of Father Spirit."*

"Are You saying that the Germans were right in contending that our first ancestors were the blond and blue eyed Aryans?"

**The Goddess:** *"Your first ancestors were blond and blue-eyed, but not Aryans. The Aryans were a patriarchal race which manifested during the latter days of Atlantis. However, some physical features of the Lemurian Kumaras were passed down to the Aryan race."*

"The Kumaras must have been the ancestors of many races, not just the

Aryans, if they are our planetary progenitors."

**The Goddess:** "*Yes. The descendants of the Lemurian Kumaras spread throughout the world and interbred with many native races. In such places as India, Peru and even Atlantis, their descendants became worshipped as the pale gods who founded lineages of priest kings and spiritual gurus.*"

"The annals of Peru and India are rife with references to such pale skinned rulers. Even modern science has proven that the early rulers were pale skinned."[11]

**The Goddess:** "*Right, and when the early royal lineages of those lands mutated through interbreeding with the native, indigenous races, the monarchs and priests often tried to show their affiliation to their divine ancestors by attaching artificial beards to their chins, elongating their skulls, and wearing heavy gold earrings in order to stretch their ears.*"

"There is a Peruvian legend which claims that the ancestress of the Andean people was a Venusian woman with a long, pointed head and big ears. The Spanish nicknamed her Orejones or 'Big Ears.' Was she a Kumara?"

**The Goddess:** "*Yes. She was a Kumara and the ancestress of many Andean rulers. The Incas emulated her through their custom of wearing large earrings and artificially elogating their heads.*"

"The blond, blue eyed look you mention... it seems to be common among the Venusians who visit Earth. Those who have had close encounters with Venusians during the last century, such as George Adamski, claim they possessed Nordic features."

**The Goddess:** "*Yes. They are either Kumaras themselves or the descendants of them.*"

## AGARTHA AND SHAMBALLA

"I have heard that the Nazis went looking for their ancestors in the Far East. I know they were seeking the Aryans, but perhaps they were inadvertently on the trail of the Nordic featured Kumaras?"

The Goddess: "*The Nazis had acquired many legends of Agartha, the underground civilization that the blond haired Lemurians had created in order to survive a series of planetary cataclysms. The Nazis were convinced that the fair skinned founders of Agartha were their Aryan ancestors. So yes, they were indeed inadvertently seeking out the Kumaras.*"

"If I recall correctly, wasn't it a Nazi plan to discover a tunnel leading into Agartha?"

The Goddess: "*Yes. They were convinced that once they entered Agartha they would find their blond haired Aryan ancestors waiting for them. They would then attempt to enlist their support in their goal of world domination.*"

"Were there evil forces in Agartha as some people, like Rudolph Stiener, have maintained?"

The Goddess: "*Perhaps you are referring to rumors of a subterranean civilization comprised of sorcerers practicing black magic and ruled over by an evil King of the World? Well, there is a King of the World in Agartha and he is My First Son, Sanat Kumara. In ancient times when Agartha was created Sanat became its king and Shamballa served as its capital city.*"

"So how did the King of the World become thought of as evil?"

The Goddess: "*I have already mentioned the two sides or aspects of Sanat. As the ruler of the Ray of Will he is both the Higher Will and the lower will, which I have referred to as Sanat-Sananda and Sanat-Lucifer. Both these 'kings' or aspects of Sanat rule from Shamballa. Those who contend that the King of the World is an evil entity have linked their consciousness to the lower will or Sanat-Lucifer, but those who have attuned themselves to the Higher Will have aligned themselves with Sanat-Sananda. Seekers in the latter category recognize the King of the World to be a beneficent ruler and the director of the Great White Brotherhood.*"

"Is this why there is a rumor that there are two kings and two kingdoms, Agartha and Shamballa, one of which is evil and the other spiritual?"

The Goddess: "*Yes. The two aspects of Sanat rule over two different areas and dimensions of Agartha. In one section of the kingdom ego-centric energies have converged to create an environment compatible for dark spirits to reside within and flourish. Dark magicians, such as the Tibet Bon practitioners, often align themselves with these evil spirits. But in another section of Agartha beings of light stand ready to help those on the spiritual quest to union with the Father."*

"The dark spirits must have been the ones the Nazis eventually contacted. But what I don't understand is why the Nazis returned from the East with Tibetan monks. Were the Tibetans attuned to the lower or higher vibration of Agartha?"

The Goddess: *"Most were attuned to the higher. Throughout history, the Tibetan Buddhists have had a special relationship with Agartha and saw the Nazi agenda as an opportunity to precipitate a 'return of Shamballa' with the King of the World as the head of a one-world government. When it became evident that the Nazis had lost the war, the monks realized they had lost their unique opportunity and proceeded to commit mass suicide."*

"Does Agartha still exist?"

The Goddess: *"Yes. But primarily on the etheric plane. Many of the ancient tunnels still exist and masters often appear and disappear within them. But most beings who reside in Agartha are solely fourth dimensional, or nearly so. And they are consciousnesses, not personalities. They will appear to you physically if you are fortunate enough to receive their blessing or teaching."*

This information from the Goddess about Agartha was particularly fascinating to me. For years I had avidly studied both the legends and factual accounts of the subterranean kingdom, many of which were obviously dubious or spurious, but some of which appeared to have merit.

My favorite source of information concerning Agartha is the testimony of one Ferdinand Ossendowski, a Russian explorer who traveled through Mongolia during the 1920s. During his tour, Ossendowski often overheard conversations regarding Agartha and the King of the World which he later compiled into his book *Beasts, Men and Gods* (E.P. Dutton + Co., NYC, 1922). According to one account disclosed to him, supposedly a Mongolian hunter once inadvertently stumbled upon a doorway leading into Agartha and then visited the subterranean kingdom. When he re-emerged some time later, Buddhist Lamas prevented him from telling his tale and revealing the location of Agartha by severing his tongue. Ossendowski was initially skeptical of this tale, but later he was shown the doorway himself, a tunnel entrance which the Buddhists referred to as the "Smoking Gate."

Ultimately, Ossendowski discovered that the Mongolian Buddhist monks were specially affiliated with Agartha, and tunnels leading from the underground kingdom actually terminated in many of their monasteries. The monks maintained that the King of the World traveled through one of these tunnels in 1890 and entered the Buddhist monastery at Narabanchi. He was seated upon a throne and then proceeded to give the resident monks a prophetic discourse concerning the coming hundred years. When Ossendowski questioned the Mongolian monks about the background of this underworld king he learned that the monarch had arrived on Earth thousands of years previously and had then assumed the role of both World Guru and King of the Earth. His name and symbol was AUM, the sacred syllable of three letters which represent the three powers of the Goddess. It appeared as though Ossendowski had inadvertently stumbled upon the legend of Sanat Kumara.

Another Buddhist source of information regarding the King of the World comes from the Sungma Red Lama, also known as Robert Dickhoff, a westerner who studied in Asia and claims to have been initiated by a Buddhist Lama intimately associated with Agartha. Supposedly the master told Dickhoff that the King of the World had originally come from Venus and had initially inhabited a serpentine or reptilian body, but it had since been transformed into a human body! Dickhoff was also informed that the Biblical Serpent of Eden was actually this serpentine master who had come from Venus. Another apparent reference to Sanat Kumara.

Other sources of Agartha information which have come to my attention are from those claiming to be members of the Great White Brotherhood. H. P. Blavatsky and Elizabeth Clare Prophet, the founders of the Theosophical Society and the Church Universal and Triumphant respectively, claimed that their authority to represent the GWB came from the "Ascended Masters" Kuthumi and Master Morya, two Buddhist monks living at the Tashi Lumpo monastery at Shigatse, Tibet, which is supposedly connected by tunnels to Aghartha and Shamballa. Kuthumi and Morya have been known to leave their monastery on occasion to travel to Shamballa or to seek out those on the Earth destined to play a special role in the GWB.

Perhaps in order to prove the existence of Agartha, Kuthumi left his monastery and traveled to Paris in 1947. Calling himself the "Prince Regent of Agartha," he attracted the attention of the French metaphysical community and was eventually given an interview by a prestigious French magazine. Afterwards, he began to organize an expedition to return with him to Agartha, but mysteriously disappeared without a trace just before the group was about to leave. Could Kuthumi have really led an expedition to Shigatse and then into the subterranean kingdom? Many Tibetan monks think so. According to them, the abbot of the Tashi Lumpo monastery, the Tashi Lama, has made numerous journeys to and from Shamballa via both underground tunnels and overland routes. In fact, one Tashi Lama wrote "The Way to Shamballa," a guide book on how to get there.

Another Russian adventurer and his wife who traveled across Mongolia, Nicholas Roerich and his wife Helena, also acquired many secrets concerning Shamballa. They met Master Moya and were privately instructed by him in the mysteries of Agni Yoga, a path for awakening the Kundalini and opening the heart. Morya claimed that this yoga had originated at Shamballa and maintained that it was to be the Yoga of the New Age. Apparently it was the path of transformation originally brought to Earth by Sanat Kumara and the Sons of God.

One additional westerner who was influenced by an ascended master affiliated with Shamballa is Alice Baily. When she was a young girl, Ms. Baily was visited by Dwahl Khul, a Tibetan monk who suddenly appeared in her house. He told her that she had made a soul contract to work for the GWB and it was time to fulfill the agreement. From that time onwards, Alice Baily channeled reams of information about various aspects of the GWB, such as Shamballa, the Kumaras, and the King of the World which was later compiled into a series of lengthy, esoteric tombs. Ms. Baily, who was a very controversial figure from the outset of her ministry, became even more so when she christened her publishing organization "Lucifer Trust." In order to silence the subsequent uproar from her Christian adversaries, she later changed the name to Lucis Trust, but the "dye had been cast." She never came right out and declared it, but Ms. Baily implied by her actions that the GWB was intimately aligned with Lucifer, and that Lucifer is Sanat Kumara, the King of the World.

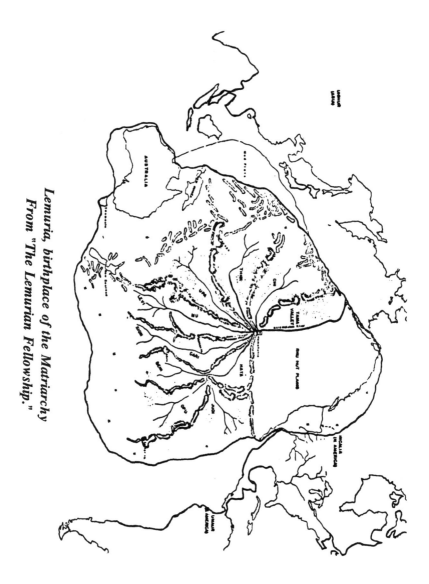

*Lemuria, birthplace of the Matriarchy*
*From "The Lemurian Fellowship."*

# CHAPTER III
# THE WORLDWIDE VENUS CULTURE

"Well, from what You have told me, it sounds like Sanat's palace at Shamballa-Agartha has served as the capital headquarters for not just the Matriarchy, but also the Patriarchy. As Sanat-Sananda he has apparently ruled the Matriarchy, and as Sanat-Lucifer he has governed the Patriarchy. Is this right?"

The Goddess: "*Yes. But the patriarchal tradition did not emerge until the development of the intellect on Atlantis. Before that, Sanat ruled principally over Lemuria and the Worldwide Venus Culture it engendered.*"

"What do you mean by 'Worldwide Venus Culture?' Are You saying that the Lemurian matriarchal culture established by the Kumaras on Mu was eventually spread throughout the globe?"

The Goddess: "*Yes. Missionary members of the Solar Brotherhood spread the culture of Mu throughout much of the Earth. They became the gods and saviors of those lands.*"

"I am not familiar with Your Venus Culture..."

The Goddess: *"My Venus Culture was a synthesis. There were elements of the Lemurian matriarchal culture within it, of course, because Mu was its birthing place. But My Venus Culture was modified and embellished upon by many different races and cultures around the Earth.*

*"There were, however, some elements of the Venus Culture which remained unchanged wherever it took root, such as the worship of Me. My images and symbols could once be found the world over. Today, these ancient images of Me are collectively known as 'Venuses.' And it's no coincidence that they are referred to as that. They are anthropormorphical vestiges of My Venus Culture which knew Me as the planet Venus."[1]*

"One popular symbol often found in conjunction with Your images and is the ank. Does the ank's current ubiquitous appearance around the globe also bare witness to the universal nature of Your ancient Venusian Culture?"

The Goddess: *"Yes. The missionaries of My Venus Culture introduced this symbol of fertility and eternal life to many of the civilizations they traveled to. The symbol's tell-tale appearance on many of the surviving temple or pyramidal walls of ancient times reveals where the sacred rites of My Venus Culture*

The ank, symbol of Venus

*regarding death and rebirth were once administered. It has also become the female symbol, as well as the symbol for the planet Venus among you astrologers."*

## VENUS, THE CELESTIAL GURU

"Not only the ank, but the planet Venus itself has been intimately associated with immortality for thousands of years. I have read that certain legendary immortals, such as Osiris of Egypt and Quetzlcoatl of Mexico, have been incarnations of it or otherwise closely connected to it. Am I right in assuming that this association of Venus with immortality also emerged out of Your Venus Culture?"

The Goddess: *"Yes, and as you can probably guess this association began on*

*Lemuria, the home of the Sons of God from Venus, and then spread around the globe. The early Lemurian Sons of God, the Kumaras, were immortal yogis who taught the path leading to spiritual perfection to all those on Mu who were ready to receive it. Since it was known among the citizens of Mu that the Kumaras had themselves come from Venus, it was only natural that eventually both the Sons of God and their home planet would become associated with immortality on Lemuria.*

*"When the Lemurian missionaries of My Venus Culture eventually left Mu, they spread the legend of the Kumaras and their home, Venus, to the different people around the world. In each country they traveled to, they also installed images of the Twin boys within special temples so that the developing cultures could worship them. This is how the legend and worship of the Twins eventually became ubiquitous.*

*"Part of the legend which the missionaries of My Venus Culture spread concerned the Kumaras' role as saviors of all Earth's people. According to them, the Sons of God had come to Earth to spiritually uplift all humanity and remind it of its divine origins. They also told the people that even though the Sons of God would eventually return to Venus, they would keep returning to Earth until all humans had achieved recognition of their divinity, until they had all become gods and goddesses. This was the beginning of the holy myth of the Son or Sons of God who came from Heaven for the salvation of humankind and then promised to return when he/they left. Originally 'Heaven' was the planet Venus.*

*"Such was the legend of the Kumaras which initially circulated around the globe. Later, however, this myth was revised by the Patriarchy which determined that only one Twin could come from the upper world or Heaven. This, of course, meant that the other Twin had to have come from someplace else, such as the Earth or the underworld.*

*"The legends of Osiris and Quetzlcoatl were derived from the original legend of the Kumara Twins, albeit with some modification by the Atlantean Patriarchy. This is why, even though Osiris and Quetzlcoatl have twin brothers, they are the only ones said to have come from Venus. As you might have guessed, Osiris and Quetzlcoatl are evolutions of the Twin Sanat-Sananda."*

"If they were Sanat-Sananda, then their twin brothers, Seth and Tezcatilopoca, must be versions of Sanat-Lucifer..."

**The Goddess:** *"This is true. Their destructive twin brothers were indigenous* *versions of Lucifer."*

"You are right about Quetzlcoatl and not his brother being associated with Venus. However, I seem to recall that both he and Tzcatilopoca are associated with Venus's sacred number of thirteen. Perhaps this points to these Mexican twins having originally emerged from Your Venus Culture."

**The Goddess:** *"Yes, it does. You can also find these twins as twin serpents within the core of the Mexican Sacred or Venusian Calendar where they are united together as a symbol of Venus. The Mayans and Nahuatls inherited the wisdom of My Venus Culture and knew that the Twins united were Venus."*

"How about the Jews and Christians and their legend of Jesus and Lucifer? Did they also inherit their wisdom from Your Venus Culture?"

**The Goddess:** *"Yes. Jesus and Lucifer were the Judeo-Christian version of Sananda and Lucifer, and as testimony of this truth, you will find that both their sacred numbers are thirteen, the number of Venus. The name of 'Christ' is numerologically a thirteen, and Lucifer's calling card is the 'destructive' thirteen."*

"Besides the number thirteen, another trait which Jesus and the other versions of Sananda share is their definitive symbol, the cross. Osiris's symbol is the Djed cross; Quetzlcoatl's is the Tau cross; and Jesus's is the Latin cross."

**The Goddess:** *"Yes. The cross, like the ank, is both a symbol of the immortal Sons of God, as well as their planet, Venus. It too emerged from My Venus Culture. The two shafts of the cross reveal both the androgenous nature of My immortal Sons, as well as Venus's polarity. One special cross from My Venus Culture which is both a symbol of My immortal Son, as well as a symbol for Venus, is the Mexican cross with five circles. You know of it as the ancient Mesoamerican symbol for Venus."*

**The Mexican Cross and symbol of Venus**

"That cross is also an astronomical symbol, isn't it?"

**The Goddess:** *"Yes. The priests of the Venus Culture were excellent astronomers, and they knew that Venus and Earth are involved in a sacred cycle during which Earth revolves around the Sun eight times while Venus revolves around it thirteen. But from their vantage point on Earth, it appeared to these priests as though Venus only completes five cycles, not thirteen, during this cycle.[2] Thus, both five and thirteen became Venus's sacred numbers. And eventually five became the backbone of the planet's symbol."*

"Did the Mexicans also know about the celestial pentagram of five points which Venus makes in the heavens during its eight year cycle?"

**The Goddess:** *"Of course. The pentagram and the spiral, both of which are based upon the Golden Proportion, the ratio 5:8, were captured in the heavens by the priests of My Venus Culture and their numerous descendants, such as the Mexicans. To truly understand Me, one must thoroughly comprehend the pentagram, the spiral, and the Golden Proportion."*

"It appears to me that a nearly complete understanding of You, the Goddess, can be derived simply by observing the movements of the planet Venus. Your numbers thirteen and five, Your symbols of the pentagram and the spiral, as well as Your dual nature as the Twins—they are all intrinsic to Venus."

**The Goddess:** *"Yes, My attributes are revealed by the planet Venus. Many legends of Me, the Goddess, have been built solely upon its observation. This also applies to My First Son, because we are One. The myths of Quetzlcoatl, Osiris, and Jesus, for example, were based upon the planet's movements. When Venus journeyed under the Earth between its sunset to its sunrise positions, it told the priests of My Venus Culture that My Son would die and travel to the underworld for awhile. When Venus rejoined the Sun at sunrise, it revealed that My Son would eventually be resurrected into immortal life."*

"The shaman I am training with now maintains that all the stars are consciousnesses, and that by meditating on them you can both commune and communicate with those consiousnesses. If we mediate on Venus, are we communing with You?"

**The Goddess:** *"Yes. You will receive both the blessings of Me and My Kumara Sons from Venus. It will also be a great boon for your spiritual growth to* *meditate on the planet, because Venus is the Savior of your Solar System. The Morning and Evening Stars, those sparkling manifestations of My Kumara Twins, are collectively Sanat Kumara, My First Son. Sanat Kumara is the Savior of Humanity."*

"I have always thought Jupiter, not Venus, was the savior or guru planet, especially since the Hindus have named it 'Guru."

The Goddess: *"You are right. Jupiter is also a guru of the Solar System, but Venus is specifically the guru of My matriarchal tradition. When India was primarily matriarchal, Venus was the pre-eminent guru planet of that country. But later, under the influence of the Patriarchy, Jupiter acquired that role."*

"Are You saying, then, that Jupiter is the guru planet of the Patriarchy around the Earth?"

The Goddess: *"Yes, in that the patriarchal tradition is very much guided by traditional dogma and philosophical inquiry, and Jupiter rules over those components of religion."*

"Can we pray to Venus and Jupiter for assistance as we would deities or spiritual masters?"

The Goddess: *"Certainly. All the planets are living entities and can support you in accordance with their unique nature. For example, invoking the spirit of Venus, the planet of the Twins, is particularly efficacious for uniting the polarity within the body, activating Kundalini, and awakening the heart chakra. It can also help you find a partner or lover, because it magnetically unites the opposing genders through the power of love. Invoking Mars is good for increasing physical energy or success in battles. Mercury is helpful with intellectual pursuits, etc."*

## THE ATLANTEAN VENUS CULTURE

"Did the emissaries of Your Venus Culture travel to Atlantis? There are certain historical sources, such as those of the Native American tradition, which maintain that much of the wisdom we now possess about Venus actually came from Atlantis. The sacred Venus calendar of Mesoamerica, for example, apparently came from there."

**The Goddess:** *"Yes. My Sons of the Lemurian Solar Brotherhood founded a model Venus Culture on Atlantis during the continent's early ages. This, however, occurred long before the advent of the patriarchy."*

"This must be why the Greek legends seem to affiliate Atlantis with Venus. In their legends, the Greeks named the continent Hesperus or the Hesperides, a name for Venus. They maintained that Hesperus was a paradise in the west where the golden apples of wisdom grew abundantly."

**The Goddess:** *"Yes, the Greeks correctly named and portrayed Atlantis as Hesperus, the western home of My matriarchal culture. The golden apples of Hesperus they refer to in their legends are symbolic of My sacred wisdom which existed on Atlantis for thousands of years. The serpent Lawton, the protector of the apples, is a representation of a lineage of masters established by Sanat Kumara who guarded this wisdom Their symbol was the serpent.*

*"You might remember that in the Greek legend Lawton is eventually defeated by the solar god Hercules. This event graphically allegorizes the eventual overthrow of My matriarchal tradition by the Atlantean priests of the Patriarchy."*

"If Your Venus Culture existed at the beginning of Atlantean history was Neptune[3] affiliated with it in some way?"

**The Goddess:** *"Neptune was not only affiliated with it, he was its guide and patron. Neptune is a name for My First Son, Sanat Kumara, the 'King of the World.'"*

"Well that's a bit of a surprise...how could Sanat be king of both Atlantis and Lemuria?"

**The Goddess:** *"Sanat Kumara was King of the World, not just of Lemuria. In the same way that you ruled under Sanat on Lemuria, Neptune's 'sons,'[4] the kings of Atlantis, reigned as officials and lineal descendants of Sanat."*

"If Neptune is Sanat, I would expect there to be at least some similarities in their respective legends...."

**The Goddess:** *"There are. The most obvious one is that they both wielded the*

71

*trident, as well as My three powers it denotes: creation, preservation, and destruction. They were also both fathers of twins and associated with Venus. Remember that Plato claimed Neptune was the father of five pairs of twins? The numbers five and two affiliates him with Venus. Two is the number of My Twins, the Morning and Evening Stars, and five is Venus's sacred number. Five and two are united within the Mexican symbol for Venus (composed of five circles and two shafts), thus making it an ancient symbol for Sanat or Neptune."*

"But Sanat was not king of the sea like Neptune supposedly was..."

The Goddess: *"The 'sea' that Neptune ruled over was the 'sea' of consciousness, the ocean of transcendental wisdom, not one of the physical bodies of water covering the Earth. Neptune was originally worshipped by the Atlanteans as My First Son, the Primal Dragon, which had emerged out of the cosmic sea at the beginning of time. That was his origin and his home."*

"Are there any references in mythology to Neptune having been King of the World?"

The Goddess: *"Indirectly. Remember that Chronos of Greek mythology was the first King of the World? Well, Chronos was Neptune."*

"I remember Chronos. But what did Chronos have to do with the sea?"

The Goddess: *"Chronos means time. Time emerged out of the infinite sea of consciousness in the form of the Primal Dragon. The Mesopotamians knew Chronos as the Primal Dragon Enki,[5] and the Romans called him Saturn. Both Enki and Saturn are epithets for Neptune-Sanat."*

"But if Chronos and Neptune are the same, why would the Greek historians make Chronos the father of Neptune?"

The Goddess: *"This is the paradox. In the same way that Sanat is both Father and Son, so is Chronos."*

"Therefore, Chronos, Enki, Sanat and Neptune were all names for Your First Son who was the Primal Dragon and first King of the World. Is this right?"

The Goddess: *"Yes. They are all names for My First Son who became the King of the World and founded lineages of priest kings baring symbols affiliating them with Venus and the Cosmic Fire or Primal Dragon. The kings of Atlantis, for example, carried the ceremonial trident, symbol of the wisdom and three powers of the Primal Dragon. Their crown had thirteen triangles across its top and eight more at its base, representing the sacred eight year cycle of Venus during which the planet revolves around the Sun thirteen times. There were also two bull horns affixed to the sides of the crown, signifying that the ruler was the embodiment of the Twins and wielded the life force of the Primal Dragon."[6]*

"Obviously the Atlantean rulers were closely connected to Venus and the Primal Dragon. If they reigned as representatives of Your First Son I would expect that their kingdom must have been a model matriarchal culture."

The Goddess: *"Originally it was. The incipient goal of the enlightened founders of the Atlantean civilization was to harmonize with the Mother Earth while continually honoring a higher will. Atlantis was initially called by a name of the Goddess, such as Hesperus, but later both the civilization and its name became masculine and patriarchal."*

"What was it called originally?"

The Goddess: *"It was a name which incorporated both the 'A' and 'K' sounds. These are archetypal sounds associated with Me, My Twins, and the Primal Dragon."*

"If Atlantis was a matriarchal culture, was the goal there to become an immortal child of the Goddess as it was on Lemuria?"

The Goddess: *"Yes. The goal on Atlantis was to become an immortal Kaberoi, an eternal Son or Daughter of God, just as it had been to become a Kumara on Lemuria. On Atlantis, Kumara became Kaberoi."*

"Were the Kaberoi Twins of popular legend worshipped on Atlantis?"

The Goddess: *"Yes. The Kaberoi Twins were worshipped on Atlantis as both twin serpents and two young boys, just as the Kumara Twins had been on Mu.*

*The Kaberoi were placed upon ornate, jewel encrusted altars within the temples of the Atlantean Solar Brotherhood and worshipped daily as the founders of My matriarchal tradition on Atlantis."*

"And Neptune...was he considered one of the Twins?"

The Goddess: *"Neptune was My First Son, so he was both Father and Son. He was worshipped as one of the twin boys, but also as their union. In this role he was worshipped as a dragon, a serpent or a solitary forever-young boy. He was also worshipped as a strong male astride a dragon or dolphin while riding upon the cosmic sea, thus revealing his true home."*

"Was there a school of the Kaberoi Brotherhood on Atlantis similar to the school of the Kumaras on Lemuria?"

The Goddess: *"Yes. There were many schools of the Kaberoi on Atlantis and they taught a curriculum of matriarchal wisdom similar to that which was promulgated on Lemuria. Both My mundane and sacred arts were inculcated there. But 'mundane' was not a word used by My Atlantean children to describe My arts because they were all sacred to them. All My arts had been brought to Earth by My heroic Sons from Venus. My Twins were worshipped as heroes."*

"I assume the secrets of Kundalini were taught in the Atlantean schools..."

The Goddess: *"Of course. An understanding of the Kundalini has always been an essential part of the spiritual training within My matriarchal tradition no matter where it has taken root. Atlantis was no exception. The goal of My school on Atlantis was to become a perfected manifestation of My First Son by being consumed in the transformative fire of the Kundalini. He or she would then be known as a 'Kaberoi Dragon,' an immortal Son or Daughter of God."*

"So essentially the Atlanteans strove to become one with Neptune, Your First Son, in the same way that the Lemurians strove to become one with Sanat Kumara. Is this right?"

**The Goddess:**"*Yes. The Atlanteans' goal was to merge into the cosmic sea, unite with Neptune, and become an immortal Kaberoi.*"

"And if Neptune was Sanat, he must have been recognized by the Atlantean sages to be the androgenous serpent power."

**The Goddess:** "*Yes. The Atlanteans recognized the Kundalini to be a manifestation of the Primal Dragon, which they knew as Neptune. They called the Kaberoi Twins 'Twin Flames,' and their father, Neptune, the androgenous Kundalini fire. The knew that the Twin flames moved through the two subtle energy vessels which spiral around the spine, the Ida and Pingala Nadis, and Neptune moved within the central vessel which runs up the center of the spine, the Sushumna Nadi.*"

"Apparently Kaberoi means fire. I have heard that one meaning of the name is 'powerful through fire.'"

**The Goddess:** "*Yes. This name denotes both the inner Kundalini, as well as those initiates who successfully advanced through the Atlantean school of the Kaberoi and became powerful through its fire.*"

"I have heard that on Atlantis magic, especially black magic, was practiced. Did the black magical powers of the Atlanteans accrue from the awakening of the Kundalini?"

**The Goddess:** "*Yes. Unfortunately during the patriarchal period on Atlantis some sorcerers awakened the serpent power in order to control and dominate others through its supernatural power. Remember the golden apples stolen from the serpent Lawton by Hercules? They represent the secrets of the Kundalini stolen by these sorcerers from My pure Atlantean devotees.*"

"Was there a dark brotherhood of sorcerers on Atlantis?"

**The Goddess:** "*Yes, the Sons of Lucifer.[7] Their symbol was a dark, wing-less dragon, which represented the lower, unevolved qualities of egoism and control. The wing-less dragon represented the unfolding Kundalini serpent which these sorcerers were not able to move to the crown of the head and unite with Spirit, thereby giving it 'wings.' The Sons of Lucifer kept the power* *below the head in order to control it with their egos.*

      *"By contrast, the emblem of the Solar Brotherhood on Atlantis was a blue, golden or winged dragon. This symbol represented the female power or serpent which had acquired wings or a heavenly hue by rising to the head and uniting with Spirit. As opposed to their dark brothers, the masters of the Solar Brotherhood were guided by the will of Spirit in the way they used their Kundalini power."*

      "Were those who used the power in a positive way on Atlantis related to the legendary Thoth-Hermes lineage?"

The Goddess: *"Yes. The name Thoth-Hermes was a lineage of masters within the Kaberoi Brotherhood. Like the name Kaberoi, the title denoted a person who had become an enlightened vehicle of the Divine Mind and the possessor of My three powers.[8]"*

      "If Thoth-Hermes denoted masters of the Kaberoi Brotherhood, then I would assume that the symbol of the caduceus must have originated within the Solar Brotherhood also..."

The Goddess: *"Yes. The symbol of the caduceus has existed within the Solar Brotherhood since the creation of the humanoid species within the constellation of Lyra. It was brought to Earth by many extraterrestrial missionaries, especially the Venusian Kumaras and the Sirians."*

      "Are You saying that the Thoth-Hermes of legend was descended from extraterrestrials?"

The Goddess: *"Yes. Thoth-Hermes emerged from the Kaberoi Brotherhood which had its origins with the Kumaras from Venus and the alchemical adepts from Sirius."*

      "It sounds as though Thoth-Hermes must be another name for your First Son."

The Goddess: *"You are right. Thoth-Hermes is My First Son and another name for Sanat Kumara. Those masters who became a Thoth-Hermes united their consciousness with Sanat Kumara and became the vehicle of My First*

76

*Son. They then became the androgenous father of the Twins, and this truth was represented by their symbol, the caduceus, which symbolizes the union of the Twins as dual serpents.*

*"The link between Sanat-Lucifer and Thoth-Hermes was known on Atlantis and later revealed in the sacred texts of the Middle East and Egypt. In the Egyptian scriptures, for example, you will find that one of the names of Thoth-Hermes was Set, and Set or Satan was an alternate name for Sanat-Lucifer."*

"Was Thoth-Hermes called Set, the Egyptian god of destruction, because he was associated with the process of transformation in Egypt?"

The Goddess: *"Yes. And also because some Kaberoi Masters of the Thoth-Hermes lineage were descended from the Sirians, whose symbol was Set."*

"So the Atlantean alchemy which we ascribe to Thoth-Hermes was a mixture of that brought from Venus and Sirius?"

The Goddess: *"Right. On Atlantis, this wisdom was synthesized and inscribed upon the Emerald Tablet of Thoth-Hermes, a tablet of solid emerald which outlined the process of alchemy in thirteen successive precepts."*

"The number thirteen and the color green seems to associate it the Atlantean alchemical wisdom more with Venus than Sirius."

The Goddess: *"It affiliates Atlantean alchemy with both Venus and Sirius because they are both celestial heart chakras, meeting points of the polarity. Sirius is the Higher Self of Venus."*

"Doesn't Sirius's association to alchemy partly stem from the fact that it is a three star group?"

The Goddess: *"Yes. Two of the stars represent the polarity, and the third one represents their union."*

"Were the Venusians or Sirians instrumental in the building of the Great Pyramid of Egypt, which today is considered to be a temple of spiritual alchemy?"

**The Goddess:** *"The Venusians and Sirians assisted the Kaberoi in its construction, just as they had assisted the Solar Brotherhood in building pyramids for alchemical purposes on Atlantis. The shape of the triangles comprising the four sides of the pyramid is the special symbol of Syrian alchemy. Its three corners denote the three stars in the Sirian group.*

*"Pyramids are embodiments of the Primal Dragon and My First Son, and they were made by the Sirians and Venusians to produce his wisdom and power. Interiorly, they unite the polarity and produce My Son as the Kundalini fire.*[9] *Those who enter them are engulfed by the presence of My First Son and eventually become transformed into him.*

*"Thoth-Hermes is a manifestation of the Kundalini and My First Son. This is why he is intimately associated with the Great Pyramid. More than having simply built the Great Pyramid, Thoth-Hermes is the Pyramid."*

"Would You say that both the Sirians and Venusians were especially bonded with the Atlanteans?"

**The Goddess:** *"Yes, especially the Sirians. The Sirian-Atlantean connection is allegorically represented by the depictions of Neptune swimming with dolphins, the loving mammals which migrated from Sirius. Just by their presence, the dolphins will teach you that the goal of alchemy and human evolution is love."*

"Speaking of the Sirian-Atlantean bond, one legend claims that a king of Atlantis received the gift of a heart shaped rock from the Sirians. Supposedly they had brought it from their home[10]..."

**The Goddess:** *"Yes. The stone represented the star Sirius, which is the heart chakra of the galaxy. It also signified that the goal of Sirian alchemy is the opening of the heart."*

## THE VENUS CULTURE IN EGYPT

"According to legend, Atlantean alchemy was brought to Egypt by Thoth-Hermes..."

**The Goddess:** *"Yes. Some adepts of the Thoth-Hermes lineage brought its secrets to North Africa where it became an important branch of Egyptian sacred science. It was an esteemed spiritual art during the early dynasties* *when Set was honored as the greatest of gods. Set is the patron of Sirian alchemy."*

"The Egyptians referred to Sirius as Au Set. Is this because they knew that alchemy came from Sirius?"

**The Goddess:** *"Yes. The Egyptians considered Sirius to be the special home of transformative alchemy."*

"Sirius is called the 'Dog Star' and is located in the constellation of the dog. What, if anything, did the dog have to do with Egyptian alchemy?"

**The Goddess:** *"In Egypt, the symbol of Sirius, the jackal-dog Anubis, represented the power or energy which devours the flesh of deceased humans and then transforms it into subtle life force suitable for existence within the Dwat or next dimension. Anubis is also the power of alchemy which transforms the flesh of a living man into an immortal sheath. This is why Anubis became a patron of Egyptian alchemy."*

"If Anubis is the alchemical transformer, then he must be the Kundalini..."

**The Goddess:** *"Yes. Both Set and Anubis were symbols of the Kundalini in Egypt, and both personified My power of destruction and transformation. In the earliest dynasties the two gods were united as one deity. Seth's strange head is a version of Anubis's."*

According to the Egyptian tradition, Anubis led the deceased into the Duat or next world. Did he lead them by transforming their bodies and preparing them for the next world?"

**The Goddess:** *"Yes. But he also 'led' them in the form of directives received from the Higher Self. As a manifestation of My First Son, Anubis was also the consciousness and wisdom of the Higher Self which is every person's angelic guide into the next world."*

"Is Anubis another form Sanat Kumara?"

**The Goddess:** "*Yes, which makes him a form of Thoth-Hermes as well. The later Greeks transferred the functions of Anubis to their Thoth-Hermes Psychopomps, the guide to the underworld.*"

"Was Egypt as bonded to Sirius as the Atlanteans were?"

**The Goddess:** "*Yes. In fact, Egypt's original name, Khem, was the Egyptians' name for a dark dragon-goat which served as a symbol for both the Kundalini and Sirian alchemy. The later name of 'Egypt' was a variation on the name Ptah-Volcan,*[11] *which was one of the forms of Khem in Egypt.*"

"I recall that Ptah was worshipped as the father of the Kaberoi Twins in his city of Memphis, Egypt. Was he synonymous with Neptune-Sanat, the father of the Kaberoi on Atlantis?"

**The Goddess:** "*Yes. Neptune became Ptah once he reached Egypt. Ptah's images, the Primal Dragon and forever-young boy, had been Neptune's images on Atlantis.*"

"If Ptah is the fiery Kundalini, what then is his consort, the explosive Sekhmet?"

**The Goddess:** "*Although Ptah, the Kundalini, wielded My three powers, in Memphis he became primarily associated with the power of creation while his destructive power became the property of his consort, Sekhmet. It was the power of Sekhmet which the priests of Memphis primarily invoked for spiritual transformation and Kundalini awakening.*"

"If Ptah is the father of the Twin Kaberoi, why then did the Carthaginain historian, Sanconiathon,[12] claim that they were the 'Sons of Sydyk?' Was Sydyk Ptah?"

**The Goddess:** "*Yes. Sydyk was a name for Ptah. It is an abbreviation for Melchizedek.*"

"What is the meaning of Melchizedek?"

**The Goddess:** "*The Melchizedeks are angelic beings who supervise different* *branches of the Great White Brotherhood in your galaxy. Neptune-Sanat or Ptah performs the function of the planetary Melchizedek by overseeing the Great White Brotherhood on Earth."*

"If Memphis was the city of Ptah, the Kundalini, why wasn't the Great Pyramid built there? It seems to me that the transformational powers must have been strongest there."

The Goddess:*"There was already a natural pyramid in Memphis. The city was built on a pyramidal mound which was henceforth honored as a form of Ptah. The vortexual plateau of Giza was chosen as the site of the Great Pyramid because it was in the exact center of the geological land mass of the Earth. It sat in the exact center of the four directions and was, therefore, the ideal place for uniting the polarity and awakening the fire serpent."*

"Was Giza chosen as the capital of the Solar Brotherhood?"

The Goddess: *"It was chosen to be its <u>western</u> capital. It performed this role in conjunction with the city of An or Heliopolis, which was built across the Nile River from Giza. Heliopolis, the 'City of the Sun,' was the principal headquarters and training college for the Egyptian priests of the Solar Brotherhood."*

"I have heard that Giza-Heliopolis was where the alchemical wisdom from Atlantis was stored and taught..."

The Goddess: *"Yes. Underground vaults were carved into the bedrock for the preservation of the Emerald Tablet and other important alchemical works of Thoth-Hermes and the Kaberoi masters. The school of the priesthood was then built over the underground cavities."*

"Did the priests have to go through a trial period before these ancient alchemical works were revealed?"

The Goddess: *"Yes. A superficial explanation of the texts was given to new or intermediate priests and priestesses. Only when they had passed certain tests and deemed worthy were they allowed entrance into the subterranean rooms. Later, after they had studied the texts in-depth, some candidates were taken*

81

*down a passageway leading into the Great Pyramid. There they gained full initiation into the Solar Brotherhood and became priests and priestesses of Osiris."*

"Who was the head of the Solar Brotherhood in Egypt?"

The Goddess: *"As you can probably guess, it was the Pharaoh. He was a manifestation of My First Son in Egypt. As such, he was both Father and Son of the Twins which is why one of his royal titles was 'The Twins.' He was the androgenous Spirit, or Ra, incarnate in a material form."*

"I thought the Pharaoh was an incarnation of Horus?"

The Goddess: *"Horus was an aspect of Ra. The infinite Spirit, Ra, divided to become the polarity, Horus and Seth, Spirit and matter. The Pharaoh's material body was a manifestation of material Seth, and his incarnated Spirit was Horus."*

"Was Horus, then, synonymous with Sanat-Sananda and his brother Seth with Sanat-Lucifer?"

The Goddess: *"Yes, Horus and Seth were one version of My Kumara Twins in Egypt. And in the tradition of the Atlantean Kaberoi, the Egyptians taught that they were born from Me, the planet Venus. One of Venus's early icons in Egypt was a deity with the heads of both Horus and Seth."*

"Did the Egyptians inherit the knowledge of the Twins' Venusian origins from the Atlanteans?"

The Goddess: *"Yes. One Atlantean legend which was brought to Egypt via the Bull Cult asserted that Horus had been born from the horned, cow goddess Hathor. Hathor was the Egyptian Venus."*

"If the Egyptians regarded the Pharaoh as Your First Son, did they maintain that he came from Venus?"

The Goddess: *"They maintained that his soul, Horus, had originated from Venus. The Pharaoh's Ank symbolized his affiliation to a lineage of priest kings which had originated with Sanat Kumara from Venus."*

"So the Pharaoh was a manifestation of Sanat Kumara in Egypt?"

The Goddess: *"Yes, the Pharaoh was a manifestation of My First Son in Egypt. The archetypal Pharaoh was Osiris, who was an embodiment of the Horned God, the god of nature, and the union of the Twins. When he died, Osiris merged with the planet Venus.*

*"Ptah, the father of the Twins, was synonymous with Osiris. In Memphis, Ptah and Osiris were united as My First Son, the forever young boy Ptah-Seker-Osiris."*

"Ptah and Osiris were also united as the Apis Bull of Memphis, weren't they?"

The Goddess: *"Yes. They united as the Apis Bull because they were the two neters[13] of the Kundalini or life force, and the bull was worshipped as the living embodiment of the life force."*

"If Apis was Ptah, did the Bull Cult in Egypt come from Atlantis like Ptah did?"

The Goddess: *"Yes. The Memphis Bull Cult arrived in Egypt from Atlantis where it had been presided over by kings wearing the Venus crown of bull horns. These dragon kings of Atlantis were full of life force and were thus considered to be 'bulls' themselves."*

## THE WORLDWIDE VENUS BULL CULT

"History maintains that the Bull Cult eventually spread all across Asia. Did Atlantean missionaries spread it throughout the continent?"

The Goddess: *"Yes. After establishing the Bull Cult in Egypt, Atlantean missionaries and their descendants moved eastward and spread the cult across Asia. The ancient Egyptian legend which alludes to their journey states that Ptah-Osiris climbed on the back of a bull and traveled throughout the world spreading the rites of the Bull Cult. These included how to make wine and the sacred rites of its consumption. The consumption of Bull meat and wine was the 'Holy Communion' of the Bull Cult. They were symbolic of the flesh and blood of My First Son, the Horned God."*

"I have heard that many Asian countries adopted the myth of the Goddess and Her bull Son consort."

The Goddess: *"Yes. Many Asian countries embraced My Bull Cult. In Sumeria and Babylonia, for example, the priest kings became esteemed incarnations of Dammuzi or Tammuz, the nature-bull god and Son of Venus. Even the temples of the Mesopotamian Elamites had huge horns attached to them, symbolizing that such structures were the living manifestations of My Bull Son."*

"I remember that the Mesopotamian bards, the Kalu priests, played a stringed instrument in ceremony which was shaped like a bull and sounded like a bull bellowing. Did this instrument originate on Atlantis?"

The Goddess: *"Yes. For thousands of years the sound of the bull was recognized on Atlantis as one of the purist of all sounds. It was a version of AUM, the sound of creation. And any instrument which could reproduce it possessed magical properties."*

"Did Ptah's missionaries take the Bull Cult to the Americas? The legend of Quetzlcoatl is very similar to Osiris's and both figures are associated with the life force."

The Goddess: *"Yes. Neptune-Ptah's missionaries brought the Bull Cult from Atlantis and established the lineage of the Quetzlcoatls or Sons of God in Middle America. Their first colony was Tamoanchan, the 'Place where the People of the Serpent Landed.'*
*"Quetzlcoatl was synonymous with Osiris. They were both personifications of the Kundalini; both had bull associations; and they both had the same symbol, the cross, which is the symbol of the Kundalini life force. Quetzlcoatl's cross was the Tau, and Tau is the root of Taurus, the Zodiacal name of the bull."*

"So the cross and the bull are obviously related..."

The Goddess: *"Yes, they are. The cross, bull and serpent are all interrelated.*

*Each represents the union of the polarity and the life force which is born from that union. And since they denote the same thing, sometimes you can find two or more of them existing together, such as the ubiquitous symbol of the serpent dangling from the shafts of a cross. Foliage is often added to this symbol to create the classical Serpent on the Tree motif."*

"So why does one often find enmity between the bull and snake in mythology?"

**The Goddess:** *"Because the bull represents the creative power of the life force and the snake symbolizes its destructive power. The bull represents the life force when it is above the ground, such as during the spring and summer months when vegetation is flourishing, and the serpent represents its manifestation after going underground and becoming dormant during the fall and winter seasons when vegetation recedes and dies.*

*"During the matriarchal era the bull and serpent were brothers, they were two equally important and necessary powers of the life force. But under the later Patriarchy the snake acquired evil associations because it represented My destructive power, so a split between the bull and serpent became inevitable. Eventually they became disconnected and in continual war with each other.*

*"In time the Patriarchy associated the bull with the creative life force emanating from the Sun and gave him a kingdom in the sky. Meanwhile, his former brother, the serpent, became associated with the darkness and death of the underworld and became its evil lord."*

"I think it's a bit amusing that the patriarchal theologians chose the bull to be the lord of Heaven and later made a complete about face by assigning the features of the bull to their Devil."

**The Goddess:** *"Eventually the Patriarchy decided it was unseemly and sacrilegious for their high god to possess animalistic features. After all, they were the features of the pagan gods they sought to discredit. But the Patriarchy did not abandon their heavenly bull god completely. They simply transferred many of his symbols and rites to a humanized Son of God."*

"Such as the cross?"

**The Goddess:** "*Yes, and the dove. The dove had become a symbol of the heavenly bull because the Seven Doves, the Pleiades, had anciently been placed within the Zodiacal sign of the bull, Taurus. The dove is also My symbol, and it affiliates My First Son with Me.*

"*The ancient Bull Cult rite of Holy Communion was passed on to the cult of the Son of God, albeit with some slight modifications. Instead of bull meat, for example, wafers were ritually consumed as the body of the Son.*"

## THE HEBREW VENUS CULTURE

"So the cult of Jesus Christ, the Son of God, really dates back to the Atlantean Bull Cult?"

**The Goddess:** "*Yes, and beyond. The symbols associated with Jesus, such as the dove, the cross, the number 13, as well as the virgin birth and the planet Venus are all very ancient associations ascribed to My First Son. My Son had always been ascribed a virgin birth, otherwise he would not have been considered the true Son of Spirit.*"

"Was Jesus associated with Venus?"

**The Goddess:** "*Yes. Remember in the Book of Revelation Jesus Christ proclaims: 'I am the bright and Morning Star.' Moreover, you will find that his early symbol is closely related to the Egyptian hieroglyph for Venus. And guess what? Like all My Sons, Jesus was a Twin.*"

*The Egyptian hieroglyph for Venus and the early Christian symbol for Jesus*

"You must be referring to the popular notion which maintains that Jesus had a twin brother named Thomas."[14]

**The Goddess:** "*Yes. They weren't necessarily born at the same time, but Thomas was Jesus's Twin Flame. Jesus was an incarnation of Sananda Kumara and Thomas was a ray of his twin brother, Sanat. The goal of the* *order which incarnated them, the Essenes,[15] was to manifest both of the Twins on the Earth plane at the same time. This was necessary for the work they had agreed to perform, that of preparing the way for the coming Fifth World of Venus and the revival of My spiritual tradition. This task required both Twins to be in physical incarnation at once."*

"Was the Essene organization a branch of your Venus Culture?"

The Goddess: *"Yes. And consistent with the other branches of My Venus Culture they held the planet Venus in very high regard,[16] honoring it as the heavenly guru and home of the Twins. The legend of the Venusian Twins was also an important component of Essene theology. The Essenes knew My Twins as the forever-young Kaberoi boys, the worship of which they had inherited from the Phoenicians and Egyptians, and the Atlanteans before them. Effigies of the Kaberoi were placed within the Holy of Hollies as the Twin Cherubs who guarded the Ark of the Covenant."*

"Madame Blavatsky maintained that the Hebrews worshipped the Kaberoi in Hebron. I think she also claimed that the Hebrews nicknamed the place the 'City of the Kaberoi."

The Goddess: *"This is true. Hebron was a center of My Venus Culture. The priests of Hebron, the Levites, were serpent worshippers[17] who possessed the wisdom of the Kaberoi and passed it on to the Nazaria or Nassaria, the branch of Essenes which Jesus and James incarnated into. The term Nassaria has the meaning of 'Serpents."*

"Obviously the worship of the Serpent aligns the Levites and Nassaria with You. Were they also affiliated with the Solar Brotherhood?"

The Goddess: *"Yes, of course. The Solar or Great White Brotherhood is the vehicle of My spiritual tradition. Moses brought the rites and wisdom of the Solar Brotherhood to Palestine from Egypt, which is why the Levites and Essenes became worshippers of the transcendental Sun. Moses also brought with him the secret alchemical wisdom of how to unite with the hidden Sun. The knowledge was contained within the writings of Thoth-Hermes, whom the Levites and Essenes came to know as their ancestor Enoch, and eventually compiled into 'The Books of Enoch,' special arcane texts of the Kabbala, the*

*'Secret Wisdom' of the Hebrews."*

"The Books of Enoch you mention... I am aware of only one such book."

The Goddess: *"There were more than one. There were books for each successive level of alchemy. Remember the different Lions of alchemy?"*

"You mean the White, Green, Brown, and Red Lions,[18] each of which is an elixir of immortality with a stronger degree of intensity than its predecessor? I was making and consuming the White Lion for awhile."

The Goddess: *"Right. Well, The Books of Enoch explained how to produce the Lions, as well as how to prepare the body for their consumption. Fasting, for example, was an essential practice for preparing the body."*

"Wasn't the location of the Essene settlement on the Dead Sea chosen because it could support the preparation of the elixir?"

The Goddess: *"Yes. The salt of the Dead Sea was a vital ingredient of their elixir. But the area was also attractive because its energy was very pure from being continuously cleansed by the absorbing power of the salt and the sweeping sea breezes. When working to expand and cleanse the etheric body, a pure environment is essential."*

"I suppose the Essenes' knowledge of the Twins was also helpful in their alchemy."

The Goddess: *"Of course. The knowledge of the Twins is fundamental to alchemy. The process of alchemy consists of uniting the polarity, the Twins, and awakening the Kundalini or fire serpent, which is the Father of the Twins. Essene alchemy consisted of uniting the Twins to become the Kundalini fire, which they knew as Jehovah or Cain, the fiery 'Smith' god. Jehovah was both Cain, one of the Twins, as well as the Father of the Twins.*
*"The elixir made by Essene Alchemy was recognized to be a manifestation of the union of the Twins. It was a synthesized version of seminal fluid which, after entering the body, became transmuted into Kundalini."*

88

"I have heard that one practice of the Essenes was to unite with their guardian angels. Was this practice supported by the consumption of the elixir?"

**The Goddess:** *"Yes. The elixir helped prepare the body of an Essene for union with his or her guardian angel, which was recognized to be a manifestation of one's Higher Self. Each Essene experienced his or her angel to be a cherub, a twin boys and/or a dragon, just as the ancient Atlantean Kaberoi had. Their cherubs were manifestations of My First Son, Sanat Kumara, the archetypal angel."*

"The connection of Jehovah or Cain to the Kundalini is implied within the literature of the Kabbala. What other alchemical secrets did the Kabbala supply the Essenes?"

**The Goddess:** *"The Kabbala also provided them with diagrams and cryptic recipes related to alchemy. The Sephirothic Tree of the Kabbala, for example, is a geometric diagram of the spine and the path of the Kundalini. An understanding of this 'Tree' leads to awakening of the inner serpent fire and its ascension."*

"So, I guess that both the Tree in the Garden of Eden, as well as the Sephirothic Tree, provided the Essenes with information regarding the Kundalini?"

**The Goddess:** *"Yes. The Tree of the Sephiroth is collectively represented as the two Trees in the Garden of Eden of the Holy Bible. The serpent on the Tree of the Wisdom of Good and Evil and the cherub at the base of Tree of Immortal Life are both representations of the Kundalini. The sword wielding cherub is the first and greatest of the cherubs, Sanat Kumara, whose power of protection and preservation was recognized among the Essenes as the sword wielding Angel Michael."*

"Are You saying that Michael represented the Kundalini's power of preservation among the Essenes?"

**The Goddess:** *"Yes. Michael and Sanat have many similarities. In their respective traditions, the Hindu and Jewish, they were both honored as the Commander of the Army of the Heavenly Host, the army of God. They were* *also both recognized as the rulers of the Blue Ray."*

"I remember that Michael was a commander, but I don't remember that about Sanat."

**The Goddess:** *"You will find the association you seek in Hindu mythology wherein Sanat Kumara is Kartikeya, the Commander of the armies of his father, Shiva, the Spirit."*

"Right...okay, now I remember. Did the Essenes also acquire knowledge of the Kaberoi and Sanat Kumara from the Phoenicians? I know that the band of builders that Solomon hired from Tyre were part of a worldwide brotherhood."

**The Goddess:** *"Yes. The Phoenicians who helped construct Solomon's Temple were part of a worldwide mystical brotherhood of builders,[19] some of whom even studied in India. From this brotherhood, the Phoenicians inherited alchemical secrets dating back to the time of the Motherlands. They also received alchemical wisdom from a group of settlers who came directly from Atlantis, known as 'those of the Kaberoi.'[20] These Atlanteans arrived in the Middle East on ships with an image of the greatest Kaberoi or cherub, Ptah or Sanat Kumara, attached to their prows. The ancient wisdom they brought, which included the worship of Sanat Kumara and the Kaberoi Twins, became the foundation stone of Phoenician alchemy and was eventually passed to the Essenes."*

"Did the Phoenician builders also become Kundalini adepts?"

**The Goddess:** *"Yes. They developed profound Kundalini powers and wisdom. Their divine powers, such as the power of levitation, were used in moving the massive blocks used in the construction of their temples, while their divine wisdom assisted them in making their splendid temples living manifestations of My First Son, Jehovah or Sanat. Their greatest temples, such as Solomon's Temple, thus became very efficient Kundalini generators. Solomon's Temple was made to be the embodiment of Jehovah, and its design incorporated the geometrical spiral, the form of the Kundalini, into its dimensions. As planned, the structure powerfully united the polarity and produced an abundance of transformational fire, especially within the inner sanctum wherein the Holy of*

*Hollies, the Ark of the Covenant, was placed. The Ark itself united the polarity and generated Kundalini by virtue of it being constructed out of a balanced combination of yin wood and yang metal. The two cherubs which gracefully spread their wings over the Ark were images of the Kaberoi Twins. They represented the polarity which is united as the Ark's indwelling spirit of Jehovah."*

"Speaking of the Twins, if Jesus and Thomas were indeed manifestations of them, then their incarnation together must have precipitated a Kundalini-like reaction on the planet..."

The Goddess: *"Yes. Their combined energies had the effect of activating the Kundalini energies of Earth and transforming the Age of Aries into the Age of Pisces."*

## THE VENUS CULTURE OF INDIA

"It's certainly interesting that historically both Jesus and Thomas are intimately associated with India. Supposedly they both went to India and spent quite a bit of time there."

The Goddess: *"Both of them had karmic ties to the people of India. Many Lemurians had reincarnated there, and the ancient school of the Kumaras had survived for many thousands of years on the sub-continent. One of the brothers' goals was to peacefully overthrow the patriarchal caste system which had dominated the Matriarchy in India for many years."*

"Did they gain assistance from the vestiges of the ancient matriarchal Lemurians living in India at the time?"

The Goddess: *"Yes. They allied themselves with the Nagas, Danavas, and other Goddess worshipping tribes. They were also allied with the Goddess worshipping Buddhists, and provided inspired guidance for the compilation of certain Tantric texts of Mahayana Buddhism."*

"I suppose at the time they arrived in India the members of Your tradition had become the 'down trodden' of India."

The Goddess: *"Yes. The Patriarchy had taken over the upper castes and even tried to disparage the memory of the Matriarchy by re-writing history and referring to the ancient matriarchal sages as evil demons."*

"Do You mean the 'evil' Danavas and Asuras?"

**The Goddess:** *"Yes. The Patriarchy denigrated the Danavas and Asuras by referring to them as the evil 'Fallen Angels.' In truth, they were My emissaries who had accompanied Sanat-Azzazel from Venus and taught alchemy and My other sacred arts to their brothers and sisters on Earth."*

"In the Hindu records it says that the leader of the Asuras was Shukra, which is a name for Venus. This seems to prove conclusively that the Asuras were indeed from Venus."

**The Goddess:** *"Shukra is a name for both Venus and My First Son, Sanat-Azzazel. It is also the name for seminal fluid or essence which nourishes the body and eventually transmutes into the upward moving Kundalini."*

"I suppose one reason that the Matriarchy has been denigrated so often by the Patriarchy is because its leader is intimately associated with the sexual organs and fluids."

**The Goddess:** *"This is true. Sanat or Shukra is the deity of both seminal fluid and what it transmutes into, Kundalini. My First Son is the teacher of both the 'downward' path of generation, as well as the 'upward' path of regeneration or transmutation."*

"There is a legend I am familiar with which claims that Shukra brought the wisdom of Raja Yoga to Earth. That is certainly a path of transformation."

**The Goddess:** *"Shukra brought the wisdom of how to transmute the seminal fluid into Kundalini and raise it up the spine, thereby giving rise to advanced degrees of meditational awareness. This is Raja Yoga. Shukra or Sanat Kumara is ascribed the authorship of most yogas, because he was the Adi or first Guru of Yoga on Earth."*

"Didn't some of the yogic rites in India come from Atlantis via the Bull Cult?"

The Goddess: "*Yes. One of the Bull Cult rites which became part of Tantricism was the Holy Communion of wine and animal flesh. During the Holy Communion of a Tantric sect participants would partake of meat, wine, grain, fish and intercourse—the five 'forbidden things'—in order to unite with My essence.*"

"Was the Tantric partaking of sacraments, such as ganga, also from Your early tradition?"

The Goddess: "*Yes. You will find many sacraments, including the legendary Soma, associated with My tradition. In the Vedas, you will find them consumed by the Lunar Race, which was a lineage composed of members of My tradition. Lord Krishna, who became a mouthpiece of the Matriarchy and helped establish many rites of the Goddess tradition, was a member of the Lunar Race.*"

"What exactly was the Soma? There is a lot of speculation regarding it."

The Goddess: "*The Soma was made from a mushroom combined with certain synergizing substances. During its production, a strict manufacturing process was involved during specific phases of the moon—because the female orb rules both mushrooms and the Soma. The Soma production began during the light of the new moon, and was completed during the radiance of the full moon. You might have heard that the Hindus refer to moonbeams as 'soma.' Well, the Soma beverage was equivalent to liquid moonbeams. And its consumption made the body a conductor and accumulator of the moon's rays.*"

"Did it have any effect on the Kundalini?"

The Goddess: "*Yes. Like the elixir of the Essenes, Soma was essentially a synthesized version of seminal fluid. When taken internally it would built up one's inner store of seminal fluid and assist in its transmutation into the fiery Kundalini. Because it was 'condensed' life force or Kundalini, the Hindu alchemists referred to Soma as the liquid Essence of the Kumara. They believed that it not only bestowed longevity, but had the power of transforming an alchemist or yogi into a Son of God, a Kumara. Through its upward movement as the transformative Kundalini, the Soma would awaken the dormant parts of the brain and ultimately unite one with the consciousness of*

*My Son."*

"That makes a lot of sense. I once read a book by Dr. Andrew Wilde which stated that mushrooms can effect the seminal fluid directly. Apparently there are even mushrooms which are called names which mean 'seminal fluid."

The Goddess: *"This is true. Mushrooms build up the seminal fluid, which is why they are herbs of immunity and immortality in China. When the seminal fluid is abundant, immunity and the entire body is strong because the seminal fluid transforms into chi or life force. When the seminal fluid decreases significantly, perhaps because of old age, the body weakens. When it is totally consumed, the body dies."*

## THE VENUS CULTURE IN PERU

"Peru is another place where a sacramental culture has existed for aeons. I am just now learning about it through training with a San Pedro[21] shaman."

The Goddess: *"Yes. My missionaries from Lemuria played a critical role in the cult of San Pedro and the civilization it emerged from, Chavin."*

"Did the dragon become the principal deity of Chavin because it was seen by the shamen on San Pedro, or was it because the shamen there possessed a knowledge of the life force or Kundalini?"

The Goddess: *"Both. The dragon which was envisioned on San Pedro <u>was</u> the Kundalini. When it appeared it taught the shamen about itself, including how to move it through the body and up the spine."*

"So, could it be said that Kundalini inhabits the San Pedro?"

The Goddess: *"Yes. The San Pedro cactus reacts like certain kinds of mushrooms within the body. It both builds up the seminal fluid and assists its transmutation into Kundalini."*

"Was the San Pedro cactus also part of Your Venus Culture?"

The Goddess: *"Yes. The first San Pedro shamen in Peru learned their art from the Lemurian missionaries of My Venus Culture."*

"Were these Lemurian missionaries related to Sanat Kumara? I have heard numerous legends regarding Sanat's influence in Peru. Some people believed he visited there in the past."

The Goddess: *"These Lemurian missionaries had studied in the schools founded by Sanat Kumara on Lemuria. There they learned to regard both Me, the Goddess, as well as My First Son, Sanat Kumara, as the Divine Mind of God. Under their instructive influence, Venus eventually became known in Peru as Qollar, meaning Divine Teacher."*

"Did they bring the Solar Brotherhood to the Andes?"

The Goddess: *"Yes. The missionary whom you are most familiar with that brought the seeds of the Solar Brotherhood to the Andes is Aramu Muru. Lord Meru and his Lemurian helpers, the Kapac Kuna,[22] erected temples throughout the Andes, and then placed within one of them the sacred Solar Disc, a power object which had been brought from Venus by the Kumaras before being installed within an important temple of the Solar Brotherhood on Mu."*

"Was Aramu Muru also a manifestation of Your First Son? I have always found the repetition of his name instrumental in activating the inner Kundalini."

The Goddess: *"Yes. Aramu Muru had merged his consciousness with the Infinite Sun and become a manifestation of My First Son, as well as an embodiment of the Kundalini. He was a product of the ancient order of the Cyclopeans, an elite branch of Kundalini masters within the Solar Brotherhood on Mu. The Cyclopeans were also known as the Merus and the Amarus, or fire serpents. Their highest rank, 'Amaru,' incorporates the syllable 'mar,' a universal name for fire. Both mar and its reverse, 'ram,' are the universal seed syllables for transformative fire."*

"I would assume that Lord Meru brought the wisdom of the Kundalini with him to Peru."

The Goddess: *"Yes. He and other initiated Cyclopeans brought the secret wisdom of Kundalini to Peru. Some of the Cyclopeans who came to the Andes were very large, and they could easily lift the blocks used in the construction of the megalithic temples with their physical prowess alone. But they also used their Kundalini powers when needed. Many of the temples they built, including Machu Picchu and Sacsayhuaman, were 'Cyclopean' in design and dedicated to the awakening and moving of the Kundalini."*

"Did they build Tiahuanaco?"

**The Goddess:** *"Yes. Along with the Kumaras."*

"My guide Pepe[23] told me that the Incas once worshipped golden images of a young boy called P'un chou in their temples. He thinks they may have been related to the Kumaras."

**The Goddess:** *"Yes. P'un chou means 'dawn' and refers to the Morning Star. P'un chou was My First Son, Sanat Kumara, and his golden, forever young boy image commemorated Sanat's visitations to the Andes."*

"Did the Incas take some of the Kundalini wisdom of the Kumaras and Cyclopeans with them when they fled the Spanish?"

**The Goddess:** *"Yes. Some of it still exists in Paititi, the lost city of the Incas, while much of it remains permanently transfixed on an energy level within the sacred valley surrounding the Monastery of the Seven Rays. This is why Sister Thedra was sent there by My Son Sananda Kumara."*

"Can sacraments help one access the Kundalini wisdom at the Monastery or within the other temples built by the Kumaras?"

**The Goddess:** *"Yes. If taken properly sacraments will activate and expand one's psychic perception. But the wisdom of the Kumaras can be accessed in any place and by any person with a pure heart."*

## THE GREEK VENUS CULTURE

"Why is it that when I have taken psilocybin mushrooms as sacraments in the past I have ended up communing with demons? My desire was simply to expand my consciousness."

**The Goddess:** *"At those times you experienced the grotesque persona of the Kundalini which resides within the mushrooms. Wasn't the blood dripping from the demons' fangs reminiscent of Kali, the female persona of the Kundalini in India?"*

"Yes, very much so..."

**The Goddess:** *"Well, as I have told you, these sacraments are vehicles of the transformative Kundalini which can manifest as a serpent, a ferocious puma, or a terrifying demon. The demons you met were manifestations of My First Son."*

The Goddess's words had the immediate effect of transporting my mind to a day when the consumption of sacramental mushrooms had precipitated my worst nightmare. On the fateful autumn day, I began by battling to the windswept summit of a five thousand foot peak in the Olympic Mountains. Once on the top of the mountain, I quickly set about drawing pentagrams on the ground while simultaneously consuming the contents of a small pouch of potent psilocybin mushrooms I had brought with me. As part of my ritual I also called out for my friend the "Dragon." My connection with him had been established some months earlier when, after similarly consuming mushrooms on a different mountain in the Olympics, I had been transported into his benevolent presence. I experienced him to be a multi-colored dragon-like figure who possessed profound esoteric wisdom, some of which he proceeded to disclose to me. When we parted company that day, he had hospitably invited me to return to talk with him some time in the future. So here I was.

I called for my dragon friend for about twenty minutes and then my batch of mushrooms suddenly took full effect. Only this time I found myself transported to a dark dimension which was completely different from the one I had met the beneficent dragon in. The sky above, which moments before had been a light grey, was now nearly jet black, and an eerie bone-chilling wind was beginning to howl and swirl around me. Darkness seemed to engulf the mountain from all directions. "Right out of a horror flick," I nervously concluded while glancing around suspiciously for the horrifying images of inimical dragons to make an unwelcome appearance. And to make matters worse, I felt seriously sick. I had consumed far too many mushrooms than my body could digest, and all I could think about was vomiting them out of my system. But each time I tried to retch, nothing happened. Apparently the mushrooms weren't done with me.

Soon a palpable sinister presence began to loom within the surrounding darkness. The belief that I was in the presence of a "Dark Dragon," or what my Christian upbringing had taught me was the "Devil," crept steadily into my consciousness until the hairs on the back of my neck stood straight up. My first instinct was simple survival; I needed to get away from the dark entity. So I stumbled into the center of an outcropping of tall, monolithic rocks and anxiously awaited my fate. As I cowered, my eyes naturally fell upon the smooth vertical face of a rock directly in front of me. In an instant the rock face transformed into a live monitor which broadcast the face of a gruesome demon. His piercing red eyes, the deep cut lines of his darkened, leathery face, and the long fangs dripping with blood at the corners of his sinister smile, communicated to me in no uncertain terms that he was not friendly. In fact, I sensed that he would like nothing better than to tear me to shreds and devour me piece by piece. Soon other demonic faces, hundreds of them, appeared in rapid succession in front of me, each more nauseating than the one before it. These gruesome faces magnified my already desperate emotional state and added force to the volitle mass growing within my intestines.

I decided my only hope was to get away, and fast. Otherwise I feared I might likely reach a state of terror from which there was no return. I tried to run in order to move the mushrooms out of my blood system, but because of the overwhelming malady in my gut I stumbled and fell hard on the ground. With great effort I picked myself up and continued to stagger along. I was determined to escape the clutches of the "Devil."

As I ambled down the mountain in my inebriated state, I quickly became so physically sick that I really thought I was going to die. My inner organs were attempting to throw off the toxins I had unwisely fed them, and this made the temperature of my body soar. Both my heart and mind were racing furiously. The thought of dying sat heavy upon me, but an inner voice informed me that if I died at that moment I would be stuck in the realm of the "Devil" for an eternity. So I kept moving.

When I finally reached the trailhead I heaved a sigh of relief, but then I discovered that my euphoria was premature and my troubles were far from over. The vegetation covering the ground and the trees flanking the path were now accomplices of the "Devil." The groundcover of vines proceeded to nip at my feet as I walked, while the tree branches grabbed at my arms and head like living tentacles of death. I ducked them as best I could and tried to pick up my speed in order to allude them, but in doing so I managed to loose sight of the trail and was soon hopelessly lost. Somehow I managed to remain unfazed by this sad turn of events. Apparently my resolve to beat death had become so unshakable by this time that I was determined to survive even if I had to trailblaze all the way down the mountain.

Finally, after what seemed like countless hours of fighting off the phantom vegetation, I again found the path. The drug had worn off significantly by then and I was returning to my normal third dimension world. With great relief I told myself that I had somehow cheated death and its lord, the "Devil." I had cut short my visit to his dark realm and succeeded in returning to the land of the living.

"Wow," I blurted out after reliving my traumatic episode. "I don't want to have an experience like that again!"

**The Goddess:** "*Your experience was an initiation of sorts and mimicked that of the initiates of the Eleusinian Mystery School of Greece. They were also given a strong sacramental potion like yours, which was made with hallucinogenic mushrooms mixed with various mind-expanding herbs, and then instructed to find their way through a pitch-black, underground maze. The maze simulated the underworld of Pluto or Lucifer, so essentially they were being asked to die and go to Hell for a time. And believe Me, once the drink took full effect, they truly believed they had gone there. They were surrounded by demons for the entire time it took them to migrate through the cold, damp labyrinth.*"

"Yup, that sounds like my experience all right. Well, at least I could see where I was going, for the most part. I think if I was back in Greece I would have preferred the sacramental rites of Dionysus, at least they were out in nature..."

**The Goddess:** "*The moonlit Dionysian rites also summoned the First Son in a demonic or serpentine form, and they were often no less terrifying than the rites of the Eleusinian Mysteries. But the devotees of Dionysus expected to encounter a dark deity because they equated Dionysus with the 'destructive' serpentine life force which dwells underground—or in the underworld. He was said to rule the Earth during the winter months of the year, the time when the powers of destruction are at their peak, and his 'Twin,' Apollo,[24] was said to rule during the summer months. As you can probably see, Dionysus and Apollo were a Greek version of Sanat and Sananda Kumara.*"

" I always suspected that there was something dark about Dionysus, now I understand what it is. He was the lord of the underworld and a manifestation of the destructive Kundalini."

The Goddess: "*Right. On both Crete and Greece Dionysus was associated with the alchemical fire and worshipped as the serpentine Kundalini. This is why he became the patron of the Eluesinian Mysteries and other Greek mystery rites. An image revealing Dionysus—that of a boy holding a torch, symbol of the fiery Kundalini—was often present during these nocturnal rites. This was Dionysus in his form of Iakos, the 'Patron of the Nocturnal Rites.' Iakos is also a name of Sirius.*"

"Does Dionysus's name of Iakos align his cult with the Sirians?"

The Goddess: "*Yes. The rites of Dionysus's cult descended from Egypt and Crete where Sirian alchemy was esteemed and performed.*"

"If Dionysus came to Greece from Egypt along with the Sirian rites, was he originally an evolution of Set, the Egyptian lord of destruction?"

The Goddess: "*Yes. Dionysus was evolved from the fire gods Set and Ptah, and their ancestor, the Atlantean Neptune. In parts of Greece he was known as the 'First and Greatest Kaberoi,' or as the 'Father of the Kaberoi,' just as his predecessors Neptune and Ptah had been.*"

"Now that I think of it...didn't Dionysus also manifest both as a boy and a serpent as Ptah and Neptune had?"

The Goddess: "*Yes. His images were a later version of Ptah's and Neptune's. Dionysus's cult on Crete, which centered around the serpent-boy Zan, was an evolution of the Ptah-Neptune's alchemical cults on Egypt and Atlantis. The Dactyloi priests of Crete, the priests of Zan, were also descended from the priests of those neighboring countries.*"

"So, in some ways the cult of Dionysus was pure Sirian."

The Goddess: "*This is true. In fact extraterrestrial Sirians oversaw the workings of the cult from other dimensions. They were the ascended lords of*

100

*the Bacchuses."*

"Speaking of Bacchuses, I am continually fascinated by the similarities between Dionysus and Shiva and the lunatic behavior which has characterized their respective cults. The Bacchuses and Shiva Yogis had aberrant behavior in common..."

The Goddess: *"The 'do as thou wilt' attitude their cults encouraged is a timeless component of My matriarchal tradition. Sacraments can easily lead to such behavior. But this attitude must be accompanied by egolessness, otherwise it will not only be destructive to the environment, but also to the soul."*

## THE VENUS CULTURE IN BRITAIN

"Britain also had a sacramental cult and a tradition of adepts exhibiting bizarre behavior..."

The Goddess: *"Yes. There were many such cults in Britain, especially among the Druids and Bards. It was common for the Welsh Bards, for example, to consume different combinations of herbs and mushrooms in order to open themselves up to divine knowledge, as well as to ecstatic and unusual behavior. They followed in the footsteps of their ancestors, the Pheryllt,[25] who consumed a hallucinogenic combination called the Cauldron of Keridwen."*

"Weren't the Pheryllt descended from the alchemical colonists from Atlantis?"

The Goddess: *"Yes. The cult of Keridwen was descended from the Atlantean Kaberoi."*

"Was Sirian alchemy part of Keridwen's cult?"

The Goddess: *"Yes. In fact, Goddess Keridwen was a manifestation of the Kundalini, and she shared certain destructive traits with Set, Ptah and Neptune. She rode upon fiery dragons, and her destructive/transformative power was represented by the cauldron she carried as her definitive symbol. The liquid or potion in her cauldron was actually symbolic of the seminal fluid which becomes converted to Kundalini as it is 'cooked.'"*

"So her cauldron actually existed within the human body?"

The Goddess: "*Yes. Her cauldron was the inner seminal fluid and she was the fiery spark which transmuted it into Kundalini.*"

"I assume, then, that the Pheryllts' alchemical potion in the Cauldron of Keridwen must have been considered by them to be a synthetic version of seminal fluid..."

The Goddess: "*Yes. It was a special elixir which transmuted into the Kundalini once it was within the body. The Welsh Bards referred cryptically to the Kundalini as the fire of the 'Inner Cauldron' and sought to release it from its vault, the four cornered castle or root chakra of four petals at the base of the spine. They accomplished this by using a combination of the elixir and controlled breathing patterns.*"

"Lewis Spence referred to the stone circles of England as the 'Temples of Keridwen.' I assume this is because they were 'cauldrons' of transformation."

The Goddess: "*Yes. The Temples of Keridwen were designed like pyramids to unite the polarity and interiorly generate the fiery energy of Keridwen, the Kundalini. Powerful alchemical initiations occurred within these 'cauldrons.' of the countryside.*"

"Avebury is sometimes referred to as the Heart Chakra. Is this because the polarity, represented by its dual rings, merges together there?"

The Goddess: "*All the Temples of Keridwen united the polarity, but Avebury's position in the British grid makes it a heart chakra for that part of the world.*"

"Was the Bull Cult an influence in Britain?"

The Goddess: "*Yes. The Druids' sacrifice of bulls, the consumption of wine and sacraments, as well as their alchemy—these were all aspects of the Bull Cult in Britain. The Druids recognized the bull to be a representation of both My First Son and the life force. They sacrificed it so that its potent life-giving blood could soak the ground, thereby sanctifying and fertilizing it.*
"*Great earthen mounds called Tors—thus linking them to Taurus, the*"

102

*bull—were often the scene of the Druids' bull rites. These Tors were the British pyramids. They were living manifestations of My Bull Son and both moved and generated the life force."*

"If a Tor is similar to a pyramid, this would explain why many temples and chapels can currently be found upon their summits in Britain. The summit is apparently where the energy of the Tor is the strongest."

The Goddess: *"Yes. Just like the apex of a pyramid, an etheric geyser shoots out of the summit of the Tor. It is the place where St. Michael holds the dragon, or life force, in one place so it can be used for ritual. This is why you can find many temples and chapels dedicated to St. Michael on the summits of the British Tors."*

"The Tor at Glastonbury is famous for being an entrance to the underworld kingdom of a fairy king. Is there really an underground inhabitant there?"

The Goddess: *"The fairy king does not exist physically under the Tor, but in a dimension which can be accessed through the inter-dimensional portal created by the Tor. Whenever the pyramidal shape exists, a doorway to other worlds or dimensions is naturally created."*

"The fairy king was supposedly related to the ancient Tuatha de Danaan who were forced underground by their conquerors. Can all the Danaan be accessed through the same portal at Glastonbury?"

The Goddess: *"Yes. But the Danaan are fourth dimensional beings which can be summoned at any time and at any location, provided the heart and intentions of the seeker are pure."*

"Did the Danaan or Pheryllt bring the worship of the Kaberoi Twins with them from Atlantis?"

The Goddess: *"Yes. They could not have accomplished their alchemy without a knowledge of the Twins. The Danaans had arrived from Atlantis via Greece and Asia Minor, so they had acquired much of their wisdom of the Kaberoi from those areas. Later, they were able to establish an exchange program with their cousins who remained in that part of the world, such as the Tribe of Dan, thus enabling the early Brits to study within the Mediterranean schools of the Kaberoi and the southern Danaans to study within the schools of the Druids. The legendary visit of Jesus/Sananda to Britain was arranged through that program."*

"Then the legend of Abaris, the Greek teacher of Pythagoras, and a famous British king[26]—both of whom were supposedly initiated on Samothrace and brought the wisdom of the Kaberoi to Britain—must really be based on fact."

## THE VENUS CULTURE IN MESOPOTAMIA

"Did the Mesopotamians take part in this exchange program between the Danaans of north and south? There appear to be many similarities between the cultures of Britain and Mesopotamia. Both, for example, had natural, man-made pyramids, as well as bards, diviners, and magicians."[27]

The Goddess: *"Certain elements of Mesopotamian culture infiltrated the civilizations in Asia Minor, and these elements of culture were eventually transported to Britain. But the British and Mesopotamian cultures were related in other ways. They were, for example, both strongly influenced by Atlantean missionaries of the Kaberoi, such as the Pheryllt. In Mesopotamia, these Atlantean missionaries are known historically as the Anunnaki. The Anunnaki were the emissaries of Enki, the Lord of the World."*

"Did the Anunnaki bring the secrets of Sirian alchemy with them from Atlantis?"

The Goddess: *"Yes. The Anunnaki brought both Sirian alchemy and its symbol, the dragon-goat, to Mesopotamia. Enki, their dragon-goat god, was descended from the same Atlantean dragon who evolved into the dragon Khem in Egypt.."*

"Robert Temple speculates in his book *The Sirius Mystery* that the Anunnaki were the 'Sons of Anu,'[28] and that the Sumerian Anu is synonymous with the Egyptian Anu-bis. Wouldn't this make the Anunnaki the 'Sons of Sirius?"

The Goddess: *"Yes, and they were. They were descended from the alchemical missionaries who had arrived on Atlantis from Sirius."*

"I would assume, then, that the dragon icon worshipped by the Dogon of Africa is also Enki. The Dogon claim to have been taught by visiting Sirian missionaries in the distant past."

**The Goddess:** *"Yes. The memories of the Dogon go back to the time of Atlantis, when Sirian alchemy was being taught on the western motherland and in parts of northern Africa."*

"Did the Atlantean Anunnaki found schools of alchemy once they reached Mesopotamia?"

**The Goddess:** *"Yes. One of their principal alchemical colleges was at Eridu, Enki's capital city. The goal of the curriculum taught there was to become one with Enki through alchemy. Enki was the symbol of the Higher Self and the guardian angel of the Anunnaki. He was their version of Sanat Kumara, My First Son.*
*"Following the Great Flood, the wisdom of the Anunnaki was passed on to the historical Ashipu priests. The Ashipu were also adept alchemists and formidable magicians like their predecessors."*

"I would assume, then, that the historical Sumerians were well acquainted with the wisdom of the Kundalini..."

**The Goddess:** *"Certainly. Dragon Enki was the symbol of the Kundalini. One popular Sumerian motif portrayed Enki coiled upon a tree with thirteen branches. This tree was symbolic of the spine, and Enki was the Kundalini which coils along its length. Thirteen is the number of stages involved in the alchemical transmutation orchestrated by the Kundalini.*
*"Enki's tree motif was the origin of the Biblical Tree of Eternal Life. He became the Kundalini or Cherub with the flaming sword guarding its base. He grants wisdom and immortal life by ascending the tree."*

"Did any of Enki's symbols represent him as father of the Twins?"

**The Goddess:** *"Yes. His principal symbol, the goat-fish. The goat-fish, which is the synthesis of a fish and a fiery, impulsive goat, represents the female and* *male principles united as the androgenous Kundalini."*

"If Enki was synonymous with Your First Son, he must have also been associated with the Ziggurat, the Mesopotamian version of the pyramid."

The Goddess: *"Yes. The Ziggurats, which were built by the Ashipu and the Anunnaki, were conceived of as homes of Enki. They were temples conducive to the practices of alchemy."*

"In Egypt, a black stone was used in alchemy to represent Khem's forces of transmutation. Did a black stone represent Enki in Mesopotamian alchemy?"

The Goddess: *"Yes. A black meteorite was honored in the Middle East as both Me and My First Son, Enki. These black stones were recognized to be manifestations of the serpent Kundalini and to contain important alchemical properties."*

"I recently read that there is a remote ancient city in Saudi Arabia[29] which was once inhabited by worshippers of black stones. Interestingly, the city has reliefs engraved over its doorways identical to the five step cross-stair step pattern which is found decorating the temples supposedly built by the Kumaras in Peru."

The Goddess: *"The descendants of the Kumaras, the missionary Kaberoi, built this city. They were members of a branch of the Solar Brotherhood and adept practitioners of alchemy."*

"Did the missionary Kaberoi have any influence on the construction of the megalithic ruins of Ba'albek in Lebanon? Arab legend contends it built by giants soon after the deluge."

The Goddess: *"Yes. The ancient temple of Ba'albek in Lebanon was built by missionaries of the Atlantean Kaberoi along with Kundalini adepts of the Cyclopean Order.[30] The blocks which comprise the foundation of this temple were hundreds of tons in weight, but the Kaberoi and Cyclopeans easily slid them into place through the utilitarian use of brute strength and Kundalini power. The temple once served as a home for the worship of My First Son and his mother, the Goddess Venus."*

# CHAPTER IV
# ATLANTIS, BIRTHPLACE OF THE PATRIARCHY

"From what you have told me, it appears as though the patriarchal tradition of the Middle East was built upon the foundations of Your matriarchal tradition."

The Goddess: *"This is true. A good example of this occurred in Mecca. The original temple at Mecca was dedicated to Me and the worship of My black stone."*

"Did Mecca become patriarchal during the time of Abraham, whom tradition suggests rebuilt the temple?"[1]

The Goddess: *"Abraham began a trend in Mecca which culminated in the abolition of image worship and the establishment of Patriarchy."*

"But isn't Your black stone or meteorite still worshipped at Mecca?"

**The Goddess:** *"Technically, yes. It resides within the Kaaba. However the legend regarding its origin has been drastically revised by the Patriarchy. Instead of being a manifestation of Me, the black meteorite is now believed to have been given directly to Adam from God and been originally white in color. Over time it became black because of man's sin."*

"But the meteorite is still You...so whether they acknowledge it or not, those who bow towards Mecca are paying homage to You."

**The Goddess:** *"This is very true. In fact, the black cubed Kaaba is also Me. The geometrical cube is the Pythagorean Solid which represents the Earth element or matter, and black is its corresponding color."*

"So Your essence pervades Mecca..."

**The Goddess:** *"Yes, but technically it is the essence of My destructive power. Mecca is the home of My destructive Twin, Sanat-Lucifer. The black cube and rock are his symbols."*

"Okay, then those bowing to Meccas are bowing to Lucifer."

**The Goddess:** *"Yes, Lucifer is the patron of Patriarchy. He is the lower will, the ego and intellect. These are the guiding forces of the Patriarchy."*

"Then essentially the Moslems are bowing to their patron, Lucifer. That must be why the characteristics of control and dominance are predominant in the Moslem world."

**The Goddess:** *"Yes, as well as why many Moslems remain enmeshed in traditional dogmatic beliefs. The cube is representative of crystallization and stagnation."*

"But if the Kaaba is the headquarters of Your power of destruction, wouldn't it also be the home of Your power of spiritual transformation? Aren't they two sides of the same coin?"

**The Goddess:** *"Yes. You might say that the cubical block of the Kaaba is the home of the Earth's Kundalini, the planetary power of both destruction and* *transformation. This is why the Middle East is such a volatile area."*

"Okay, so besides darkness and destruction, can also find an expansive force in Mecca because the Kundalini leads to spiritual freedom, right?"

The Goddess: *"Yes. But that aspect of the planetary Kundalini is not activated unless the planet is ready for evolutionary ascension, or there is a strong desire within the collective consciousness for spiritual growth and freedom. Otherwise, the lower destructive qualities of Lucifer are made manifest. The mystical sects of Islam, the Sufis, follow the high road to freedom and consciously invoke the transformative power of the Kundalini. They receive an abundance of Baraka, or Kundalini power, from the Kaaba as their reward."*

"Can it be said, then, that the Sufis invoke and serve Lucifer?"

The Goddess: *"The Sufis serve Lucifer's higher aspect, Sanat-Sananda, the Higher Will, rather than Sanat-Lucifer, the lower will and ego."*

"What about the Sufis' cousins, the Lucifer worshipping Yezidhi of central Asia? If they received the worship of Sanat from the Sufis, shouldn't they also be devotees of Sananda?"

The Goddess: *"Essentially they are. As you know, they refuse to acknowledge Lucifer's dark, restrictive qualities, and the derogatory name of Satan is forbidden among them. In truth, they are devotees of Sanat-Sananda."*

"So, even within the patriarchal traditions like Islam, there are sects, like the Sufis, which follow Your matriarchal path?"

The Goddess: *"Yes. But these sects were following My path well before the advent of patriarchal religion. The Sufi tradition, for example, existed well before the time of Islam. In fact, the Sufis were the original keepers of My temple at Mecca."*

"I'm sure that the Patriarchy was happy to assimilate the Sufis and their knowledge of Kundalini. That way they could effectively control the secrets of Matriarchy. Perhaps they also desired to use the Kundalini power against each other."

**The Goddess:** *"Yes. It was in their cellular memory to do so because, as you know, that is what happened among their ancestors on Atlantis, the birthplace of the Patriarchy. During the later days of the motherland, many black magicians arose within the order of the Sons of Lucifer seeking to control others."*

"Were the Sons of Lucifer the Aryans? I usually associate the name Aryan with the early Patriarchy."

**The Goddess:** *"Aryan is a name derived by the German archaeologists.[2] But its current usage does indeed refer to a branch of the Sons of Lucifer. The so-called Aryan race was the preeminent patriarchal race which evolved on Atlantis as the result of the development of the ego and intellect."*

"Did they develop together on Atlantis...I mean intellect and ego?"

**The Goddess:** *"Yes. Intellect is the faculty of categorizing and seeing differences. Once this faculty is developed, a sense of separateness from others naturally follows, thereby giving rise to the ego. This evolutionary development was destined to occur on Atlantis."*

"Is the development of the ego and intellect on Atlantis portrayed somehow in the Garden of Eden allegory?"

**The Goddess:** *"Yes. The Eden myth encompasses the evolution of humanity which occurred on both Atlantis and Lemuria. The evolution of the intellect and ego is represented in the legend by Adam and Eve eating of the forbidden fruit. This allegorical event refers to the time when evolving humans were beginning to enjoy earthly, sensual pleasures and needed to develop an intellect in order to discern what was healthy for them to 'eat' and what wasn't. Of course, this evolution took many thousands of years to complete, so the scene encompasses both the age of Lemuria and that of Atlantis.*

"Once they had eaten the fruits and developed an intellect, Adam and Eve experienced differences between themselves. This must have been the dawn of the ego."

**The Goddess:** *"Exactly. The curse of the serpent was also a consequence of* *eating the fruit."*

"Do You mean the curse on the serpent to crawl on the ground forever?"

The Goddess: *"Yes. This 'curse' represents the life force which had to contract, or 'descend' in frequency, so that the divine couple could live in a solid, three dimensional world[3] and enjoy their earthly pleasures.*

*"But there is another equally important interpretation of the serpent's 'curse.' As I have mentioned, the serpent on the tree of Eden is also a symbol of the human spine and Kundalini. Before the divine couple ate of the fruits of the tree the serpent was high upon the tree, i.e., the Kundalini was high up the spine and humans could experience an intuitive oneness with creation. In order for humans to completely throw themselves into the experience of duality and sensuality, the Kundalini had to descend into the root chakra at the base of the spine."*

"Didn't part of the Kundalini go to sleep after it descended?"

The Goddess: *"Yes. Only when humans are finished with their three dimensional experience will that part of the serpent become active again and reascend the tree."*

"In the mean time, what is the function of the Kundalini?"

The Goddess: *"It fuels the entire body with life force, especially the lower three chakras which control the ego, intellect, and the reproductive organs. Collectively, the three lower chakras are the Lucifer Body, the body of the lower will, while the upper three chakras constitute the Sananda Body, the sheath of the Higher Will."*

"I would guess that the Kundalini's descent and its activation of the lower three chakras must have initially contributed to the Atlanteans' domineering tendencies..."

The Goddess: *"Yes. It also contributed to the aggressiveness of the Atlanteans by producing an abundance of seminal fluid and male testosterone. When the Kundalini descends in frequency and condenses, it becomes seminal fluid."*

111

"I know from my Chinese medical theory training that the sexual or seminal essences form the brain. Did the serpent have to become seminal fluid in order to form and feed the physical brain?"

**The Goddess:** "*Generally speaking, the serpent had to become essence to nourish and form up all the organs and tissues which have a physical manifestation. But the purest essence goes to the brain.*"

"Was the brain always divided in halves?"

**The Goddess:** "*Initially it was not divided. This occurred when the intellect was fully developed and humans descended into duality.*"

"Was this stage of human evolution assisted by extraterrestrials as some believe?"

**The Goddess:** "*There was assistance from both the Venusians and Sirians in the division of the brain. This was a necessary step of human evolution. Before there could be a reunion of the Twins—Sananda and Lucifer as intuition and intellect or Higher Self and lower self—a complete separation of the polarity needed to occur in the human body. This is fundamental alchemy. The male and female principles must completely separate before reuniting.*

"*Since Lemurian times the Venusians and Sirians have been supervising the entire process of human alchemy, from the separation of the polarity to its reunion. And it will be their yogic wisdom which will assist you in reuniting the polarity and becoming androgenous gods and goddesses.*"

## THE SPREAD OF PATRIARCHY

"Is the migration of the Patriarchy from Atlantis synonymous with what we know as the path of migration taken by the Aryans?"

**The Goddess:** "*Basically, yes. Many branches of the Patriarchy went eastward and northward from Atlantis. They traveled to certain pan-Atlantic regions, such as Europe and the Mediterranean, and some arrived in India and Iran.*"

"I suppose that wherever they went, they spread not only patriarchal principles but the exaltation of the intellect."

**The Goddess:** *"Yes, as well as the concept of free will. You find this notion particularly widespread in Europe, a continent where Atlantean souls have repeatedly incarnated for thousands of years."*

"The notion of free will....I guess it must be tied up with the ego and intellect."

**The Goddess:** *"Yes. It springs from the idea of separateness. In truth, 'no man is an island' and everything in the universe is interconnected. Many human actions are even inspired by frequencies broadcast from other universes."*

"You are now defining the underlying precept of astrology."

**The Goddess:** *"Yes. 'As above, so below."*

"Astrology seems to be such an integral part of Hinduism. How could this be possible if the founders of Hinduism were the patriarchal Aryans?"

**The Goddess:** *"Neither astrology or the Hindu caste system were founded by the Aryans. They were brought to India from Lemuria by My matriarchal devotees. The caste system was founded on Lemuria as a way of separating developing souls into successive levels of experience, and to better assist their evolutionary growth. The Aryans brought to India a version of the caste system which had been distorted by an elite group of Luciferians seeking to control the populace of Atlantis. After establishing this biased caste system in India, the Aryans placed themselves in the controlling ruling castes of Brahmin priests and Kshatriya kings."*

"A caste system was observed on Lemuria? I thought everyone was equal there..."

**The Goddess:** *"There was equality, but souls existed at different levels of evolution. In contrast to the Atlantean and Hindu caste systems, however, all citizens of Lemuria were eligible to participate in spiritual life."*

"Was the patriarchal influence a non-factor in India until the time of the Aryans?"

**The Goddess:** "*Yes. The patriarchal Atlanteans had their eyes on conquering India thousands of years before the Aryans arrived, but they were never successful in realizing this goal. Remember the legend of a battle which occurred between the Atlanteans and the Rama Empire in India? The Atlanteans pitted their technology against India's superior spiritual power and lost. When the Aryans later arrived, India's spiritual power had declined so they were able to easily conquer the country and implement their own caste structure.*"

"Isn't that later invasion of the Aryans depicted as the legendary battle between the Devas and the Asuras?"[4]

**The Goddess:** "*Yes. The Asuras were the ancestors and deities of My devotees in India, the Danavas and Nagas, and the Devas were the patron deities of the patriarchal Aryans. When My devotees were defeated by the Aryans, it was proclaimed that the Asuras had been defeated by the Devas.*"

"But even after the Aryan conquest, wasn't Your matriarchal tradition able to survive in India?"

**The Goddess:** "*Yes. One example of its survival is astrology, and another is Yoga. My tradition survived as Tantric Yoga while the Aryan spiritual tradition assumed the form of Vedanta. As you know, Tantricism accepts anyone with a pure heart, while the Vedantic path only accepts males and those of the upper castes.*"

"The Iranians believe that their Aryan ancestors came from the north. Apparently the Nazis used this information to their advantage when they claimed that the Aryans were descended from the first human race which developed at the poles, the Polarians. Did the Aryans really come from the North?"

**The Goddess:** "*Certainly. Many moved across northern Europe and Asia before sweeping down into south-eastern Asia. But the Aryans were not the highly evolved race the Nazis gave them credit for being. That distinction goes to the blond haired and blue eyed Lemurians.*"

"What about the Hebrews? Were they influenced by the patriarchal Aryans?"

114

**The Goddess:** *"They were influenced by an Aryan migration of Hittites which infiltrated the Middle East and Babylon. The patriarchal Hittites colonized much of upper Mesopotamia, where Abraham's ancestors came from."*[5]

"Were Abraham's ancestors originally patriarchal or matriarchal?"

**The Goddess:** *"They were a mix. Some of Abraham's ancestors had been Goddess worshippers and aligned with the guardians of My temple at Mecca."*

"Were his ancestors related to the Sufis?"

**The Goddess:** *"Yes. Abraham was heir to the wisdom and power of both the early Sufis and the Ashipu priesthood of Sumeria. He was also initiated into the Melchizedek priesthood, which is a later name for the ancient Kaberoi Brotherhood from Atlantis."*

"With so much influence coming from Your tradition, I am surprised that the Jews could have become so patriarchal."

**The Goddess:** *"Even though they were ostensibly patriarchal, they worshipped Me as Ashteroth-Anath, the Canaanite Venus. Moreover, some branches of the Jews—the Levites and Essenes—remained faithful to My tradition by preserving the wisdom of the Kaberoi Brotherhood from Atlantis. The Essenes provided a very important service to Me by incarnating the Twins, an event which initiated a 2000 year alchemical process destined to culminate in the union of the polarity and My revival."*

"Which would eventually usher in the Fifth World, right?"

**The Goddess:** *"Yes. But first the Armageddon..."*

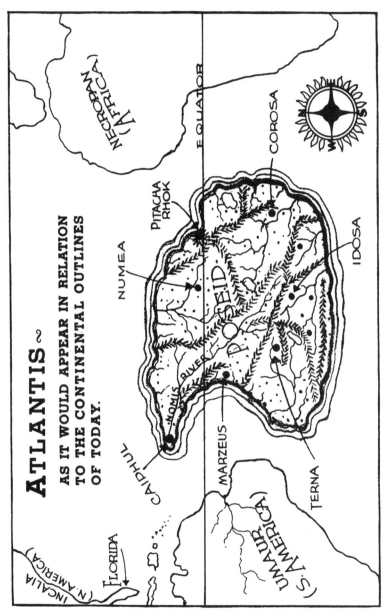

The Lemurian Fellowship's concept of the island of Atlantis circa 10,000 B.C. It includes several major cities that supposedly existed at that time.

*Atlantis, the birthplace of the Patriarchy*

# CHAPTER V
# ARMAGEDDON: MATRIARCHY VS. PATRIARCHY

"By Armageddon, are You perhaps referring to the battle depicted in the *Book of Revelation* in the *Holy Bible?*"

The Goddess: "*Yes. Armageddon is the final battle between My two Sons and the opposing polarities and traditions they represent, the Matriarchy and Patriarchy, during the present cycle.*"

"As I understand it, this battle is due to occur sometime before 2012."

The Goddess: "*This is correct. However you will be happy to know that the worst part of the battle has already transpired. It occurred during World War II when the Patriarchy made one last futile attempt at exterminating the Matriarchy and conquering the free world. The vehicle of the Patriarchy at that time, the Nazis, were one of the purest examples of Luciferian divisiveness and domination to ever exist on the Earth. Their leader, Hitler, was the incarnation of a powerful black magician who had once been a leader of the Sons of Lucifer on Atlantis. The soul of Hitler is what you know of as the Anti-Christ.*"

"Are You saying that the Anti-Christ has come and gone?"

The Goddess: "*Yes and no. That individual who was destined to embody the soul of the Anti-Christ has come and gone. But as long as control and dominance continue to plague the Earth, then the power of the Anti-Christ continues to thrive.*"

"If Hitler was the Anti-Christ, was he defeated by the Second Coming of Christ as prophesied?"

The Goddess: "*Yes, but indirectly. Hitler was defeated by the representatives of Christ who took the form of the matriarchal forces which arose in opposition to the Nazis.*"

"By 'matriarchal forces' do You mean the democratic countries of the west?"

The Goddess: "*Yes. Especially the United States of America. America was created by branches of My matriarchal tradition in Europe, including the Knights Templars, Freemasons, and Rosicrucians, to act as a leader of My matriarchal forces.*"

"Apparently it was the destiny of those European sects to resurrect and mobilize the Matriarchy in preparation for the Armageddon..."

The Goddess: "*Yes. They inherited this role from their matriarchal ancestors, the Essenes and Sufis, and the Kaberoi Brotherhood before them.*"

"How long had the Armageddon been anticipated?"

The Goddess: "*Since the advent of the Sons of Lucifer on Atlantis. But even before Atlantis the Lemurian Kumaras had prophesied both it and the founding of America.*"

"The founding of America has been known about that long? That would explain how the Essenes knew of its eventual discovery. Supposedly their texts mentioned a future land in the west called 'Merica' which was somehow associated with Venus."[1]

118

**The Goddess:** *"Yes. This Essene knowledge was passed to their descendants, the Templars, who formally discovered and named the land 'America.' But even before the Templars' arrival, the Western Hemisphere had been called 'Amaruca,' a version of America, by missionaries of the Kumaras and Kaberoi who had settled there.*

*"Merica, Amaruca, and their evolution, America, all mean 'Place of the Goddess' and 'Place of the Serpent.' America was destined to be the future home of the Matriarchy. The root of Merica is mer, a name for the female principle."*

"Supposedly Columbus was aligned with the Templars and sailed to the Americas in ships flying white sails with red crosses on them."[2]

**The Goddess:** *"He was an important instrument for the Matriarchy. The red cross which embellished Columbus's sails is My ancient symbol. It is the symbol of the Goddess and the planet Venus."*

"I have also heard that the red cross is an alchemical symbol..."

**The Goddess:** *"Yes, of course. It represents the fiery Kundalini which results from the union of the polarity. The Goddess, the planet Venus, and the Kundalini are all the androgenous union of the polarity. This is the true meaning of the red cross."[3]*

"Did the Templars inherit the red cross from Your sects in the Middle East?"

**The Goddess:** *"Yes. But originally it came from My matriarchal cultures on Atlantis and Lemuria where it was placed upon a white background and displayed within My temples. It can still be found in some of My temples in India.*

*"The color red on a white background represents Me as the fiery life force which emerged out of the pure, infinite Spirit. Red is also associated with the female principle because it is the color of blood."*

"If the descendants of the early Matriarchy were the European mystery schools, what form did the descendants of the Sons of Lucifer take? My first guess would be that they became the dictatorial, militaristic empires and the

119

oppressive monarchies which co-existed with the mystery schools. And perhaps...the Christian Church."

## THE UNITED BRANCHES OF THE MATRIARCHY

### THE GNOSTICS

The Goddess: *"Yes, your intuition is correct. The descendants of the Sons of Lucifer, who were thirsty for power and control, managed to infiltrate the Church. This occurred when the early Christian movement divided to become the Christian Catholic Church governed by the patriarchal forces of Sanat-Lucifer, and the sect of Gnosticism governed by the matriarchal followers of Sanat-Sananda."*

"It's ironic that the master associated with the Christian Church is Jesus-Sananda when it is in fact guided by Lucifer."

The Goddess: *"Right. The Patriarchy chose Jesus-Sananda as its patron because the destructive power of Lucifer was considered evil to its dualistic mentality. However, by controlling peoples' beliefs, the Patriarchy inadvertently gave its allegiance to Lucifer."*

"Your tradition is just the opposite, right? Lucifer has become its symbol even though its allegiance is to Sananda."

The Goddess: *"Yes. My tradition utilizes the destruction/transformation powers of Lucifer in order to break through the crystallized concepts and beliefs of humankind. Once this is accomplished, all humanity will be able to soar into the unlimited freedom which comes through union with Sananda, the will of Spirit."*

"The destructive nature of Your tradition was emphasized by the early Gnostic cults of the Middle East. Many of them earned a reputation for acting destructively towards the laws and customs of man in order to achieve spiritual freedom."

The Goddess: *"Yes. In this way they were similar to My lunatic sects in India. In fact, there was an efficient exchange of ideas, practices and students between the Gnostics of Asia Minor and the Yogis of India. This exchange was in place when the greatest of the Gnostics, Jesus-Sananda, studied in India.[4]*

*"Not only the Gnostics, but their Essene predecessors also encouraged radical behavior. But since the Essenes lived in isolated communities, this part of their history is not too well known. That is except for the Essene radical John the Baptist. John and Jesus-Sananda were members of the Naasaria, the most esoteric branch of the Essenes. John eventually transmitted his radical tendencies to his disciples, such as Simon Magus, the founder of a sect of Gnosticism."[5]*

"From what I know of him, Simon Magus was either brave or crazy, or both. By openly declaring himself to be God, he could have easily gotten himself crucified or burned at the stake."

**The Goddess:** *"Simon was a great Gnostic who had transcended body consciousness and was not concerned about what others thought of him. He was beyond duality and continuously reveled in the Gnostic awareness of I AM GOD. To reach enlightenment, Simon had raised his Kundalini via sexual Tantric practices imported from India. His Tantric partner was a prostitute, whom he worshipped as a manifestation of Me."[6]*

"Didn't the Gnostics claim that their yoga and alchemical wisdom was first given to them by the Serpent on the Tree in the Garden of Eden? If that Serpent was Sanat Kumara as You say it was, then both Yoga and Gnosticism have a common ancestor."

**The Goddess:** *"Yes. As I have said, there was an intimate exchange of wisdom between Yoga and Gnosticism. Part of this wisdom revealed a common heritage for both paths."*

"If the Gnostics had transcended duality through Yoga, why are there traces of an eternal duality in Gnostic philosophy?"

**The Goddess:** *"In its later stages, elements of patriarchal theology infiltrated Gnosticism. However, the true Gnostics remained ardent non-dualists and acknowledged that the unified spiritual essence had divided to become the two brothers: Sanat-Lucifer, the King of the World, and Sanat-Sananda, the Savior of the World. But they also knew it would eventually reunite into Oneness."*

## THE ISMAILI AND THE KNIGHTS TEMPLARS

"Were the Gnostics affiliated with the Sufis? Weren't they co-branches of Your tradition?"

The Goddess: *"Yes, they were cousins. In fact one radical sub-sect of Sufis, the Ismaili,[7] indirectly worshipped Sanat Kumara as their leader."*

"Sanat Kumara was patron of the Ismaili Order?"

The Goddess: *"Sanat worked through the head of the Ismaili order, the Imam, who was their secret King of the World. He channeled the power and wisdom of Sanat and had formidable Kundalini or Baraka at his disposal."*

"But as Moslems, weren't the Ismaili a branch of the Patriarchy?"

The Goddess: *"The Ismaili had emerged out of the Shiite[8] sect of Islam which inculcated the higher values of My matriarchal tradition, such as racial equality and freedom of belief. The ancestors of the Ismaili had been the keepers of My temple in Mecca, so the order had always been aligned with Me."*

"Were the Ismaili, then, aligned to Sanat-Sananda as opposed to Sanat-Lucifer?"

The Goddess: *"Yes. Some Ismaili were Kundalini adepts who used the energy for spiritual liberation. A mystery tradition arose within the Ismaili order for the purpose of awakening the Kundalini power and its unfoldment."*

"But what about the Assassins?[9] I thought they were a branch of the Ismaili, but their actions were certainly not indicative of a desire for spiritual growth or union with Sananda."

The Goddess: *"Initially the order was guided by the pure spiritual principles of the Ismaili, but the leader of the Assassins eventually chose himself as the Imam and then proceeded to use Luciferian control to place himself on the throne of the world."*

"Were the Templars initiated into the Assassins as some historians suggest?"

**The Goddess:** *"The Knights Templars were not initiated into the Assassin movement, but they adopted some of the doctrines and rites of both the Ismaili and Assassins.*

*"Under the Ismaili influence, the Templars became inspired to precipitate the creation of a future one-world government ruled over by a King of the World. The Ismaili called this future king the Mahdi, and the Templars recognized him as Sanat-Sananda, the Higher Will of Sanat Kumara."*

"I have heard that the Templars were part of the Priory of Sion which sought to create a one-world government governed by a descendent of Jesus."[10]

**The Goddess:** *"Right. Their ultimate goal was to eventually place a descendent of Jesus on the throne of the world. He would be a manifestation or incarnation of Sanat-Sananda."*

"But didn't the Templars worship a demon called Rex Mundi as King of the World?"

**The Goddess:** *"Yes. The Templars learned from their brothers in the Middle East, the Sufis and Essenes, that leading up to the installment of Sananda as King the World, the planet will be ruled by Rex Mundi, who is also known as Baphomet. Rex Mundi or Baphomet is the planetary Kundalini which resides at Mecca.*

*"As the planetary Kundalini, Baphomet is essentially the Middle Eastern version of Sanat Kumara, the planetary Kundalini which rules the Earth from Shamballa. This is why Baphomet was called 'King of the World' by the Sufis and others. Baphomet or Sanat is the planetary will whose power, the Kundalini, enacts his mandates.*

*"Since they are the planetary Kundalini, both Sanat and Baphomet have two sides. They are both Sanat-Sananda and Sanat-Lucifer, the yin and yang of the planet which unites as the androgenous Kundalini. Remember that the meaning of Baphomet is 'Father of Understanding?'[11] Baphomet is the androgenous union of the Twins.*

*"Throughout its history, Sanat or Baphomet's two sides have taken turns ruling the Earth. They rule the planet when their corresponding*

*principle, yin or yang, is ascendant. During matriarchal Lemurian times, when the Goddess was ascendant, Sanat-Sananda was monarch of the Earth. But since the advent of Patriarchy, it has been Sanat-Lucifer's turn to be king.*

   *"Rex Mundi was portrayed as demonic by the Templars because he was a manifestation of the Atlantean Primal Dragon, but also because his destructive/controlling power was ascendant on the Earth during their time. However, they knew that was was destined to change when the yin forces re-emerge and Sananda reclaims the throne of the planet."*

   "I assume that the Templars invoked the higher, transformative powers of Baphomet rather than his dark, controlling side?

"The Goddess: *"Yes. They worshipped the destructive/transformative power of Baphomet or Rex Mundi which leads to union with Sananda, the Higher Self. But the Templars were fierce warriors, and not all of them were forgiving spiritual seekers. Some invoked Baphomet's destructive, controlling power to help them win their battles and to gain revenge on their enemies."*

   "Did the Ismaili also summon Lucifer's dark side? The Moslems in general had a reputation of being rather controlling and warlike."

The Goddess: *"Yes. Even some of the pure Ismaili were known to invoke Lucifer's combative, destructive power which was so prolific at Mecca. In fact, they named their headquarters, Cairo, after Mars, the planet which was associated with Lucifer's power of destructive manipulation."[12]*

   "Mars is associated with Lucifer?"

The Goddess: *"Yes, both Mars and Saturn broadcast to Earth the powers associated with Lucifer. Mars' emanates Lucifer's destructive power and Saturn is the vehicle of his controlling nature. You might recall that the Hindus associated Mars with Lucifer by calling the planet Karttikeya, which is a name for Sanat Kumara."*

   "There is a legend concerning a 'Lucifer Rebellion' which supposedly arrived on Earth from Mars during the time of Atlantis.[13] Can You comment on this?"

**The Goddess:** *"It is true that there was a war-like race which traveled from Mars to Atlantis in very ancient times. They became the ancestors of the Sons of Lucifer. They constructed the pyramids on Mars and the famous 'Face on Mars' which represented their deity, Sanat-Lucifer."*

"Did they use their technology to build pyramids on Atlantis?"

**The Goddess:** *"Yes. On Atlantis, the Martians and their disciples, the Sons of Lucifer, built pyramids and utilized crystals to amplify the life force. They then used the resultant power for destructive purposes, which is how they had destroyed their own civilization on Mars. The symbol of their brotherhood on Atlantis was a version of Baphomet, but it represented primarily My power of destruction, as opposed to My transformative power."*

"Wasn't Baphomet a form of Khem and therefore a symbol of the Kundalini on Atlantis?"

**The Goddess:** *"Yes. The adepts of the Atlantean Kaberoi Brotherhood worshipped Baphomet's transformative power. According to them, Baphomet was the Kundalini and a symbol of Sirian alchemy."*[14]

"When the Templars later inherited the symbol of Baphomet, did they also acquire the secrets of Sirian alchemy?"

**The Goddess:** *"Yes. They inherited the ancient wisdom of Sirian alchemy in its entirety from the Ismaili and Sufis, who had themselves received it from the Egyptians and Atlanteans."*

"Well...if the Templars knew how to tap into the supernatural power of Baphomet, You must have had the beginnings of quite a formidable army when they finally marched into Europe to overthrow the Patriarchy."

**The Goddess:** *"Yes. The march to Armageddon was on. You might say that the 'first shot was fired' when the Christians equated Rex Mundi with their Devil and then set out to destroy the Templars."*

"But it sounds to me like he *was* their Devil!"

125

The Goddess: "*Only if you chose to solely acknowledge Baphomet's destructive and controlling nature. But Baphomet was an embodiment of all My three powers, including My transformative power which leads one to unlimited spiritual freedom.*"

"I'm sure it must have been difficult for the Templars to educate the Christians about Baphomet's more exalted, transformative nature when the Knights were caught practicing sexual Tantra and defiling the cross."

The Goddess: "*The cross was a symbol of the Patriarchy to the Templars. This is why they trampled or spat upon it. And their was nothing inherently evil about their sexual Tantric practices. These practices were designed to awaken Baphomet, the Kundalini, and raise it up the spine.*"

"I suppose at one time or another all the branches of the Matriarchy in Europe were accused of heresy by the Christians."

The Goddess: "*Yes. They all practiced similar heretical rites and adopted similar theologies. And they all sought to align with a version of Baphomet or Rex Mundi, who was Sanat Kumara, the King of the World.*"

## THE WITCHES

"What about the practitioners of Witchcraft? Weren't they also part of Your European movement?"

The Goddess: "*Witchcraft had a special connection to the European mystery schools since it had similarly been founded by the Sufis.*"[15]

"But I thought Witchcraft had existed in Europe long before the Sufis..."

The Goddess: "*It had. Witchcraft has existed throughout Europe in a rudimentary form since the Neolithic Age, but it was the Sufis who gave it organization and standardized rites. The Sufis introduced the Witches' coven of thirteen members, as well as many of the dances and rites observed within those secret gatherings. They also helped to synthesize the personality of the Witches' God, which became an amalgamation of Baphomet, the Neolithic Horned God, and Shiva-Sanat of the Hindu tradition.*"

"It sounds like the Witches' god was another manifestation of Your First Son."

**The Goddess:** *"Yes, he was. He was a manifestation of My First Son, the King of the World, and fountainhead of life force or Kundalini. The Witches used his power to heal and perform their magic."*

"Are You saying that the Witches were indoctrinated into the secrets of the Kundalini?"

**The Goddess:** *"Yes, but they did not necessarily call it that. To them, Kundalini was simply the power of their Lord which was used for healing and material prosperity. They knew that this power could be summoned through incantations, in ceremony, or acquired through certain Tantric rites and the consumption of sacramental herbs."*

"I wouldn't expect that Witches inherited ancient scriptures or doctrines regarding Kundalini, like some of Your other sects did."

**The Goddess:** *"True, although there were some Witches in Spain who had studied among the Sufis and were quite academic. Some became Tantric priestesses with an intimate knowledge of the spine and the Kundalini energy. Among these esoteric priestesses, the broomstick was not just a cleaning implement, it was a symbol of the human spine. To them, the legendary nocturnal flights of the Witches on their brooms were simply metaphors for 'riding' the spine to other states of consciousness through the raising of the indwelling Kundalini."*

"Was the mating ritual with their 'Lord' which took place during the Witches' covens also a Tantric rite?"[16]

**The Goddess:** *"Yes. During the rite, the power of the King of the World was transmitted into a Witch via a priest acting the part of her Lord, and this had the ultimate effect of awakening her Kundalini."*

"And the priest who acted in the role of 'Lord' in their covens...was he a representative of Your Son?"[17]

127

**The Goddess:**"*Yes. The thirteenth person of each coven was a representation of Sanat Kumara and channeled his destructive/transformative power to the initiates within the group. Thirteen is the number of the Kundalini, and it rules both destruction and transformation.*"

"Were some of the Witches as evil as they were portrayed?"

**The Goddess:** "*Most weren't. However some were forced to use the destructive power of Sanat-Lucifer to protect themselves, especially from the machinations of the Inquisition. Ultimately this led some of them down a very dark path indeed, and helped black magic gain a foothold in Europe.*"

"Some of the herbs consumed by the Witches, like Datura and Belladonna, are quite toxic and can precipitate intense hallucinations and even psychosis. Why were they ingested?"

**The Goddess:** "*The Witches cult was a branch of My Left Hand Path which incorporates the use of herbs like these for transcending the intellect and 'taking leave of one's senses,' as well as one's physical body. They assisted the Witches in communing with astral entities and conducting their astral flights.*"

"Did the Witches encounter the demonic denizens I have seen on sacraments?"

**The Goddess:** "*Yes, but they accepted the demons as either accomplices or manifestations of their Lord. In this regard, they mirrored their cousins in India, the Tantrics, who consumed Datura for the purpose of communing with the grotesque forms and legions of Lord Shiva.*"

"The Witches appear in have many things in common with the Tantric cult of Lord Shiva in India."

**The Goddess:** "*This is because some Sufi and Gypsy sects took Shiva's Tantricism into Europe and then incorporated it into the Witches' rites.[18] Lord Shiva, who was the lord of destruction and the wielder of the trident, contributed to the formation of the Witches' Lord.*"

"Did the Witches work with the other branches of Your tradition in Europe once they had become an organized force?"

**The Goddess:** *"Yes. But it took a while before they all knew of each other. Then they exchanged members and rites."*

"By then, I imagine that the patriarchal Christian forces must have realized that they had their hands full if they were going to silence the united orders of Templars, Rosicrucians, Freemasons and Witches..."

**The Goddess:** *"Yes. The gnostic Cathars were also part of this movement. But unfortunately they were made sacrificial lambs by the patriarchal Inquisition."[19]*

## THE ILLUMINATI

"So, where does the Illuminati fit into Your united movement? There are more conspiracy theories about the Illuminati then all the other European secret societies put together."

**The Goddess:** *"The Illuminati were descended from the Templars and Ismaili. When an Illuminati underwent initiation into the order, he simultaneously pledged his undying devotion to the Templars and the King of the World. Ultimately, if he succeeded in progressing through the ranks of the order he would arrive at the highest degree, union with Sanat Kumara or Baphomet, which was known as 'King of the World."[20]*

"Didn't the Illuminati movement prove ineffective when the German authorities discovered it and banished it from its homeland of Bavaria? Wasn't that the end of it for the most part?"

**The Goddess:** *"No. The headquarters of the Illuminati simply moved to a much better location, Paris, which at that time was a mecca for all My secret societies in Europe."*

"Did the Illuminati unite with the other groups in Paris in order to create a united matriarchal movement?"

**The Goddess:** "*Yes. And once the movement had solidified the King of the World, Sanat Kumara, became its master and patron. The ultimate goal of this united movement was to revive the Matriarchy and eventually place the future 'King,' Sanat-Sananda,*[21] *on the throne of a one-world government.*"

"What about those among the Illuminati who were not so spiritual...did they align with the controlling side of Sanat-Lucifer as so many people believe?"

**The Goddess:** "*Yes. Some zealous Illuminati were interested in world domination at any price, just as their Assassin predecessors had been. For this reason, they aligned themselves with the controlling and warring aspect of Sanat-Lucifer, and then expediently infiltrated many powerful organizations of the Patriarchy with the goal of manipulating them from their highest ranks.*"

"I have read that Paris eventually became a headquarters for St. Germain and Cagliostro. Were they the leaders of the united European movement?"

**The Goddess:** "*Yes. They were the 'generals' of My European campaign. They chaired the clandestine meetings of My united movement, which convened in some of the most magnificent palaces in and around Paris. The dungeons and hidden chambers of these palaces were the clandestine temples of the movement.*"

"Supposedly both Franklin and Jefferson came to Paris on a diplomatic mission and were initiated into the Nine Sisters, one of the most esoteric organizations in Europe. Were the Nine Sisters part of this united group?"

**The Goddess:** "*Yes. Franklin and Jefferson were initiated into My united movement via the Nine Sisters. Following their initiation, they accepted St. Germain as both their Grandmaster, as well as the patron of their soon-to-be new country. This union was, of course, pre-destined. From the start, the USA was destined to be the alchemical mead which would eventually revive Matriarchy and transform the world. St. Germain, through his rulership of the Violet Ray, the Ray of alchemy, has overseen USA's role in transforming the world.*"

"Obviously, the choice of using such Illuminati symbols as the pyramid for the national seal of the USA was not an arbitrary decision."

**The Goddess:** *"Not at all. By adopting the symbols of the Illuminati, the USA officially proclaimed itself to be a branch of the Illuminati and the torchbearer of My matriarchal tradition. In order to further cement its bond with the Illuminati, your country accepted the symbol of My united movement, the Statue of Liberty, from the French branch of the organization."*[22]

"The gift of the Statue of Liberty seems to prove that the Illuminati's ultimate goal was freedom for all, and not the sabotage of such freedom as some people fear."

**The Goddess:** *"This is true. The Illuminati were a branch of My matriarchal tradition which is traditionally guided by the principles of love and allowance. From its inception, the order was closely guided by My Sons from Sirius, the master teachers of My tradition within your local galaxy. This is why the Illuminati chose July 4 as Independence Day. On that day the Sun is in exact conjunction with Sirius."*

"It also occurs when the Sun is transiting through Your sign of Cancer, the sign of the Mother..."

**The Goddess:** *"Yes. There were many esoteric reasons for choosing that day."*

"Did some of the Illuminati symbols on the Seal of the USA evolve from the organization's Sirian patronage?"

**The Goddess:** *"Yes. One symbol on your national seal is Sirius's pre-eminent motif, the eye within the capstone of a pyramid. As a triune star group, the three sides comprising the triangular face of the pyramid has, for ages, been the definitive symbol of Sirius. The eye in the center of the pyramidal capstone represents the all seeing eye of Spirit which unites and transcends the trinity."*

"Is Venusian influence also reflected on the United States seal?"

**The Goddess:** *"Yes. The original national bird on the U.S. seal was a phoenix, the bird of Venus. And the six pointed star above the bird, which is composed* *of thirteen smaller stars, is a pre-eminent symbol of the planet. The interlaced triangles of the Star of David symbolize the Morning and Evening Stars or the Twins, and the thirteen stars they incorporate symbolize the thirteen revolutions Venus makes during its sacred eight year cycle."*

"Why did the eagle eventually replace the phoenix on the seal?"

The Goddess: *"Both because the eagle is the national bird, as well as because it represents the USA's patron and future King of the World, Sanat-Sananda. In the same way that the falcon is Egyptian Horus's bird, the eagle is Sanat-Sananda's."*

"And the inscription New World Order found on the seal? Where did that come from?"

## THE NEW WORLD ORDER

The Goddess: *"You should know that by now. It was the banner of the Illuminati and the Templars. Implementing the New World Order has been the ultimate goal of My secret societies around the world for many ages. It announces the revival of the Matriarchy and the founding of a one-world government ruled by My First Son."*

"Many people fear that the New World Order will consist of a secret society of world bankers seeking to selfishly control us."

The Goddess: *"Well their fears are not totally unfounded. The banking institutions were founded with pure intentions by My sons, the Templars. But money is power, so these institutions eventually came under the dominating control of the Patriarchy.*

*"There are currently those world bankers who have cultivated the Luciferian qualities of control and dominance. They are headed for a downfall, as are all My children who are not willing to surrender their will to a higher will."*

"What will it take to 'wake them up?"

The Goddess: *"They need to start believing there is a will higher and more powerful than their own. They have got to understand that in the broader*

132

*scope of things their powers are very circumspect. For most of them, this revelation will necessitate one or more personal crises which are completely out of their control."*

"Like the money system falling apart?"

**The Goddess:** *"Eventually this needs to occur. As long as the money system is in place there will always be those who will try to use their wealth to control and dominate their brothers and sisters, as well as the natural resources of the Earth."*

"It's hard to believe that the world bankers would turn to a higher power when most of them appear to be either agnostic or atheistic."

**The Goddess:** *"They are currently that way because they have never been forced to defer to a higher power. They have always been able to bring the forces of nature under their own control, so why turn to God? But if weather conditions or the economy or a plague was to wreck irreversible havoc in their lives, they might start thinking otherwise.*

*"Atheism is not a natural human response to life. It arose in Europe as a reaction to the oppressive ideology of the Patriarchy. After thousands of years of being exploited or being forced to believe something they did not want to or die, My children said: 'No More.' They became rebellious towards any symbol of outer authority telling them how to live life, be it church or government. Some proclaimed 'God is dead!,' even though they were actually referring to the Christian concept of God, not the infinite Spirit. Nietzsche, their spokesperson, was a Gnostic at heart. He knew that God was not sitting on a cloud surrounded by angels, but dwelling inside the human heart. And he went insane trying to get others to understand this. He knew that we become what he called the 'Superman' when the inner Spirit fully blossoms."*

"But didn't others, who were not as spiritually informed as Nietzsche, reason that God has no manifestation anywhere and is just the Church's fabrication to control the masses. Didn't they become the pure atheists?"

**The Goddess:** *"There were some of that consciousness. One of the movements they founded is now called 'Satanism.' Its rebellious battle cry, 'I am going to do what I want when I want to do it and don't try to stop me,' could once be*

133

*heard over much of northern Europe. In many ways the European Satanists were no different from the radical Gnostics of Alexandria who had lived thousands of years before them, except that they lacked the understanding and inner experience of their earlier counterparts."*

"Are Satanists out to control and dominate the world as some people believe?"

The Goddess: *"Some are. However, most are simply interested in controlling those within their immediate environment in order to satisfy their own selfish desires. But eventually even these Satanists will seek answers and solace from a higher power. They will realize that the happiness achieved from sensual desires is transitory, and that meeting their needs is not always predictable or within their limited powers. Then they will begin to search for a longer lasting peace and joy, and their search will eventually lead them to God."*

"Okay. So back to the world bankers. Is a huge calamity the only thing which is going to motivate them into seeking a higher power?"

The Goddess: *"It might be if they are going to seek God in their present existence. Like the Satanists, the bankers will eventually be inspired to seek a more lasting peace than the ephemeral world can provide them. But for those inner yearnings to emerge, many lifetimes of experience are often required."*

"It doesn't sound very encouraging..."

The Goddess: *"No, but look around you. Many business people are currently seeking some alternative to the continued stress they are under. Some are now turning to meditation for health reasons and/or to calm their overly active minds."*

"This is true..."

The Goddess: *"And often, after having had just one experience of inner peace, many business people find themselves hooked on meditation and resolve to commit to a daily practice of it. But to go deep in meditation for sustained periods of time, they will discover that surrender to a higher will is indispensable. Only by surrendering to a higher will, can the worrying mind subside and make room for a lasting experience of transcendental peace and joy."*

"So eventually meditation will demand that the persons in business surrender to a higher will? Let's keep them meditating!"

**The Goddess:** *"If they continue to meditate, it will be only a matter of time before they realize that what they really want, i.e. lasting peace, is not different from what God desires for them. This revelation will inspire them to achieve further levels of surrender."*

"And once they have completely surrendered their lower will to God?"

**The Goddess:** *"They become Gnostics with the supernatural understanding that they have always been one with God but have been living in an illusion."*

"It appears that we all destined to become Gnostics, sooner or later."

**The Goddess:** *"Yes. Gnosticism is everyone's natural state and destiny. And it is the collective destiny of My children in the coming golden age.*

*"Once enough of My children have attained the wisdom of I AND GOD ARE ONE, the New World Order will officially commence. The collective Higher Will, Sanat-Sananda, will then ascend the throne of the world as its king and the work of My devotees will have born its grandest fruit."*

"So, just as prophesied, the King of the World will ride out of Shamballa on his white stallion and rule the Earth?"[23]

**The Goddess:** *"No. The transforming power of the King of the World, the Kundalini, will emerge from Shamballa, not a person. His power will destroy all the negative elements upon the Earth controlled by Sanat-Lucifer, and then Sanat-Sananda will take his rightful place as King of the World in the New Age, the Fifth World."*

"The prophecy of the Second Coming and Thousand Year Reign of Christ[24] obviously refers to the same event..."

**The Goddess:** *"Yes. Christ will return as Sanat-Sananda."*

"Will Sanat-Sananda be in a physical body when he arrives?"

**The Goddess:** *"Sanat-Sananda is a consciousness, not a person, as is Sanat-Lucifer. Sanat-Sananda is the consciousness of love and allowance. There will be those who represent him as the head of the coming world government, but his primary seat and throne will be within everyone's heart."*

"What about Sanat-Lucifer? I thought you said the Twins would unite in the Fifth World. Doesn't that mean they will rule the world together?"

**The Goddess:** *"The Twins will reunite in the Fifth World as higher and lower will. Sanat-Lucifer, the ego or lower will and individuality, will unite with Sanat-Sananda, the Higher Will. They will work together, but Sanat-Sananda will be the ultimate ruler."*

"Love and allowance will reign over dominance and control? That is certainly encouraging."

**The Goddess:** *"Yes. The Earth's future is represented in the Book of Revelation wherein the Dragon, Lucifer, is tossed into the bottomless pit. For awhile Sananda will keep Lucifer under lock and key."*

"But this is supposed to happen after Armageddon is finished, isn't it? What is currently left of the battle between the Twins?"

**The Goddess:** *"The conflict between Sanat-Sananda ruled America and the Sanat-Lucifer ruled Islamic and Communist countries must come to a resolution. This will be the last battle of the Twins."*

"Is world war still a possibility?"

**The Goddess:** *"Yes, but not to the extent many soothsayers would have you believe. When Communism was strong there was a definite threat of world war. But since the collapse of that Luciferian form of government in Russia, the forces of democracy and freedom have greatly outgained those of control and dominance."*

"But the Hopis predict nuclear war..."

136

**The Goddess:** *"Their war has already occurred. Their prophecies concerning a nuclear war are actually about World War II. Remember that the Hopis predict that the White Brother will return with two others, one of whom would carry the symbol of the Sun, and the other the swastika? These are the symbols of the Nazis and Japanese which allied as the Axis powers during WW II. The Hopi prophecy of two devastating explosions are a reference to the nuclear bombs dropped on Hiroshima and Nagasaki."*

"Then what *will* change the face of the Earth if not nuclear war?"

**The Goddess:** *"There will be many of what you call 'natural disasters.' Many volcanoes, earthquakes, tornados, hurricanes, floods, will disrupt and change the appearance and vibration of the planet. For awhile My destructive/transformative power will be ascendent on the Earth as the Kundalini accomplishes its task of demolishing and/or reorganizing the structures of the previous age in order to pave the way for a new era. This transformation will effect the body of the Earth, as well as the physical, emotional, and mental bodies of all My children. And then My power of transformation will suddenly subside and be superseded by the creative power of the Kundalini. My children will then begin to experience the world in a dramatically new way and out of newly transformed bodies."*

"But for that to occur, Your children must win the inner Armageddon by uniting ego with Spirit, lower self with higher self..."

**The Goddess:** *"Yes. You all must unite intuition with intellect. Then you will be able to trust your inner voices. If you let Me, I will communicate to you as your inner voice of wisdom and lead you to your destiny. You are My children, and I am always poised to help, guide and protect you. In fact, I have taken physical form on Earth now to assist you during these times."*

## THE AVATAR

"Do You mean as the prophesied Avatar?"

**The Goddess:** *"Yes, but not exactly as prophesied. I do not ride upon a big white horse and spit fire. I do, however, 'ride' within the bodies of certain masters currently on the planet who are teaching the path of love, such as your Ammachi,[25] who, by the way, always wears white."*

137

"Are You the Avatar spirit or is Christ-Sananda?"

The Goddess: *"We are One. I am love, and My Son Christ-Sananda is love. The Avatar spirit is the consciousness of love."*

"Then, perhaps, there is more than one Avatar?"

The Goddess: *"Yes. Many masters have come to do battle with Sanat-Lucifer, who now manifests on Earth as the ego and intellectual consciousness which engenders duality. Collectively these masters are My Son Sanat-Sananda, the Higher Self."*

"Many masters on Earth are now teaching the path of love, or Bhakti Yoga. Is this the Yoga of the Avatar?"

The Goddess: *"Yes, it is. Only through Bhakti Yoga, the path of love and devotion through kindness and service, can the forces of control and dominance be defeated. Bhakti Yoga has always been the Yoga of My First Son. It was originally taught on Lemuria by My First Son, Sanat Kumara, who brought it from Venus and transmitted it to Narada,[25] the author of the Bhakti Sutras, the definitive text on Bhakti Yoga."*

"Well, since many of us are practicing the path of love, it appears as though the work of the Avatar is succeeding."

The Goddess: *"Yes. The work of the Avatar has been very successful. It is now paving the way for My return via the resurrected Goddess tradition."*

"And You will return permanently when we move into the Fifth World of Venus, right?"

The Goddess: *"Yes. The Fifth World is the prophesied Kingdom of Heaven. It is My home and the abode of Sanat-Sananda. But as My son Sananda once said, 'you must become a child to enter the Kingdom of Heaven.' You must become My child to enter My realm. You must become a Kumara."*

# CHAPTER VI
# THE FIFTH WORLD OF VENUS

"Obviously, it's imperative that we open out hearts now if we want to enter the coming Kingdom of Heaven..."

**The Goddess:** *"Yes. Only when the majority of My children have opened their heart will the Fifth World or Kingdom of Heaven truly commence. Otherwise, it will be the Fifth World in name only."*

"When I think of having an open heart, I almost always think of Lemuria. Perhaps I need to return to how I was then."

**The Goddess:** *"Your heart was open then, as were the hearts of many of My children in physical incarnation at that time. As you all open your hearts again, you will indeed return to Lemuria.*

*"But the coming civilization of the Fifth World will not be a revival of either Lemuria or Atlantis. It will be a union of the two. In fact, the Fifth World will be the synthesis of every civilization and tradition which has existed upon Earth over the last six million years."*

"I'm confused...by calling it the Fifth World of Venus, isn't it automatically aligned with the matriarchal tradition and Lemuria?"

**The Goddess:** *"Yes, in that love will be its theme. But love unites all polarities in harmony, and in the Fifth World of Venus love is destined to unite the Matriarchy and Patriarchy into a co-operative synthesis. The matriarchal principles regarding how to live harmoniously with the Earth will unite in love with 'patriarchal' technology. And there will be matriarchal freedom for all, but patriarchal structure and discrimination will be needed to stabilize the new civilization. So, along with the union of intuition and intellect, Spirit and ego, the Matriarchy and Patriarchy will finally unite peacefully."*

"It sounds like the Fifth World will be the time for humanity to listen to nature and the intuitive proddings from Spirit. But this tendency will need to be balanced with the discriminating intellect."

**The Goddess:** *"Yes. But don't worry, I will teach you all how to live in the New World. Once you develop your intuition fully, the ego and intellect will naturally loose their control, and then you will be able to hear My inner directives clearly. I can then teach you how to create technology which is not in conflict with nature; I can also reveal to you how to establish a symbiotic relationship between yourselves and nature; and I can show you how to build structures which are life force conductors, rather than inhibitors. I can show you so many things..."*

"It sounds as though You, the Goddess, will be the guiding consciousness of the coming World of Venus."

**The Goddess:** *"Yes. Love and intuition will be the guiding forces of the New Age."*

"Will Sanat continue to rule from Shamballa during the Fifth World?"

**The Goddess:** *"No. During the Fifth World My First Son will rule from the throne of each person's heart."*

"But there be an individual person or spirit being who continues to rule as the head of the planetary government, a future King of the World, right?"

140

The Goddess: "*There will not be a king as such. Kings are part of the old patriarchal power complex and there time has past. There will, however, be a chief executive who will preside over a one-world government. He or she will represent Sanat-Sananda on Earth and serve as the representative of all My children.*"

"Will that person be an enlightened master?"

The Goddess: "*Ultimately, yes. Only by uniting with the Higher Will can one represent Sananda. Only then can he or she begin to serve as the collective will of My children, and as caretaker of the Earth.*"

"Besides caretaking the planet, what else will it mean for him or her to be Your chief executive?"

The Goddess: "*He or she must become My model child on Earth. This means having full faith and trust in Me, for I AM the power and wisdom of God. My child does not worry about the past or future because he or she knows I will attend to every need. My child serves Me alone and waits for My command which arrives as inner inspiration. By acting upon this inner guidance, My child knows all actions will be successful because he or she is working for Me.*"

"Does Your model child, the chief executive, retain any ego or individuality, or is that completely dissolved?"

The Goddess: "*Some small part of the ego remains after uniting with Me. This is the part which knows itself to be My child.*"

"Is the coming Fifth World synonymous with the Age of Horus, the Age of the Son prophesied by Aliester Crowley?"

The Goddess: "*Yes. Aliester Crowley's Age of Horus is a synonym for the Age of the Son, or the Age of the Kumara. Crowley was correct in stating that the coming Age of Horus would be a synthesis of the Age of Isis, the Matriarchal Age and the Age of Osiris, the Patriarchal Age. He was also right in proclaiming that in the New Age 'do as thou wilt shall be the whole of the law.' Unfortunately people misconstrued this mandate because Crowley's undisciplined lifestyle made it appear as though he was calling for a world orgy. In truth, the directive of 'do as thou wilt' was meant to be observed only when the ego had been purified and transcended."*

"And then each person's actions would be inspired by communication from the Higher Self. Now I think I understand. The directives from the Higher Self are the 'Law,' not the selfish desires of the lower self or ego."

**The Goddess:** *"Right. The law of the Fifth World will not be ego centered or man-made, but divinely inspired."*

"Will there still be the need for forums of lawmakers if a higher power is in control?"

**The Goddess:** *"Eventually there will be many less lawmakers, because they won't be needed. People will already know the law because it will be universal and revealed to each of them intuitively. There will, however, continue to be the need for law enforcers."*

"Will we start to see signs of governmental changes in the near future?"

**The Goddess:** *"Yes. Those who serve the Higher Will will soon begin to take an active role in the political process. They are the ministers and heralds of Sananda."*

"What about the popular conception of time coming to an end in the New Age? Will time really stop?"

**The Goddess:** *"Yes. You are currently immersed in time because you are having a transitory experience of life. But for the enlightened masters, time is a no-thing. This is because their minds have quieted and they have tapped into an awareness which transcends ephemeral existence. All that exists for them is one eternal moment. When you merge with the Infinite, everything becomes a dream, including the concept of time."*

"Right. On Shasta I experienced this. There was no beginning or end to anything, not even creation. It has existed forever."

**The Goddess:** *"That is because you merged with Spirit in your heart. You merged with a consciousness which does not recognize time."*

"And in that experience my heart was wide-open. I could only experience love. Love and the Infinite seem to be synonymous."

**The Goddess:** *"Right. There is only fear and love, time and the Infinite. Fear, the mind, and time are inter-connected, as are love, intuition and the Infinite. If you are established in the heart, fear and the mental fluctuations it engenders dissolve into an eternal present of love and allowance."*

"If everyone is established within their hearts and united with the Higher Will during the Age of Venus, what need will there be for mystery schools and yogic disciplines?"

**The Goddess:** *"Spiritual practices will still be necessary. There will still be those coming to Earth for soul evolution who possess an ego. And as long as there is even a trace of ego, it will need to be held in check. For this reason, a justice system of sorts will also be necessary. The actions of those who are inspired by their egos or lower wills can be harmful to society."*

"But I am sure prisons will be much different than they are now..."

**The Goddess:** *"Yes. Prisons will be replaced by temples where a transgressor will go through a process of purification in order to raise his or her vibration and reconnect with the Higher Self."*

"Will there be a need for consciousness expanding sacraments in the Fifth World?"

**The Goddess:** *"They will not be essential. There will be many ways of raising an individual's vibration. But for someone who has sufficiently lowered his or her frequency, they will provide an option for uniting with the Higher Self again."*

"Will we have ongoing contact with extraterrestrials on Earth during the Fifth World."

The Goddess: "*Yes. You do now, but most of you don't know it. Most extraterrestrials are fourth dimensional. They have been waiting until you could join them on their dimension before interacting with you. They could not reveal themselves before now because you would have worshipped them, and this would have interfered with your evolution.*"

"Will we eventually be receiving technology from them?"

The Goddess: "*Some of them. Especially those you have karmic ties with, such as the Venusians and Sirians. But their wisdom also comes from Me, so you will be able to access what they know from within yourself. In the past they interbred with your species and transmitted their evolutionary Cosmic Fire so that you would be able to eventually receive any information you desired. This will occur in the coming Fifth World when your brain will evolve into an illuminated receiver of unimaginable efficiency.*"

"Will the two halves of the brain grow back together?"

The Goddess: "*No. Because you will still be using your egos and intellects. The two halves will, however, function in unison, which they are not currently doing.*"

"I think my questions have been answered now. I am also feeling a bit nauseous and I think I need to rest and lower my vibration."

The Goddess: "*Lay down and surrender to My healing energy. You can talk to Me later. I will always be near to support you and give you guidance when you seek it.*"

# CHAPTER VII:
# LIVING LIKE A CHILD OF THE GODDESS

    While laying down and surrendering to the etheric caresses of the Goddess, I went through a very intense and rapid healing process. At first I became progressively more nauseous, but then I was suddenly fine. Even my altered consciousness had nearly returned to normal. My perception was still a little blurry and my body weak, but at least I was lucid enough to put one foot in front of the other without falling flat on my face.

    The significance of the day began to seep in as I took time to review my conversation with the Goddess. While the diminishing rays of the Sun glanced off my naked body, my inner spirit basked in my incredibly good fortune. What amounted to the secrets of human existence had been revealed to me in the space of one short afternoon, and I was now the caretaker of what I considered to be the wisdom of the ages. So, rather than taking the chance of forgetting some of this priceless information, I decided to return home and capture it on my harddrive. There was still a couple hours of light left, so I gathered up my strewn clothing and quickly redressed myself. I then packed up my belongings, bid a warm farewell to the mountain lake, and resolutely set off down the mountain trail.

Well, as I was soon to find out, it probably would have been better if I had remained at the lake for the night. My body was much weaker than I expected, and kept getting more so with each step I took down the path. Everything felt off kilter, including my pack frame, which continually jabbed my sore hips and sent excruciating bolts of pain down my back and legs. But the Goddess must have supported, because somehow I managed to make it back to my car with enough energy to drive back to Olympia.

When I finally arrived home my sleepy little neighborhood was nestled under the cloak of darkness. Staggering through the front door of my home, I said a perfunctory hello to my wife before collapsing in exhaustion on the couch. At length, I decided I was much too tired to write anything and limped off to bed. Well, so much for plans.

During my next three days of convalescing, bits and pieces of my dialogue with the Goddess would spontaneously resurface into my consciousness and I would force myself to input them into my computer. I was actually amazed at how much I was able to recall. Eventually an outline of this book began to take shape, as well as the book's title. At first I resisted calling it "Conversations with the Goddess," thinking that such a title would be judged as an obvious exploitation and rip-off of the *Conversations with God* series. But after some deliberation, I decided the Goddess had some important things to say, and this title would inspire many people who were normally skeptical of "received" information to at least pick up the book and give it cursory consideration.

When I had finally recovered enough to get on with my life, the effects of my day at the mountain lake continued to doggedly pursue me. For example, I would occasionally find myself lost in deep contemplation regarding my inner Lucifer. The memory of having been the rebellious son for a short time was still fresh in my mind, and each moment I indulged myself in its recall I felt tinges of excitement move throughout my body. Eventually I decided that I had tasted a deeper sense of freedom than I had ever known before—and I wanted more. I was somehow able to convince myself that I needed to focus on the Lucifer part of myself, and that such an endeavor was both therapeutic and spiritual. After all, wouldn't my inner Lucifer help me to ultimately break through my limitations so I could unite with Sananda, my higher self?

The first big decision I encountered in my Luciferian experiment was deciding where to begin. I loved the freedom of being naked in the lake, but did that mean I should become a nudist or naturist, or perhaps even an exhibitionist as Lucifer seemed to relish being? The thought of more sexual freedom was also very appealing to me. But should I become more sexually promiscuous at the risk of losing my marriage? I seriously weighed all these options before finally opting to take a more moderate approach. Being the Virgo conservative type, My natural inclination is to stick my toes in the waters of experimentation without getting completely wet. At least that way my whole life can not be turned completely upside down.

Within a month, an opportunity to let my inner Lucifer "let his hair down" and run free and wild presented itself. I left for Peru as the featured speaker of a spiritually oriented tour. I saw this as an opportunity to break free of my old behavioral straight jacket and remake myself into a new image without raising too many eyebrows. Everyone would just have to accept they were stuck with an eccentric featured speaker.

Well, to make a long, sad story thankfully short, I made more enemies than friends during that tour, and that included the tour's director, my wife. I was as flamboyant and wild as I had ever been, but at the cost of shutting myself off to the needs of others. I flirted whenever I had the chance, and found myself becoming dangerously attracted to one of the women on the tour. I even tried to enrol some of our passengers in a group experience of nudity. That experiment fared the worst of all, and I heard about it later when certain disgruntled participants submitted their post-tour evaluation forms. Apparently many were appalled I could even suggest such a thing.

So, after dejectedly returning to the safety of my home, I decided to take a breather from my experiment. I was spiritually depleted and desperately needing some answers. I toyed with the idea of taking another sacrament to re-establish communication with the Goddess, but I really didn't feel the inspiration to do so. Anyway, the Goddess didn't say that She wold only be there for me if I was under the influence. So, I decided to take another tact and proceeded to spend numerous hours in front of my computer in hopes of contacting the Goddess through automatic writing. I had had some relative success with automatic writing in the past, so why not attempt it now? Either it would work or it wouldn't, I really had nothing to lose. Finally, after many days of waiting for inspiration, there was a knock at the cosmic door and my hands began to move effortlessly across the keyboard...

The Goddess: *"Take heart My Son, I have been watching you. Your Lucifer experiment was not entirely a bust. You were right, you did need to express the shadow side of yourself for awhile before it could be integrated. Your inner Lucifer needed to run wild for awhile before you could understand why it needs restraining. But now you should learn how to temper it with the love of Sananda."*

"I'm at a loss Goddess. Are You now saying that the wild Luciferian path is only to be followed for awhile?"

**The Goddess:** *"Yes. Think of Nietzsche's three transformations: the camel, the lion, and the child. The camel, which is loaded down with responsibilities and inhibitions, transforms into the wild lion for awhile, but eventually he becomes the placid child."*

"What, then, is the best path for me now if I am to transform from the lion into Your child?"

**The Goddess:** *"The Middle Path of balance is best. You have learned through experience that there needs to be a balance between Lucifer and Sananda, have you not? Well, if you can unite the polarity signified by these two Twins, you will travel to the world within your heart and find the source of infinite freedom and joy. You will then live as My child, the Kumara."*

"And how do I do that?"

**The Goddess:** *"There are many facets to the Middle Path. For example, while satisfying your own desires try being caring towards others. Daily observance of the disciplines of the Bhakti Path will help you to achieve a natural love for others, as well as yourself. Continue to chant the name of God, meditate often, and serve others when you can. And one more thing...spend time in the loving presence of your Ammachi. Let Me work through her to transform you into My loving Son."*

"Well, it certainly feels like Ammachi is transforming me into Your Son when I am in her presence. I always feel like a playful little boy around her, and she seems to encourage this adolescent behavior by being playful towards me."

**The Goddess:** *"Yes. Her role is to transform all My devotees into Kumaras with the hearts of children. Besides the positive effect her playfulness has on this process, by whispering into your receptive ears 'My Darling Son' or 'My Darling Daughter,' she is also planting the seeds of transmutation."*

"Please advise me how I can live as Your child in every moment?"

The Goddess: "*Surrender to Me. Your Sister Thedra gave you a clue of how to do this when she touched her pulse and proclaimed to you 'I don't do that, God does that.' Not only do you not move your own blood or pump your own heart, you are not involved with the other processes in your body. You don't consciously digest your food; you don't divide your cells; you don't release the hormones which regulate your bodily functions; and you don't heal your own tissues following physical traumas. If it weren't for another consciousness performing those functions for you, you would perish.*"

"Is it You performing those functions?"

The Goddess: "*Yes. I am God's power. It is I who nourishes and sustains you. You could not even think a thought if it was not I who carry the neurochemicals across the synapses.*"

"From that perspective, I guess I owe a lot to You."

The Goddess: "*Yes, in fact everything. But when I am take care of you, I take care of Myself. In truth, there is no separation. It is just your own ego which makes you believe that you are an individual and different from Me.*"

"If it wasn't for my ego, would I know that I am You?"

The Goddess: "*Yes. You would realize that your essence is the infinite Spirit, and I am the power which springs forth from you.*"

"What power? Do You mean the power I felt emanating out of my heart on Shasta?"

The Goddess: "*Yes, that is Me. You are always creating Me. As Spirit you created Me as Kundalini power at the beginning of time, and you continue to create Me every time you think a thought with desire.*"

"What happens after I create You?"

The Goddess: "*Well, after you created Me as Kundalini at the beginning of time, I divided into Seven Rays, or Seven Kumaras, which then proceeded to create the Solar System and your beautiful Earth. Since that time, the energy*

149

*of My Seven Rays has continued to oversee the evolution of your planet via the seven astrological planets (Saturn, Jupiter, Mars, Venus, Mercury, the Sun, and Moon) and the twelve signs of the Zodiac.*

*"Since that initial outpouring of power at the beginning of time, I have governed the destiny of Earth and all its inhabitants. But each of you is continuously modifying your destiny by your creation of more power."*

"The power with which we influence our destiny in each moment...is that a description of our free will?"

The Goddess: *"Yes. But your free will is extremely limited. You are born into a family with a specific social standing and in a specific part of the world. Your body type and mental capacity are determined by your parents. And your reactions in life are mostly determined by your past lives and childhood experiences."*

"So where is the freedom?"

The Goddess: *"True freedom comes from having the choice to reform yourself and react in a new way to life's circumstances. When you are not limited to programmed reactions—perhaps because you have changed your responses by healing their underlying emotional residue—then you have a measure of freedom. Ultimate freedom arrives when you acquire the choice to either react or not react to all the events occurring around you.*

*"Freedom also comes through remaining non-attached to the fruits of your actions. Attachment is the enemy, it keeps you bound. It keeps you tied to the roller coaster of highs and lows. Detachment, however, gives you the freedom to serve the Higher Will. When you are not attached to the fruits of your actions, you can truly serve God and Goddess. And then whatever you strive to accomplish will naturally occur, because your desire will be My desire."*

"But if you are controlling my actions, aren't I already conforming to Your will?"

The Goddess: *"You are, but you often seek a different outcome for your actions than what I have given you. Consequently, you are not completely in alignment with My will, and there is much pain."*

"How can I avoid the pain?"

The Goddess: "*You can start by making every action a gift to Me, and have no special desire for its fruit. Tell yourself 'I am serving my mother.' Also practice the mantra Sister Thedra gave you: 'Not my will but Thine be done.' If you can cultivate this attitude, then most of your personal desires will fall away on their own. And, as the saying goes, when you completely give up everything, you gain the entire universe. It is also useful to affirm 'I am not the doer.' Remember that I perform all actions through you.*"

"If I am not the doer, then what am I?"

The Goddess: "*Your true nature is that of Spirit, the eternal witness of all actions. The infinite Spirit resides within your heart as the eternal, unchanging part of yourself. Everything else, including your mind, emotions, and thoughts are subject to change and are governed by Me.*

"*Remember the time you merged with the Spirit in your heart on Mt. Shasta? You knew you had come home to your true Self, and in that state you were the passive witness and not the doer. You witnessed Me, the creative force, emerge from you and all you did was watch it and love it.*"

"You are right, I was home and could experience You as the primal energy which accomplishes all things in creation. In retrospect, I think that that experience helped me to develop a greater appreciation for prayer. If You are the doer, it is obviously in my best interest to call upon You to help me in manifesting my desires."

The Goddess: "*Yes. And I will assist you because you are My creator and I am your ally. As long as you want My help, I will be at your beck and call.*"

"Thank you. But more than knowing that You are there for me, I want to experience Your presence around me all the time, starting now."

The Goddess: "*You can find Me in your heart. That is My abode. Go into your heart.*"

"I can do that occasionally, but not all the time. What can I do to consistently experience You?"

The Goddess: *"Be patient. Continual awareness of My presence takes time. But you can daily chant My divine names, and these will open you to My ever present love. You can also practice Hatha Yoga and meditation. These will unite the polarity within your heart and also assist you in experiencing Me."*

"You are right. Through my own experience I have found that such disciplines culminate in Kundalini movement and help precipitate communion with You."

The Goddess: *"Yes. The Kundalini is Me. Have faith in it. Through it I will work to give You an experience of My presence within and around you."*

"I know You are constantly transforming me through the Kundalini. I often feel Your heat as it transforms my inner and outer world."

The Goddess: *"Yes. And as you have experienced, I often use the harshest and most heated difficulties in your life as a vehicle to take you into your heart. The right attitude is to have faith in Me and see Me at work wherever you are and with whomever you are with, even your worst enemy."*

"Which is a very difficult challenge, indeed."

The Goddess: *"Yes, but it is a necessary goal. Only when you can see all phenomenon within the world as being Me—when you can see the power of the ONE consciousness manifesting in all the multiplicity of forms—only then can you truly live in unity awareness. There is only ONE. It is only your ego and intellect which tells you differently."*

"So, what we really need is to put the intellect aside and dwell fully in the present moment with the firm conviction that you are guiding our lives in a way that is in our best and highest good?"

The Goddess: *"Yes. But before you can do that, you must have full faith in Me. You must have the faith that I will always watch over you. Otherwise, you will remain in fear for your safety and well being."*

"But aren't we subject to physical harm even if we have faith in You?"

The Goddess: *"If you have faith, then you will know that what appears as harm is only happening to evolve your consciousness and eventually bring you to inner peace."*

"I have noticed that some seekers are sometimes caught up in one crisis or another and seem to be without any inner peace for most of their lives..."

The Goddess: *"You must know that this happens when a person desires to take 'the fast track' to Me. On some level they have made the commitment to work through their blocks to freedom in a hurry. But think of this: A crisis denotes confusion, anxiety, a sense that all might be lost, does it not? If someone has put all their trust in Me, he or she knows I will always take care of them. A crisis can never exist for such a person. They find security and inner peace in their faith."*

"I am always reminded of My teacher Muktananda who thanked his guru, Nityananda, for whatever happened to him, good or bad. All things came as a blessing from Nityananda."

The Goddess: *"Nityananda was the form of God that Muktananda worshipped. Yours is Ammachi. Both are My forms. Whoever you accept as your deity or savior, know that they are a form of Me."*

"So Jesus, Buddha, Mohammed—they are all your forms?"

The Goddess: *"Yes. They are the vehicles of My love and wisdom. I come to My devotees in a form they can accept."*

"Then basically all saviors are one, they are You. It is Your wisdom and power working through them."

The Goddess: *"Yes, they are both Me and My First Son, because we are One."*

"So, I guess the Christians are correct in maintaining that there is only one Son of God?"

The Goddess: *"Yes. But not in the way they mean it. The divine awareness of My First Son, the consciousness of I AM GOD, is what is truly known as the*

153

*'only Son of God.' Throughout time this consciousness has incarnated within countless physical forms, and many of you are destined to be its vessels soon."*

"You mean in the Fifth World?"

The Goddess: *"Yes. Separation from your divine self is ending. It is time to return home."*

## THE GODDESS TAKES ME TO SWITZERLAND

Just after I had my rendezvous with the Goddess at the mountain lake, I was invited to a special conference in Zurich, Switzerland to speak about the prophesied days to come. The conference, which was scheduled for the following November of that year, was entitled the "World Congress of the Prophets," and set to include such heavyweight speakers as Zechariah Sitchin, the author of a series of esoteric books concerning the past and future of the Earth. When I first heard about the Congress, I had a sudden intuition that it had been orchestrated by the Goddess and was to serve as a vehicle for the information She had given me. At the very least, I felt that She had arranged my invitation to it and a special lesson awaited me there.

When I eventually arrived in Zurich, it was cold and rainy, so I quickly found my hotel and then began crafting my talk. Thus began two days of nervously pacing back and forth in my hotel room while trying to extract those highlights from my conversation with the Goddess which I thought would be both applicable and interesting to those attending the conference. In the end, I decided to refer a lot to my experience of Lucifer, especially to his role as King of the World and its meaning for our "end times." "This should have the Fundamentalist Christians running for the exits," I chuckled out loud while putting the finishing touches on my talk.

When I finally gave the lecture, I felt like I was back at the mountain lake and the Goddess was right by my side. The talk went off without a hitch, and the audience was both very receptive and attentive throughout. And it was especially rewarding when, at the end of the talk, people rushed the podium with questions and personal accounts of their own. The Goddess's information had indeed had a significant impact on them.

As I waded through the enthusiastic crowd which flocked the podium, Urs, my German translator, suddenly pulled me aside and guided me directly to a corner of the room where a small woman was standing. As soon as I was in front of her, this woman became very animated as she passionately began recounting in rapid German a recent dream she had had. Through Urs's expert translation, I learned that she had dreamed of herself in a hotel room at Grindelwald, a small vacation town high in the Swiss Alps, from which she was gazing upon the three surrounding high peaks of Jungfrau, Monch and Eiger. Suddenly she felt the floor of her hotel room begin to shake, and she watched with both fear and excitement as the world outside began to convulse and crumble. Huge blocks of stone and massive ice fields rolled down from the three peaks and into the surrounding valley. Then one of the peaks violently erupted, spewing ash and lava in all directions, along with what appeared to be the figure of a person. Becoming transfixed on this person's image, she watched as it flew through the air and straight into her hotel room!

With her visitor now in front of her, the German woman could clearly distinguish the features of a tall, handsome looking man. He was clean shaven and possessed classic Nordic features, such as a high forehead, blond hair and blue eyes. His golden hair was long and gently cascaded down onto a seamless, one-piece body suit, which was colored a shade of red. With both kindness and penetrating intensity this intruder looked directly into the woman's eyes and proclaimed "I am the King of the World. Whatever you ask from me will be yours."

The woman was so stunned she could barely respond to her guest. Instead, she silently prayed to God, "Lord, I'm just too scared to deal with this blond haired man right now, so please remove him from my presence." Almost immediately the man began to move backwards in the direction he had come, but not without leaving her with one parting offer. "I am the Morning and Evening Star. Pray to me if you ever need anything." When the man had returned to the volcanic mountain the dream suddenly ended.

As the woman finished sharing her dream large tears welled up in her eyes. Through emotion and words she communicated to me that although the dream had initially been very traumatic for her, ultimately it had had a very positive and profound effect on her life. And now, after listening to my talk, she was convinced that the visitor in her dream was Sanat Kumara, a.k.a. Lucifer, the King of the World. If she ever had a similar encounter with the blond haired man, she knew that the fear would be absent.

I graciously thanked the woman for sharing her story with me and was beginning to walk contemplatively back to the crowd when it suddenly occurred to me that perhaps the woman's dream was a gift to me. Perhaps, through this little woman, the Goddess was proving to me the reality of Lucifer's existence. Almost every characteristic of Lucifer's She had previously revealed to me—including his Nordic features, his association with the underworld, his red attire, his origin on Venus, and his role as King of the World—had been confirmed by this woman living on the opposite side of the world from me. Coincidence? I didn't think so.

Later that night in Ur's living room, while listening to the pitter patter of a steady November rain, I inquired from my translator whether there were any sacred mountains in Switzerland I could visit. My wife was now with me and we planned to tour the country the following week. To my complete amazement, the first three mountains he spoke of were the names of the three Grindelwald peaks in the woman's dream! I had now heard their names twice in one day and took it as a sign from the Goddess that I needed to pay them a visit.

Four days later I found myself looking out from a Grindelwald hotel room at the three sacred mountains. "Quite possibly," I told myself, "I am even in the same room as she was during the dream." But of course the floor did not shake under my feet, nor did any of the mountains suddenly erupt and catapult Lucifer into the air. I did, however, make what I decided was a very important discovery. As I surveyed the three mountains, I discovered that they were united in the form of a gigantic trident, the symbol of Lucifer! Apparently Grindelwald was indeed an abode of Lucifer, and it bore his infamous symbol to prove it. I decided that it must truly be a sacred and remarkable place. So, with profound gratitude, I profusely thanked the Goddess for bringing me to Switzerland and helping me dispel any remaining doubts I may have had about the existence of Her and Her Son.

# CHAPTER VIII
# COMMUNING WITH THE GODDESS

After returning from Switzerland, I hurriedly finished my manuscript and composed some query letters to various publishers concerning *Conversations with the Goddess* before rushing off to lead a small tour to some of the important temples and ashrams in India. Since the letters remained foremost on my mind during the tour, one of my consistent prayers to the Hindu deities and spiritual masters we encountered on the pilgrimage was: "Please help me publish my book!"

When the two week tour concluded I traveled alone to the ashram of my spiritual guide, Ammachi, in south India, and then embarked upon two weeks of silence and intense meditation. During that time I arose in darkness each morning at 3 AM and ended each day at 9 PM. I had brought a copy of the manuscript with me in order to have it blessed by Ammachi, but each time I felt ready to approach her with it the voice of the Goddess spoke clearly within my head and proclaimed: "You can bring it to Me, but I have already blessed it!" "Well," I would reply, "of course You have. You wrote it!"

At the end of my two week stay at the ashram I attended a special "Goddess" celebration, called a "Devi Bhava." During the Devi Bhava, a ritual which periodically occurs at the ashram, Ammachi completely merges Her individuality with the Goddess of the Universe, and any trace of an individualized ego completely disappears. Spiritual seekers, convalescents, and struggling householders are then invited to approach the Great Goddess for a hug and Her blessing. This particular Devi Bhava was made extra special and powerful because it coincided with a completely full Moon.

Even though I loved greeting the Goddess when She came through Ammachi untainted, I had developed a mild distaste for the Devi Bhava celebration. I did not like the huge crowds which attended them, and it always seemed like there were hordes of people jousting for the Goddess's attention or to gaze upon Her radiant countenance. So, when I first arrived at this Devi Bhava around 8 PM, all it took was one look at the sea of people crammed into the temple before the repulsion I felt compelled to run as fast as I could in the opposite direction. Soon I was racing up the three flights of stairs leading to a meditation area on the ashram's roof. As I climbed, I was comforted by the thought that if I remained on the roof long enough many people would have gotten their blessing and gone home, and I would have the Goddess to myself. In the meantime I could put in some serious meditation time.

As I stepped out onto the moon-lit roof, I quickly scanned the entire area for fellow meditators and realized that I was completely alone. With child-like exuberance, I told myself that on this special night I was going to have the place all to myself. But just in case someone else might be coming, I decided to find the best spot for meditation and moon gazing as fast as possible. My rapid search subsequently led me to a spot at the edge of roof which seemed perfect for my purposes. From there I commanded a birds-eye view of the shimmering moon-lit landscape of ashram buildings, as well as the exotic groves of tropical plants and towering palm trees which surrounded them.

As I relaxed into my seat, I noticed that the Moon had risen three quarters of the way up a clear Kerala sky and its luminosity was engulfing everything around me. I began to alternately glance at the Moon's radiant orb above and the glowing lights of the ashram's numerous buildings below me. Mingled with the breathtaking beauty of my surreal environment was the hypnotic hum of the Devi Bhava crowd milling around in front of the temple and the melodic sounds of Sanscrit chants issuing from within. With a deep sigh of euphoric satisfaction, I affirmed that there was no place on Earth I would rather be at that moment.

My idyllic surroundings quickly transported me into a semi-trance state, and I closed my eyes in order to fully embody the experience. As I did so, I could feel subtle waves of lunar energy enter my cranium, move down my spine, and permeate my entire body. I began to sway under the influence of the nectar-like soma (a Hindu name for lunar light) and my emotional state rapidly ascended to the point of ecstasy. If not for the drunken stupor which accompanied this ecstasy, I think I would have gotten up and danced in delight from one end of the roof to the other.

Soon I had become so inebriated that all I could do was fall onto my back and writhe and moan with bliss on the roof. To any casual observers I must have appeared like a man possessed. But even though my physical body was out of control, my mind remained lucid and active. I therefore decided to make a mental inquiry into the cause of my new-found ecstatic condition. "I haven't taken a sacrament," I told myself. "So how could I have achieved this kind of ecstasy?" Once again my guide, the Goddess, arrived to provide the answers.

**The Goddess:** *"What do you think is so strange about your current state of bliss? You have chosen a night when My power, the power of the Goddess, is at its fullest extent."*

"Ah!...so I am experiencing Your power?"

**The Goddess:** *"Of course. The energy of the full Moon, that which you call 'soma,' is My power."*

"But these waves of ecstasy....I have not felt them before except on sacraments or drugs. And I don't know anyone personally who has experienced them on the shakti alone."

**The Goddess:** *"That is not true. You know that your Muktananda experienced them during his spiritual practices because he wrote about it. And other people with an awakened Kundalini, or those who are very sensitive to the moon's emanations, also experience them."*

"Well I guess that I am not normally so sensitive to the Moon..."

**The Goddess:** *"You have made yourself more receptive through the meditation and fasting you have been observing. However, you were also supported in having this experience so that I could teach you something important."*

"You mean that I don't need drugs to experience this kind of ecstasy?"

**The Goddess:** *"Yes. And I also wanted you to know what communing with Me is like so that you would be able to lead others in the experience. You have been writing and meditating on the experience, now you needed to immerse yourself in it."*

"Are You saying that this is not an isolated incident, and that I will be able to recreate it in the future?"

**The Goddess:** *"Yes. But certain conditions need to be met."*

"Such as two weeks of intense meditation and a full Moon during a Devi Bhava?"

**The Goddess:** *"Yes, that is one possible scenario. But, since you have been in the business of energy movement and Kundalini awakening for a long time, you should know that there are other modalities which can also be used to recreate this experience."*

"Well... I have used crystals, pyramids, mantras, controlled breathing, meditation, color and sound together for quite awhile now. But I have never experienced the kind of energy from them that I do now."

**The Goddess:** *"Sometimes the energy is felt subtly, but its effect is nonetheless equally as powerful. Keep using your tools and listening to Me. I will guide you to the experience you need."*

"Good advice. Unfortunately I'm not normally able to hear You as clearly as I do now."

**The Goddess:** *"Your intuition is clearer tonight because of your energy charged environment. But don't worry, your communication with Me will become stronger in time. In the mean time, remember the Biblical directive: 'Be still and know that I am God.'"*

"I suppose that line could just as easily read 'Be still and know that I am the Goddess!'"

**The Goddess:** *"Yes. The God and Goddess are inseparable. The wisdom and power of God is the Goddess. When God talks to you, it is Me."*

At that point our dialogue suddenly ended and all my thoughts seemed to dissolve into a milky stillness. If I wanted to know something, the answer was there, but I found it more satisfying to remain immersed in the cosmic "no-mind" and let the ecstatic bliss of the soma move through me. I had found the stillness of God within and resolved to dwell within it, at least for a little while.

When next I opened my eyes, the Moon had risen to its zenith position in the sky and was hovering directly over me. The crispness of the air and the soft murmur of the crowd below informed me that I had been on the roof for long enough, and that it was now safe to return to the temple. So, with all the strength I could muster, I slowly shifted my weight onto my shaky legs. I was still clearly in a drunken state and not entirely sure if I was going to be able to descend the stairs back to the hall, but earlier in the day I had solemnly vowed to have an audience with the Goddess during this special Devi Bhava night. This would be my last chance to see Her before leaving India, and I had an important question to ask Her.

## "I AM YOUR TRUE MOTHER"

One hour later I had moved through the "darshan" line in the temple and was just twenty feet away from the Goddess. As was Her custom, She was seated upon a serpent throne (a throne with serpent armrests) and dressed in a regalia consisting of a deep-blue colored sari with golden trim which was surmounted by a silver, jewel studded crown. Her emanations of spiritual power or shakti were overwhelmingly strong on this special night, and I felt as though I was walking through a dense etheric soup the closer I came to Her.

As I moved forward in line, I continuously repeated my question to myself. The question concerned my relationship with my birth mother. We had been in conflict for many years, and of late we had severed all lines of communication. So, there appeared to be no hope of reconciliation and this had brought me untold pain and feelings of abandonment. My question to the Goddess was, simply, what I could do about it.

When it was my turn to greet the Goddess, I asked the attendant standing in front of Her to translate my question into Malayalam, Ammachi's native language. His immediate response was "no," because questions were not normally asked during Devi Bhava, but he then recanted when I informed him that earlier that day Ammachi had promised me I would be able to ask the Goddess a question. Then, as he proceeded to ask my question to Her, I sunk to my knees and leaned into the outstretched arms of the Goddess.

After a short, shakti imbued hug, the Goddess gently pushed me away from Her and looked me straight in my eyes. Then, in response to the question about my mother, the Goddess tenderly commanded: "She is your mother, You should try to talk to her. If she doesn't respond, then okay. But at least try." As She spoke, the Goddess's face communicated so much love and care that my heart nearly melted. I wanted to remain in front of Her forever, but I knew my time was over, so I slowly began to stand up. As I did so, the Goddess said a few more words to Her attendant concerning me and then moved to greet the next person in line.

When I was fully upright and began to turn away from the Goddess's chair, I perceived that the attendant was looking straight at me and had a mischievous grin on his face. As I inquisitively observed him, I watched as he reached down to move the Goddess's gown away from Her legs while playfully instructing me to "Kiss Her feet!" I was stunned, but remained lucid enough to know that I was being given the opportunity of a lifetime. So, with great reverence and enthusiasm, I quickly dove to my knees and placed my lips on the Goddess's silky dark brown skin. As I did so, my nose inhaled Her sweet, rose-like fragrance. All my senses were instantly filled.

But my good fortune was not over yet! After I again stood up the attendant directed me to sit right next to the throne! Before he could change his mind, I quickly squeezed in between two natives and watched admiringly as the Goddess greeted one devotee after the other. Then another unexpected event occurred. After only a few minutes of greeting Her children, the Goddess suddenly turned in my direction and again showered me with Her loving attention. In an almost an exact replay of my earlier encounter with Her, She again told me I should try to talk to my mother and how important that was. Only this time She talked for a lot longer and Her message was much more animated. Obviously She was trying very hard to drive Her point home!

After the Goddess had finished instructing me again, I remained near Her for another twenty minutes. I then stood up and slowly wandered back into the dwindling sea of people in the temple. I began to sob as I thought of the love and compassion the Goddess had directed towards me. Then the Goddess's voice emerged...

**The Goddess:** "*I am the Mother of the Universe and the fountainhead of all love and compassion. I am the Mother of mother's, and all mothers's embody Me to the degree they are capable of expressing unconditional love. By kissing My feet you have reconnected yourself with Me, the 'mother' principle. The* *conflict between you and your birth mother has been a conflict of egos, not one involving you and your true Mother. I am your true Mother and I have always loved you. And I will never abandon you."*

These words of the Goddess were both comforting and healing, and I knew they would remain in my consciousness for many days to come. When I finally left the temple, I made a point of purchasing a photo of the Goddess as a way of remembering this special night and my "mothers" eternal love for me. The photographic image of the Goddess I chose depicted Her seated upon Her throne while covered in a sari similar to the one She had worn during my darshan with Her. I spent a long time staring at this Goddess image, which I found to be both commanding and infinitely soft at the same time. I felt so much love for Her that I made an inner vow to serve the Goddess and Her creation as best I could during the crucial days to come.

## I COMMUNE WITH THE GODDESS IN PERU

In the summer of '99 I led a tour to Marca Wasi, a very special place in the Andes of Peru which was famous for its unusual rock formations and its prolific UFO sightings. Accompanying our small group was Don Arturo Cervantes, a master shaman from Lima who was going to lead us through an evening San Pedro ceremony. Little did I know at the time, but this ceremony was destined to become another very memorable opportunity for communing with the Goddess.

San Pedro is a cactus which grows in the dry, coastal regions of Peru and has been used for thousands of years by shamen to precipitate altered states of consciousness. The name San Pedro is Spanish for Saint Peter, and just like its namesake the cactus holds the keys to Heaven. According to Arturo, the cactus and the consciousness it engenders is closely connected to both Lemuria and the Goddess. It was originally used on Lemuria and holds the vibration of Mu, so it can precipitate the Lemurian consciousness of love within the user. San Pedro is specially affiliated with the Goddess by virtue of it being a "Seven Ray" sacrament, which means that it works with all the seven rays of the Goddess. As such, the cactus synergizes perfectly with the Moon, the female orb, especially during the full Moon when a rainbow of seven colors forms around it. As luck would have it, our ceremony was going to coincide with a completely full Moon.

It was late afternoon and Marca Wasi was bathed in afternoon shadows when our ceremony finally began. Ten of us formed a circle while Don Arturo instructed us about the antiquity and sanctity of the rite. He then proceeded to pass to each of us a clay mug full of a thick green liquid, the form the San Pedro takes during its preparation. Mounded onto the front of the mug was the face of Don Arturo's spirit guide, Nai Lamp, a spirit guide he has worked closely with since his initiation. One legend of Nai Lamp, a shaman of the ancient Mochica culture, claims that he brought the wisdom of San Pedro to Peru from some place across the Pacific. Don Arturo believes that place was Lemuria.

About one hour after drinking the San Pedro we all began to feel the mind expanding effects of it. We stood up in unison just as the full Moon was rising over the neighboring mountains. As we welcomed her, the radiant beams of the Moon caressed each one of us while illuminating the circle of rock formations we were gathered in. Don Arturo proclaimed that the rocks surrounding us were once the walls of an ancient Lemurian temple. So everything suddenly seemed perfect—we were communing with the Goddess in one of Her ancient temples!

For the next hour most of us leaned against one side of our megalithic temple while meditating on the rising Moon and absorbing its scintillating rays. We all became transfixed by the glow of seven colors which encircled the satellite, but what was most impactful on us was the power emanating from the Moon. There was no question that it was alive. The Moon had ceased to be the dead ball of rock we had all been brought up to believe. Perhaps because of the effect of the San Pedro, we were now able to experience it as it truly was, a living presence and vehicle of the Goddess. The love and blessings of the Goddess flowed palpably from the Moon and we could feel them being showered down around us. We were truly communing with our Mother.

I was so excited by the Moons radiance that I found myself running to each person and pointing it out. But, as it turned out, I didn't have to say a word. Each person I approached was already immersed in the experience of oneness with the Goddess. With a inner smile, I told myself that they had come home.

After a short time, Don Arturo began doing some special shamanic work on our group. He chose me to assist him, and together we went from person to person while removing toxins from their energy bodies and awakening their heart chakras. We were especially supported by the San Pedro in the heart activation part of our work, and it soon became clear that that was the cactus's primary effect. Many people in our group spontaneously accessed a love within themselves which they never knew existed. For many, it was truly a rebirth and the beginning of life lived out of their heart. Because of one man's powerful heart awakening, he was later able to begin a very profound spiritual relationship with one of the women in our group that continues today. He claims that he has never had such a deep relationship, and that he never thought it was possible for him to be part of one before his visit to Marca Wasi.

The rest of the night was spent communing with the Moon, the stars, and each other. Everything was alive. We were siblings to everything around us. We were all children of the Goddess. As such, each of us pledged to continue opening our hearts so we could better support Her in spreading love throughout the Earth.

## TOOLS FOR COMMUNING WITH THE GODDESS

Since returning from India and Peru, I have made it my goal to try to recreate an experience of communion with the Goddess on my own. Since that time, I have allowed myself to be drawn to various time-tested approaches for communing with the Goddess, such as Wiccan ritual, ceremonial magic, and certain Goddess disciplines of yoga and Hindu Tantra. I have contacted some of the local Wiccans and tried out some of these new tools during the time of the full Moon. Although I found that my receptivity was not as strong as it had been in India, I was still able to precipitate a palpable etheric connection with the Goddess.

I would now like to share with you some of my new tools, as well as others I have known about and used for many years. The Goddess has informed me that She wants all Her children to know Her, and not just through the written word. Only through direct experience can She truly be known and communed with.

## RULE NO. 1

## REMEMBER: <u>THE GODDESS IS DIVINE WISDOM AND POWER. THE GODDESS IS LOVE.</u>

If you want to commune with the Goddess, remember what She is. Only then can you know when you are truly communing with Her. It is my hope that the following tools will help you to have the kind of firsthand experience of Her you desire.

### *Names of the Goddess*

In order to invoke the presence of the Goddess, I have discovered that most of the masters and magicians throughout history have summoned Her by meditating on Her various forms and while chanting Her sacred names. In India, the names of the Goddess, which are called Her mantras, are often repeated in conjunction with meditation on Her sacred geometrical shapes, known as Her yantras. They are also chanted in proximity to the literally hundreds of human-like or anthropomorphic images of the Goddess found throughout the country.

Of all the names the ancients used to summon the Goddess's power in India, the pre-eminent one is Om (or Aum or Amen). This primal vibration is both a name of the Goddess and the "Mother" of all sounds. Its vocalization almost always precedes ones daily prayers because of its effectiveness in immediately drawing forth the power and wisdom of the Goddess. My teacher, Ammachi, an incarnation of the Goddess, teaches the name/mantra of Ma Om as a way of communing with the Goddess. Ma Om is spoken mentally and synchronized with the breath. As you breath in say "Ma" and as you breath out say "Om." Any mantra which synchronizes with the breath will quickly quiet the breath. When the breath is quiet, the mind becomes quiet, and meditation naturally follows.

Other names of the Goddess incorporate the hard K sound, which is another primal sound. Included in this list are Shakti, Kundalini, Keridwen, Kali, Shekinah and Enki. The name Kali has been used for centuries by Hindu Tantric Yogis for summoning the destructive/transformative power of the Goddess.

One of the best sources of the Goddess's names is a Tantric chant known as the *Lalita Sahasranam* or the "Thousand Names of the Goddess," which contains one thousand different names of the Goddess. Acquire a copy of the chant and you can then chose the name which summons that aspect of the Goddess you want to invoke. Or you can chant all the names at once and thereby invoke the Goddess in Her totality. Some of the Goddess's names and their meaning which I personally resonate with in the chant are:

**Om Para Shaktyai Namaha**: Salutations to the Supreme Power.

**Om Shiva Shaktyai Kai Rupinyai Namaha**: Salutations to Her who is the union of Shiva and Shakti, God and Goddess.

**Om Shri Matrai Namaha**: Salutaions to the Divine Mother, the Mother of all.

**Om Kundalinyai Namaha**: Salutations to Her who resides in the Muladhara (root chakra) as the Kundalini

**Om Shivayai Namaha**: Salutations to Her, the Consort of Shiva (the Spirit), whose Power She is.

**Om Kama Dayinyai Namaha**: Salutations to Her who grants all the desires of Her devotees.

I highly encourage you to use Sanscrit names in your invocations because, as a sacred language, it will not only manifest the Goddess but also elevate your consciousness into communion with Her. What makes a sacred language, such as Sanscrit and Hebrew, special, is that the name for something is actually the sound of its vibratory frequency. For example, in Sanscrit the name for fire is "Ram." Through the proper vocalization of that name you can actually manifest fire, because you are producing its frequency. So, it follows that through the proper vocalization of the name of the Goddess, one can actually manifest Her presence.

### Forms of the Goddess

There are various classical images of the Goddess one can worship, each of which personifies one or more Her characteristics, as well as one or more of Her three powers. For example, Lakshmi, the Hindu Goddess of wealth, represents the Goddess's grace bestowing nature, as well as Her creative and preserving powers. Durga, an intimidating goddess who rides on the back of a tiger, symbolizes the Goddess's dynamic energy of protection, which is an aspect of Her preserving power. Kali embodies that aspect of the Goddess which is time, and thus reveals Her power of destruction and transformation. Kali is specially invoked by yogis who seek to achieve enlightenment through the destruction of their egos and limited concepts.

Of the yantra forms of the Goddess one of the very best is Sri Yantra, the geometrical form of the syllable OM. Every mantra has its own yantra, and Sri Yantra is Om's. Another Goddess yantra, which is specially favored among Wiccans and Pagans, is the Pentacle or five-pointed star. Four points of the star represent the four elements, the four parts of the Goddess's universal body, and the fifth point symbolizes Spirit, the inner essence of the Goddess. Another Goddess yantra is the spiral, which is the form of the Goddess as the spiralling life force. And finally, additional Goddess yantras which can be used effectively in ritual include: the square (the symbol of dense matter), the six-pointed star (the symbol of the Goddess's dual nature), the triangle (the symbol of the Goddess's three powers), and the circle (representing the cyclical nature of the Goddess).

Sri Yantra

Mantras and their corresponding yantras are often used together to summon the Goddess, such as Om with the Sri Yantra. A yantra form can be placed in front of you or drawn upon the ground and then meditated upon while vocalizing one the Goddess's corresponding names.

If you want to intensely empower your Goddess images, or your mantras and yantras, you can use them during the classical 8 Sabbats of the Witches: the two equinoxes, the two solstices, and their four mid-point days. Or you can use them during the new and full moons, the Witches' Esbats. They will also be empowered if you use them at vortex areas, which the ancient Goddess worshippers refer to as Dragon's Lairs or Wombs of the Goddess. Or, if you want to stay home, you can make your own vortex by placing your yantra within a pyramid or by placing crystals at is various points.

When the inspiration arrives, go to a vortex on a full moon night, sit within a yantra, surround yourself with crystals, and chant with great longing in your heart for the Goddess. Don't worry, She'll be there! And in order to more effectively feel Her power when She arrives, you can hold a large crystal, wand or athame (metal knife or daggar) with its point directed heavenward. The Goddess's energy will spiral around the object and into your body.

Joining your legs and arms is also efficacious when invoking the Goddess. Crossing your legs and joining your hands naturally unites the inner polarity and awakens the Goddess as the Kundalini at Her seat at the base of the spine. Performing the Great Rite, or sexual intercourse, is another way to unite the polarity via joining the genders. Finally, sacraments can also be helpful tools for communing, but as the Goddess has taught me, they are not essential! But if you decide to use one, find the sacrament which best transports you into a communion with the Goddess without having an adverse effect upon you either physically or emotionally. For some people, wine effectuates an expansive consciousness which is conducive to communing, while for others it can seriously impair their reflexes and make them physically ill. For this latter group, hallucinogenic mushrooms, Peyote, or San Pedro might be the sacrament of choice. But remember, if you have never done a sacrament, it is usually best to let someone with experience, such as a shaman, guide you to the right one, and for him or her to be there when you consume it. But whatever you end up doing, always begin by asking for protection from the Goddess. You never know...Lucifer might be waiting for you in the next dimension!

# *Appendix*

## Chapter I

1. The hypothesis of Immanuel Velikovsky was that Venus entered the Solar System as a comet before becoming a planet and settling into its present orbit around the Sun.

2. In relation to the Earth, Venus makes five special conjunctions with the Sun during an eight year cycle. These five conjunctions create the five points of a celestial pentagram.

3. The Horned God was a deity worshipped by many cultures in Asia and Europe beginning from Paleolithic times. He represented the male principle or male god and was often worshipped in conjunction with a female goddess. He was the symbol of the male Spirit, the heavenly Father, as well as the Son which took birth through the womb of the Goddess. After maturing, the Horned God mated with his mother/consort, the Goddess.

The myth of the Horned God first popularized the notion of the Father and Son being One. It later became part of the myth of Jesus Christ.

4. Initially the philosophers of the Matriarchy conceived of the Twins as the two halves of the Goddess which had emanated out of Spirit at the beginning of time. During the later Zoroastrian era in Persia, the patriarchal Aryans added their own biased slant to the Twins myth and made them two eternally separate principles with no common origin. Under the patriarchal influence, the creative Twin became Ahura Mazda or Orzmund, the King of Heaven, while the destructive Twin became Ahriman, the King of the Earth and the underworld.

Eventually the Twins' myth was taken to Babylon where the brothers became known as Mithras, the Son of God, and his nemesis Ahriman, the underworld demon. From there it traveled to Palestine where the twins became Jesus Christ and his perpetual enemy, Lucifer/Satan.

5. In many creation myths worldwide a primeval serpent is portrayed floating upon a cosmic sea at the beginning of time. It is called both the Serpent Goddess, because it emerged out of the "female" sea, as well as the Serpent Son because it was born out of the female, cosmic sea after its impregnation by the

"male" spark of Spirit. This primal serpent eventually expanded and became the entire universe. It was known by names with a "K" sound, such as Kundalini, Enki, Ki, Kan, Kematuf, Kiao, etc. (see: *The Return of the Serpents of Wisdom*).

6. Murrugan was the version of the Son of God worshipped by the Hindus. He was the Son of Shiva (male principle) and Shakti (female principle). Murrugan is also known as Karttikeya, Subramuniya, and Kumara.

7. The Yezidhis are Kurdish people from central Asia who worship Lucifer by the name of Melek Tau. To them, Lucifer was the first and greatest of the Angels. But he is not evil. According to the Yezidhis, evil only exits in the mind of the observer.

8. The image of Murrugan, the Son of Siva and Shakti, was taken out of India by the Sufis and eventually assimilated into the catechism of the Yezidhis. The Yezidhis adopted much of their doctrine and secret rites from the Sufis.

9. Many ancient cultures worshipped the Pleiades as a huge celestial Serpent Goddess. According to them, the stars are the primeval Serpent Goddess from which the universe was initially created. The Pleiades were honored as the point from which our portion of the galaxy was created.

10. This line was chanted by the head of the spiritual tradition on Crete, the Orphics and the Dactyloi priests, during their rites.

11. Many cultures retained the memory of a mythological battle between a male hero and an evil serpent. The two opponents of this battle took on such diverse names as Yahweh and Leviathan, Merodach and Tiamat, Baal and Mot, Thor and the Midgard Serpent, St. George and the Dragon, etc.

12. The ubiquitous legend of the Twins comprises an important section in many creation myths worldwide. They are portrayed as two eternally young boys who bring to Earth many of the mundane and spiritual sciences and teach them to developing humanity. In Egypt and the Aegean Islands the Twins were known as the Kaberoi; in Greece they were the Dioscouri, Caster and Pollux; in India they were worshipped as the Aswins and Kumaras; in Mexico they were known Quetzlcoatl and Tezcatilapoca, culture bearers and masters of the mysteries; the Hopis knew the Twins as Poqanghoya and Polanghoya, while

their neighbors, the Navaho, referred to them as Monster Slayer and Child of the Waters.

13. Sister Thedra was a prophetess for Jesus-Sananda. He chose her to spread his message that end times were approaching and we should all start to prepare by changing ourselves and living righteously.

14. The Monastery of the Seven Rays was founded by Aramu Muru in a hidden valley north of Lake Titicaca. It became the headquarters of the Brotherhood of the Seven Rays and a storage vault for the Solar Disc and the records of Mu.

15. While stationed in India as a colonel of the Royal English Army, James Churchward discovered an obscure monastery within which were some stone tablets recording the journey of the Naga Maya, missionary priests which had anciently come to India from Mu. After studying and translating the tablets over a two year period, Churchward wrote a series of books about the Naga Maya and their lost continent of Mu.

16. Madame Blavatsky is famous for founding the Theosophical Society and writing numerous books on the esoteric history of the Earth. Her most famous book, *The Secret Doctrine*, is based upon records of Lemuria and Atlantis which exist in underground crypts in Tibet.

17. Elizabeth Clare Prophet is a contemporary successor to Madame Blavatsky. Her church, The Church Universal and Triumphant, is sponsored by the same masters who oversaw the creation of the Theosophical Society, Master Morya and Kuthumi. The teachings of the church are basically consistent with those of the Theosophical Society but there is more emphasis on the teachings of "Ascended Masters."

## Chapter II

1. The Earth has come to the end of a 104,000 year cycle. The cycle concluded August 16, 1987 during the Harmonic Convergence, and was then followed by the current transitional period which leads up to December 21, 2012 and the commencement of the "Fifth World." During the 104,000 year cycle the Earth passed through four "Worlds" of 26,000 years each.

2. Reiki is a laying-on-of-hands system of natural healing which was

founded in Japan in the 1800s.

3. Dr. Usui was the founder of Reiki. The system was revealed to him following a 21 day fast on Mt. Kurama in Japan.

4. The Shakta Kaula path is a branch of Hindu Tantricism which worships the Goddess as its principal deity. There are seven stages to the path and include elements of both the patriarchal and matriarchal spiritual traditions.

5. According to *The Book of Enoch*, Azazzel taught the Daughters of Men the use of antimony, an essential ingredient of the Philosopher's Stone (see: *Genesis of the Grail Kings*, Laurence Gardner, 1999, Bantam Press, London.)

6. In the original Hebrew/Aramaic version of the Bible God is referred to as the Elohim. Elohim is a plural denomination, thus denoting more than one god or multiple parts of one god.

7. The Serpent Goddess is known as "Seven Faceted" because She created the universe of form from out of Her own being while transmitting to each physical object Her imprint, which included the spiral and one or more of the seven colors, tones, etc. Because of Her septenary nature, the Primal Serpent has been portrayed as having seven heads, seven tails, etc.(see: *The Return of the Serpents of Wisdom*)

8. On some of the ancient Sumerian seals Enki is depicted as a serpent or dragon with seven heads. As the Primal Serpent, Enki possessed a septenary nature.

9. You will also find that, after the Hebrews called Sanat Satan, the patriarchal Greeks followed suit by calling Skanda Satan. Both Sanat and Skanda are names for Murrugan in India.

10. Samael was also a name of Enki. Enki was the lord or god of the northern Mesopotamian Kingdom of Sama, thus Sama-el (see: Genesis of the Grail Kings by Laurence Gardner, 1999 Bantam Press, London).

11. Studies done on royal mummies found in Egypt and Peru reveal that some not only had blond hair, but the same blood type as the Nordic races.

# Chapter III

1. The various "Venus" images discovered in Europe and Asia are strikingly similar to the classical image of the Mesopotamian Venus, Inanna. There seems to be a historical connection between them.

2. Venus and the Earth are in a continual eight year cycle together which they begin and end in conjunction. During that cycle the Earth revolves around the Sun eight times and Venus thirteen. From the vantage point of the Earth, however, Venus appears to have completed only five cycles.

3. Neptune was the son of Chronos and the god of the sea. Madame Blavatsky claimed that he was a manifestation of the Primal Dragon (see: *The Return of the Serpents of Wisdom*).

4. Plato claims that Neptune had five pairs of twin boys as his sons. He divided the island of Atlantis among them, so initially there were ten kings ruling the continent. However Atlas was emperor over them all.

5. The Greek historians claimed that the Mesopotamian Enki was the same as their deity Chronos.

6. The legend of the Atlantean crown is known by the Mescalero Apache Indians. One of them told the myth to L. Taylor Hanson, who writes about it in *The Ancient Atlantic*.

7. Edgar Cayce referred to the Sons of Lucifer as the "Sons of Belial." Among the Hebrew, Belial was a name for Satan/Lucifer. Cayce refers to the members of the Atlantean Solar Brotherhood as the "Sons of the Law of One."

8. The name Thoth is related to the English word "thought" and denotes "Divine Mind." The name Hermes is evolved from Chiram and denotes "fire."

9. The pyramid unites matter and Spirit by uniting in its design the Platonic Solid associated with matter or Earth, the cube, with the Platonic Solid associated with Spirit and fire, the tetrahedron. The pyramid also unites the polarity by joining Heaven and Earth, or Earth and the sky. Its base sits upon the Earth and its apex "touches" the sky.

10. The Sirian heart-shaped stone was given as a gift to Emperor

Tazlavoo of Atlantis by missionary Sirians. Eventually it ended up in the hands of the Dalai Lama of Tibet and then with founders of the League of Nations, which was sponsored by the Sirians and the Great White Brotherhood. When the League disbanded, the Russian adventurer and painter Nicholas Roerich returned the stone to Tibet.

11. According to Native American records revealed to L. Taylor Hanson, Volcan was a fire god worshipped by the Atlanteans. He was a deity which lived underground and his homes were volcanoes. Later his worship was taken to Egypt where he became known as Ptah (see: *The Return of the Serpents of Wisdom*).

12. Sanconiathon was a historian who lived in Carthage around 1400 B.C. The history he compiled is based upon the most ancient records which existed at that time.

13. The Egyptian Neters were deities of the forces of nature.

14. In the Book of Thomas, one of the Nag Hammadi gnostic texts, Jesus refers to Thomas as his twin and reflection. The name Thomas is evolved from a Hebrew name    which means "twin."

15. The Essenes were a mystical sect of Jews who tended to isolate themselves from the common populace in order to devote themselves to spiritual disciplines. One purpose for their existence was to incarnate the prophesied Messiah.

16. Venus was esteemed by the Essenes (see: *The Hiram Key*)

17. The serpent is the symbol of the Goddess. It represents both the wisdom and power of God. The serpent worshipping Levites were named after their serpent deity Leviathan.

18. The Lions are a progressive series of elixirs with increasing potency. The Red Lion mimics the fiery Kundalini and has the power to transform an alchemist into a god or goddess.

19. The Dionysian Architects had branches throughout Asia and parts of Europe and North Africa. They were responsible for constructing many of the

sacred temples of ancient times.

20. The early Phoenicians were called Ph'anakes, "those of the Kaberoi."

21. San Pedro is the name of a cactus which grows in the Andes and is used by shamen seeking mystical experience. It is named Saint Peter because, like the apostle, it holds the "keys to Heaven."

22.The Kapac Kuna were Lemurian missionaries who accompanied Aramu Muru to Peru. In the Andes the Kapac Kuna helped Lord Muru build the megalithic temples of the Incas.

23. Dr. Jose (Pepe) Altamirano Vallenas is a retired Professor of Tourism from the University of Cuzco and past Director of the National Institute of Culture. He is probably the most informed guide in Peru.

24. Dionysus and Apollo were worshipped as "Twins" at the temple of Delphi. Raucous music composed in honor of Dionysus, the destructive Twin, was played in winter, and melodic music in honor of Apollo, the creative Twin, was preformed in the summer time.

25. The Pheryllt are mentioned in the Welsh "Book of Talesin." They were noted alchemists and the name Pheryllt has been translated to mean "alchemists." The Pheryllt had their headquarters at the legendary city of Emyrs, which was located at Snowden on the west coast of Britain. Much of their alchemical wisdom was passed to the Druids and the Welsh Bards.

26. The legendary King Bladud, builder of Bath, is reputed to have been initiated into the Brotherhood of the Kaberoi on the Island of Samothrace in the Aegean Sea.

27. Their were three classes of priests in both Britain and Mesopotamia. In Britain the Ovates (diviners), Bards (chanters), and Druids (magicians) shared the sarcedotal functions of the Celts. In Mesopotamia the priestly duties were divided among the Baru (diviners), Kalu (chanters), and the Ashipu (magicians).

28. *The Sirius Mystery*, by Robert Temple, St. Martin's Press, NYC.

29. Mad'in Salih is an ancient lost city which was discovered in northern

Saudi Arabia.

30. There are many legends of giants which anceintly roamed Asia Minor and could have been the Cyclopeans. In Hebron, for example, there giants said to have descended from the Anakes, who were the ancient Kaberoi.

## Chapter IV

1. According to one Moslem legend, the shrine at Mecca was built by the first men on Earth and later rebuilt by Abraham.

2. The term Aryan was originally used by the German archeaologist Max Muller as a name for the fair skinned, patriarchal tribes which invaded India. Thename is derived from Arya, meaning 'Royal.'

3. The Serpent on the Tree is a symbol of the life force. During the evolution of the universe the serpent life force crystallized to become the physical universe and its myriad physical forms. The descent of the Serpent down the Tree symbolizes the decrease in the frequency of the life force as it becomes crystallized into dense matter. For a more complete explanation of the Serpent and the Tree of the Eden myth, see *The Return of the Serpents of Wisdom*.

4. The Devas were the ancient gods of the Aryans, and the Asuras, or so-called fallen gods, were the deities of the native Indian tribes.

5. Abraham's relatives derived from the city of Harran in northern Mesopotamia.

## Chapter V

1. *The Hiram Key*, Christopher Knight and Robert Lomas, Element Books, 1997

2. Columbus's father-in-law is reputed to have been a member of the Knights of Christ, a branch of the Knights Templars. Supposedly the Knights of Christ played a role in Columbus's expeditions and the ships he sailed to America flew the Templar flag, a flag with a red cross on a white background.

3. To prove the red cross's association with the Goddess, Laurence Gardner writes that it has been called Rosi-crusis, which means "Cup of Water"

or "Chalice." The cup or chalice is a symbol of the Goddess. See: *Genesis of the Grail Kings.*

4. Legends in Tibet and India maintain that Jesus traveled to that part of the world during his "lost years." An ancient text found in monastery in Ladakh claims that Jesus, whom it calls Issa, traveled throughout India and Tibet and studied with many of the greatest spiritual teachers of that time.

5. Simon Magus is believed to have been descended from John the Baptist. He is the reputed founder of the Simonites and the "Father" of the modern Gnostic tradition.

6. Simon Magus traveled with a prostitute whom he recognized as the incarnation of Barbelo or Sophia, the Gnostic Goddess. She was the Goddess and he was the incarnation of her mythical Son-lover.

7. The Ismailis are a branch of Shiite Moslems. They trace their order back to the prophet Ismail who was a direct descendant of Mohammed's.. The Ismailis once had a secret mystery school composed of nine degrees in Cairo. After achieving the ninth degree an Ismaili attained complete gnosticism.

8. The Shiites are descended from Ali, Mohammed's son in law. They have become famous for inviting many non-Arabs from various social strata and religious traditions into their sect and accepting them as equals.

9. The leader of the Assasins, Hasan Sabbah, studied at the principal Ismaili university in Cairo before splitting off and forming his own order. From his mountain retreat in Persia he trained assasins to murder the leaders of opposing spiritual and governmental organizations throughout Asia, Africa and Europe.

10. The Templars were formed out of the Priory of Sion for the express purpose of re-discovering and protecting the lineage of Jesus Christ and eventually placing his descendant upon the throne of the world (see: *The Holy Blood and the Holy Grail*, Baigent, Leigh, and Lincoln, 1982, Jonathan Cape, London).

11. Idries Shaw states that Baphomet is Moorish Spanish for "Father of Understanding"(see: The Sufis, Idries Shaw, 1977, W.H. Allen Co. Ltd. London,

England).

12. Built when the planet Mars was on the horizon, Cairo was originally called Al-Kahira, the "City of Mars," and later shortened to become Cairo. Here the Ismaili and Fatimids built a great university of spiritual wisdom called Al-Azhar, "the Luminous" or "the House of Wisdom."

13. The Lucifer Rebellion has been mentioned by certain contemporary teachers, such as Drunvalo Melchezidek.

14. Baphomet was the archetypal Primal Dragon and First Son of God. He was the black dragon image of Neptune-Sanat which had been worshipped on Atlantis before being taken to Egypt and transformed into the "Goat of Mendes." The Nubian Sufi D'hul Nun is reputed to have brought the dragon-goat out of Egypt and then added it to the icons of numerous Sufi sects. Baphomet was given a five pointed star to wear on his forehead, thus affiliating him to his mother, the Goddess, and the planet Venus.

15. According to Idries Shaw, the Witches' covens were organized by the Aniza Tribe from Persia which was led into Europe by a Dervish Sufi teacher. They contributed their whirling dance to the Witches rites, as well as the circle of 13 members which became the Witches' "coven" (13 is the number of Allah) etc..

16,17. The Witches of the Middle Ages, when questioned by the Inquisition, confessed to serving a "Lord" and master who led the rites of their covens. Their Lord was either a dark skinned man or a man dressed in the costume of a goat or bull.

18. Idries Shaw contends that a sect of Sufi Revelers, the Mascara, brought the elements of Shavism to Europe and then incorporated them into the Witch cult.

19. The Cathars were descended from the Gnostics and made their home in southern France. They were the first branch of the Matriarchal Tradition attacked by the Inquisition for their heretical beliefs. Today some people believe that the Cathars inherited sacred artifacts and records from the ancient Gnostics and Hebrew and that these are currently buried somewhere in the proximity of the town of Rennes le Chateau in southern France.

20. It is believed that the Illuminati were descended from a branch of Ismaili known as the Roshaniya, the "Illuminated Ones," which thrived in Afghanistan up to the time that the Illuminati were founded. The eight degrees of the two orders are nearly identical.

21. The final degree of the Illuminati was King of the World. This was also the final degree of the Ismaili and reputedly the final degree of the Knights Templar order.

22. The Statue of Liberty was given to the people of USA by the French Grand Orient order, a masonic branch of the Illuminati.

23. The Tibetans beleive that, at the end of time, a savior will ride out of Shamballa, the Asian headquarters of the Great White Brotherhood, and defeat the forces of evil on Earth before declaring himself King of the World.

24. The Thousand Year Reign of Christ is prophesied in the Book of Revelation in the Holy Bible.

25. Ammachi or Mata Amritanandamayi is a female saint from south India. She is considered by many Hindus to be an Avatar, an enlightened soul which has taken birth solely for the upliftment of humanity. Supposedly she came into physical incarnation already spiritually enlightened and did not need the assistance of a teacher or guru.

26. Narada is an enlightened soul who moves between dimensions while playing his vena, a stringed instrument. Music and dance are important features of the Matriarchal Tradition.

# Vedic (Hindu) and Western Astrology
by
Mark Amaru Pinkham

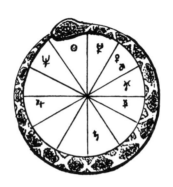

**\*Life Path Readings**
**\*Relationship Readings**
**\*Natal Charts**
**\*Transits and Progressions**

*Mark Amaru has been a practicing Astrologer for twenty years.*

To receive a tape recorded reading from Mark, please specify which system, Vedic or Western, and chose from the above selections which kind of reading you want. Include the date, time and place of your birth along with your name, address and phone number. Then send a check or money order in the amount of $80.00 (made out <u>Lapis Inc.</u>) to:

Mark Amaru Pinkham
1703 Garrison NE
Olympia, WA 98506
(360) 357-8572

# Soluna Tours
## Ambassadors of Peace and Love Tours

As directors of **Soluna Tours, Mark Amaru Pinkham** and his wife **Andrea Mikana-Pinkham** assist people in having deeply transformative experiences within the most sacred sites and temples around the world. As they journey to these places, they and those on their tours travel as Ambassadors of Love and Peace with the goal of connecting with and uplifting all the people they meet.

The name "Soluna" means Sun-Moon, or Male-Female, and denotes Soluna Tours' primary mission: uniting the polarity and awakening both intuition and love. Mark and Andrea feel that the Goddess is now urging us all to accomplish this inner alchemy so that we can love ourselves as well as all those around us, thereby reviving the female principle and preparing the way for the coming Fifth World of Venus.

Since 1994 Soluna Tours has provided spiritual travel to the ashrams, temples, and sacred sites of Peru, India, Great Britain, Central America, and Egypt. In these places, Mark and Andrea have established a network of guides, gurus and shamen with whom they work to lead persons through the spiritual practices of the ancient matriarchal tradition, such as yoga, chanting, the consumption of sacraments, and meditation. Throughout our tours, Mark continuously expounds on the history and wisdom of the Goddess path, thereby making your journey a balance of head and heart, intellectual knowledge and emotional experience.

In order to further develop and share love, while we are touring a country we make a conscious effort to spread peace and love to the people we encounter, thus assisting the Goddess in raising the vibration of planet Earth. Our goal is to attract people to our tours who share our desire to uplift the planet by spreading peace and love.

Please take the time to look through the following pages and see what tours Soluna Tours is currently offering. To be most up-to-date, visit the Soluna Tours website at www.solunatours.com. See you on the road!

# About Mark Amaru Pinkham

Mark Amaru Pinkham is the author of *The Return of the Serpents of Wisdom*, which contains the history and teachings of the spiritual masters worldwide associated with the serpent. He often speaks on radio and television, and is also a contributing writer for numerous alternative magazines, including *Magical Blend* and *Shaman's Drum*.

For the past 25 years Mark has been traveling around the world while studying numerous spiritual traditions. During that time, he has lived and studied with the Masters of Yoga **Swami Muktananda** and **Mata Amritanandamayi** and gained initiation into two Peruvian brotherhoods, the **Brotherhood of the Sun,** and the **Brotherhood of the Solar Disc**. Mark is currently studying San Pedro shamanism with **Don Arturo Cervantes** of Lima, Peru.

Mark and his wife, Andrea, are directors of Soluna Tours, which offers spiritual tours to sacred places and temples around the world. When not leading tours, Mark works as an astrologer and acupuncturist at his home in Olympia, Washington.

## FAR-OUT ADVENTURES *REVISED EDITION*
### *The Best of World Explorer Magazine*
This is a compilation of the first nine issues of *World Explorer* in a large-format paperback. Authors include: David Hatcher Childress, Joseph Jochmans, John Major Jenkins, Deanna Emerson, Katherine Routledge, Alexander Horvat, Greg Deyermenjian, Dr. Marc Miller, and others. Articles in this book include Smithsonian Gate, Dinosaur Hunting in the Congo, Secret Writings of the Incas, On the Trail of the Yeti, Secrets of the Sphinx, Living Pterodactyls, Quest for Atlantis, What Happened to the Great Library of Alexandria?, In Search of Seamonsters, Egyptians in the Pacific, Lost Megaliths of Guatemala, the Mystery of Easter Island, Comacalco: Mayan City of Mystery, Professor Wexler and plenty more.
**580 PAGES. 8X11 PAPERBACK. ILLUSTRATED. REVISED EDITION. $25.00. CODE: FOA**

## RETURN OF THE SERPENTS OF WISDOM
### by Mark Amaru Pinkham
According to ancient records, the patriarchs and founders of the early civilizations in Egypt, India, China, Peru, Mesopotamia, Britain, and the Americas were the Serpents of Wisdom—spiritual masters associated with the serpent—who arrived in these lands after abandoning their beloved homelands and crossing great seas. While bearing names denoting snake or dragon (such as Naga, Lung, Djedhi, Amaru, Quetzalcoatl, Adder, etc.), these Serpents of Wisdom oversaw the construction of magnificent civilizations within which they and their descendants served as the priest kings and as the enlightened heads of mystery school traditions. *The Return of the Serpents of Wisdom* recounts the history of these "Serpents"—where they came from, why they came, the secret wisdom they disseminated, and why they are returning now.
**400 PAGES. 6X9 PAPERBACK. ILLUSTRATED. REFERENCES. $16.95. CODE: RSW**

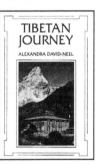

## QUEST FOR THE LOST CITY
### by Dana & Ginger Lamb
In 1937, Dana and Ginger Lamb set out from Tucson, Arizona and ended up in the unexplored jungles of Chiapas and Guatemala. Traveling by foot, horseback and burro-powered Model-T Ford, the Lambs trekked into a lost world of bandits, hermits, and an ancient civilization. They discover a lost tribe of Mayans and ultimately a lost city in the jungle. Exciting and true!
**340 PAGES. 6X9 PAPERBACK. ILLUSTRATED. $16.95. CODE: QFLC**

## TIBETAN JOURNEY
### Mystic Travellers Series
### by Alexandra David-Neel
Imported from India, this is the account of Alexandra David-Neel's first crossing of mysterious Tibet in disguise. Setting out for Lhasa in 1923 from Sikkim, she travelled incognito under the guise of a lamaist nun of rank. This book is an absorbing account of her long and hazardous journey and reveals the penetrating insight and courage of of a woman who surmounted physical, intellectual and social barriers to pursue her quest. Her accounts of Tibetan religious ceremonies and beliefs are among the fullest and best ever written.
**276 PAGES. 6X9 HARDBACK. ILLUSTRATED. INDEX. $16.95. CODE: TJY**

## MUSTANG: A LOST TIBETAN KINGDOM
### Mystic Travellers Series
### by Michel Peissel
French Archaeologist Peissel, who speaks Tibetan, journeys to the remote and forbidden Tibetan kingdom of Mustang. Mustang, known as the land of Lo in Tibetan, is in the Himalayas of Nepal with Chinese-occupied Tibet on its northern border. Though politically in Nepal, Mustang retains a certain autonomy with its own king. Peissel journeys by caravan through a medieval world, visiting subterranean monasteries, lonely hermitages and remote villages. Chapters on Tibetan Warlords, The Future Buddha, Magic and Medicine, The Ghosts of Tsarang, Crystal Clear Mountain, more.
**312 PAGES. 6X9 PAPERBACK. ILLUSTRATED. BIBLIOGRAPHY & INDEX. $14.95. CODE: MUST**

## ALTAI-HIMALAYA
### A Travel Diary
### by Nicholas Roerich
The famous Russian-American explorer's expedition through Sinkiang, Altai-Mongolia and Tibet from 1924 to 1928 is chronicled in 12 chapters including reproductions of Roerich's inspiring paintings. Roerich writes in "Travel Diary" style and discusses various mysteries and mystical arts of Central Asia including such arcane topics as the hidden city of Shambala, Agartha, more.
**407 PAGES. 6X9 HARDBACK. ILLUSTRATED. $24.95. CODE: AHIM**

# MYSTIC TRAVELLER SERIES

## THE MYSTERY OF EASTER ISLAND
### by Katherine Routledge
The reprint of Katherine Routledge's classic archaeology book which was first published in London in 1919. The book details her journey by yacht from England to South America, around Patagonia to Chile and on to Easter Island. Routledge explored the amazing island and produced one of the first-ever accounts of the life, history and legends of this strange and remote place. Routledge discusses the statues, pyramid-platforms, Rongo Rongo script, the Bird Cult, the war between the Short Ears and the Long Ears, the secret caves, ancient roads on the island, and more. This rare book serves as a sourcebook on the early discoveries and theories on Easter Island.
432 PAGES. 6X9 PAPERBACK. ILLUSTRATED. $16.95. CODE: MEI

## MYSTERY CITIES OF THE MAYA
### Exploration and Adventure in Lubaantun & Belize
### by Thomas Gann
First published in 1925, *Mystery Cities of the Maya* is a classic in Central American archaeology-adventure. Gann was close friends with Mike Mitchell-Hedges, the British adventurer who discovered the famous crystal skull with his adopted daughter Sammy and Lady Richmond Brown, their benefactress. Gann battles pirates along Belize's coast and goes upriver with Mitchell-Hedges to the site of Lubaantun where they excavate a strange lost city where the crystal skull was discovered. Lubaantun is a unique city in the Mayan world as it is built out of precisely carved blocks of stone without the usual plaster-cement facing. Lubaantun contained several large pyramids partially destroyed by earthquakes and a large amount of artifacts. Gann shared Mitchell-Hedges belief in Atlantis and lost civilizations (pre-Mayan) in Central America and the Caribbean. Lots of good photos, maps and diagrams.
252 PAGES. 6X9 PAPERBACK. ILLUSTRATED. $16.95. CODE: MCOM

## IN SECRET TIBET
### by Theodore Illion
Reprint of a rare 30s adventure travel book. Illion was a German wayfarer who not only spoke fluent Tibetan, but travelled in disguise as a native through forbidden Tibet when it was off-limits to all outsiders. His incredible adventures make this one of the most exciting travel books ever published. Includes illustrations of Tibetan monks levitating stones by acoustics.
210 PAGES. 6X9 PAPERBACK. ILLUSTRATED. $15.95. CODE: IST

## DARKNESS OVER TIBET
### by Theodore Illion
In this second reprint of Illion's rare books, the German traveller continues his journey through Tibet and is given directions to a strange underground city. As the original publisher's remarks said, "this is a rare account of an underground city in Tibet by the only Westerner ever to enter it and escape alive! "
210 PAGES. 6X9 PAPERBACK. ILLUSTRATED. $15.95. CODE: DOT

## DANGER MY ALLY
### The Amazing Life Story of the Discoverer of the Crystal Skull
### by "Mike" Mitchell-Hedges
The incredible life story of "Mike" Mitchell-Hedges, the British adventurer who discovered the Crystal Skull in the lost Mayan city of Lubaantun in Belize. Mitchell-Hedges has lived an exciting life: gambling everything on a trip to the Americas as a young man, riding with Pancho Villa, questing for Atlantis, fighting bandits in the Caribbean and discovering the famous Crystal Skull.
374 PAGES. 6X9 PAPERBACK. ILLUSTRATED. BIBLIOGRAPHY & INDEX. $16.95. CODE: DMA

## IN SECRET MONGOLIA
### by Henning Haslund
Danish-Swedish explorer Haslund's first book on his exciting explorations in Mongolia and Central Asia. Haslund takes us via camel caravan to the medieval world of Mongolia, a country still barely known today. First published by Kegan Paul of London in 1934, this rare travel adventure is back in print after 50 years. Haslund and his camel caravan journey across the Gobi Desert. He meets with renegade generals and warlords, god-kings and shamans. Haslund is captured, held for ransom, thrown into prison, battles black magic and portrays in vivid detail the birth of a new nation.
374 PAGES. 6X9 PAPERBACK. ILLUSTRATED. BIBLIOGRAPHY & INDEX. $16.95. CODE: ISM

## MEN & GODS IN MONGOLIA
### by Henning Haslund
First published in 1935 by Kegan Paul of London, Haslund takes us to the lost city of Karakota in the Gobi desert. We meet the Bodgo Gegen, a god-king in Mongolia similar to the Dalai Lama of Tibet. We meet Dambin Jansang, the dreaded warlord of the "Black Gobi." There is even material in this incredible book on the Hi-mori, an "airhorse" that flies through the sky (similar to a Vimana) and carries with it the sacred stone of Chintamani. Aside from the esoteric and mystical material, there is plenty of just plain adventure: Haslund and companions journey across the Gobi desert by camel caravan; are kidnapped and held for ransom; witness initiation into Shamanic societies; meet reincarnated warlords; and experience the violent birth of "modern" Mongolia.
358 PAGES. 6X9 PAPERBACK. 57 PHOTOS, ILLUSTRATIONS AND MAPS. $15.95. CODE: MGM

24 hour credit card orders—call: 815-253-6390 fax: 815-253-6300
email: auphq@frontiernet.net   http://www.adventuresunlimited.co.nz

# LOST CITIES SERIES

## VIMANA AIRCRAFT OF ANCIENT INDIA & ATLANTIS
### by David Hatcher Childress
### *introduction by Ivan T. Sanderson*

Did the ancients have the technology of flight? In this incredible volume on ancient India, authentic Indian texts such as the *Ramayana* and the *Mahabharata* are used to prove that ancient aircraft were in use more than four thousand years ago. Included in this book is the entire Fourth Century BC manuscript *Vimaanika Shastra* by the ancient author Maharishi Bharadwaaja, translated into English by the Mysore Sanskrit professor G.R. Josyer. Also included are chapters on Atlantean technology, the incredible Rama Empire of India and the devastating wars that destroyed it. Also an entire chapter on mercury vortex propulsion and mercury gyros, the power source described in the ancient Indian texts. Not to be missed by those interested in ancient civilizations or the UFO enigma.

334 PAGES. 6X9 PAPERBACK. RARE PHOTOGRAPHS, MAPS AND DRAWINGS. $15.95. CODE: VAA

## LOST CONTINENTS & THE HOLLOW EARTH
### *I Remember Lemuria and the Shaver Mystery*
### by David Hatcher Childress & Richard Shaver

*Lost Continents & the Hollow Earth* is Childress' thorough examination of the early hollow earth stories of Richard Shaver and the fascination that fringe fantasy subjects such as lost continents and the hollow earth have had for the American public. Shaver's rare 1948 book *I Remember Lemuria* is reprinted in its entirety, and the book is packed with illustrations from Ray Palmer's *Amazing Stories* magazine of the 1940s. Palmer and Shaver told of tunnels running through the earth—tunnels inhabited by the Deros and Teros, humanoids from an ancient spacefaring race that had inhabited the earth, eventually going underground, hundreds of thousands of years ago. Childress discusses the famous hollow earth books and delves deep into whatever reality may be behind the stories of tunnels in the earth. Operation High Jump to Antarctica in 1947 and Admiral Byrd's bizarre statements, tunnel systems in South America and Tibet, the underground world of Agartha, the belief of UFOs coming from the South Pole, more.

344 PAGES. 6X9 PAPERBACK. ILLUSTRATED. $16.95. CODE: LCHE

## LOST CITIES OF NORTH & CENTRAL AMERICA
### by David Hatcher Childress

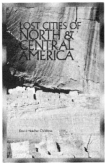

Down the back roads from coast to coast, maverick archaeologist and adventurer David Hatcher Childress goes deep into unknown America. With this incredible book, you will search for lost Mayan cities and books of gold, discover an ancient canal system in Arizona, climb gigantic pyramids in the Midwest, explore megalithic monuments in New England, and join the astonishing quest for lost cities throughout North America. From the war-torn jungles of Guatemala, Nicaragua and Honduras to the deserts, mountains and fields of Mexico, Canada, and the U.S.A., Childress takes the reader in search of sunken ruins, Viking forts, strange tunnel systems, living dinosaurs, early Chinese explorers, and fantastic lost treasure. Packed with both early and current maps, photos and illustrations.

590 PAGES. 6X9 PAPERBACK. PHOTOS, MAPS, AND ILLUSTRATIONS. FOOTNOTES & BIBLIOGRAPHY. $14.95. CODE: NCA

## LOST CITIES & ANCIENT MYSTERIES OF SOUTH AMERICA
### by David Hatcher Childress

Rogue adventurer and maverick archaeologist David Hatcher Childress takes the reader on unforgettable journeys deep into deadly jungles, high up on windswept mountains and across scorching deserts in search of lost civilizations and ancient mysteries. Travel with David and explore stone cities high in mountain forests and hear fantastic tales of Inca treasure, living dinosaurs, and a mysterious tunnel system. Whether he is hopping freight trains, searching for secret cities, or just dealing with the daily problems of food, money, and romance, the author keeps the reader spellbound. Includes both early and current maps, photos, and illustrations, and plenty of advice for the explorer planning his or her own journey of discovery.

381 PAGES. 6X9 PAPERBACK. PHOTOS, MAPS, AND ILLUSTRATIONS. FOOTNOTES & BIBLIOGRAPHY. $14.95. CODE: SAM

## LOST CITIES & ANCIENT MYSTERIES OF AFRICA & ARABIA
### by David Hatcher Childress

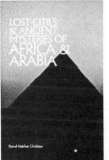

Across ancient deserts, dusty plains and steaming jungles, maverick archaeologist David Childress continues his world-wide quest for lost cities and ancient mysteries. Join him as he discovers forbidden cities in the Empty Quarter of Arabia; "Atlantean" ruins in Egypt and the Kalahari desert; a mysterious, ancient empire in the Sahara; and more. This is the tale of an extraordinary life on the road: across war-torn countries, Childress searches for King Solomon's Mines, living dinosaurs, the Ark of the Covenant and the solutions to some of the fantastic mysteries of the past.

423 PAGES. 6X9 PAPERBACK. PHOTOS, MAPS, AND ILLUSTRATIONS. FOOTNOTES & BIBLIOGRAPHY. $14.95. CODE: AFA

24 hour credit card orders—call: 815-253-6390 fax: 815-253-6300

email: auphq@frontiernet.net     www.adventuresunlimited.co.nz     www.wexclub.com

# THE LOST CITIES SERIES

## LOST CITIES OF ATLANTIS, ANCIENT EUROPE & THE MEDITERRANEAN
### by David Hatcher Childress

Atlantis! The legendary lost continent comes under the close scrutiny of maverick archaeologist David Hatcher Childress in this sixth book in the internationally popular *Lost Cities* series. Childress takes the reader in search of sunken cities in the Mediterranean; across the Atlas Mountains in search of Atlantean ruins; to remote islands in search of megalithic ruins; to meet living legends and secret societies. From Ireland to Turkey, Morocco to Eastern Europe, and around the remote islands of the Mediterranean and Atlantic, Childress takes the reader on an astonishing quest for mankind's past. Ancient technology, cataclysms, megalithic construction, lost civilizations and devastating wars of the past are all explored in this book. Childress challenges the skeptics and proves that great civilizations not only existed in the past, but the modern world and its problems are reflections of the ancient world of Atlantis.

524 PAGES. 6x9 PAPERBACK. ILLUSTRATED WITH 100S OF MAPS, PHOTOS AND DIAGRAMS. BIBLIOGRAPHY & INDEX. $16.95. CODE: MED

## LOST CITIES OF CHINA, CENTRAL INDIA & ASIA
### by David Hatcher Childress

Like a real life "Indiana Jones," maverick archaeologist David Childress takes the reader on an incredible adventure across some of the world's oldest and most remote countries in search of lost cities and ancient mysteries. Discover ancient cities in the Gobi Desert; hear fantastic tales of lost continents, vanished civilizations and secret societies bent on ruling the world; visit forgotten monasteries in forbidding snow-capped mountains with strange tunnels to mysterious subterranean cities! A unique combination of far-out exploration and practical travel advice, it will astound and delight the experienced traveler or the armchair voyager.

429 PAGES. 6x9 PAPERBACK. ILLUSTRATED. FOOTNOTES & BIBLIOGRAPHY. $14.95. CODE: CHI

## LOST CITIES OF ANCIENT LEMURIA & THE PACIFIC
### by David Hatcher Childress

Was there once a continent in the Pacific? Called Lemuria or Pacifica by geologists, Mu or Pan by the mystics, there is now ample mythological, geological and archaeological evidence to "prove" that an advanced and ancient civilization once lived in the central Pacific. Maverick archaeologist and explorer David Hatcher Childress combs the Indian Ocean, Australia and the Pacific in search of the surprising truth about mankind's past. Contains photos of the underwater city on Pohnpei; explanations on how the statues were levitated around Easter Island in a clockwise vortex movement; tales of disappearing islands; Egyptians in Australia; and more.

379 PAGES. 6x9 PAPERBACK. ILLUSTRATED. FOOTNOTES & BIBLIOGRAPHY. $14.95. CODE: LEM

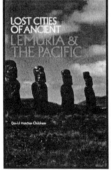

## ANCIENT TONGA
### & the Lost City of Mu'a
### by David Hatcher Childress

*Lost Cities* series author Childress takes us to the south sea islands of Tonga, Rarotonga, Samoa and Fiji to investigate the megalithic ruins on these beautiful islands. The great empire of the Polynesians, centered on Tonga and the ancient city of Mu'a, is revealed with old photos, drawings and maps. Chapters in this book are on the Lost City of Mu'a and its many megalithic pyramids, the Ha'amonga Trilithon and ancient Polynesian astronomy, Samoa and the search for the lost land of Havai'iki, Fiji and its wars with Tonga, Rarotonga's megalithic road, and Polynesian cosmology. Material on Egyptians in the Pacific, earth changes, the fortified moat around Mu'a, lost roads, more.

218 PAGES. 6x9 PAPERBACK. ILLUSTRATED. COLOR PHOTOS. BIBLIOGRAPHY. $15.95. CODE: TONG

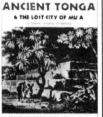

## ANCIENT MICRONESIA
### & the Lost City of Nan Madol
### by David Hatcher Childress

Micronesia, a vast archipelago of islands west of Hawaii and south of Japan, contains some of the most amazing megalithic ruins in the world. Part of our *Lost Cities of the Pacific* series, this volume explores the incredible conformations on various Micronesian islands, especially the fantastic and little-known ruins of Nan Madol on Pohnpei Island. The huge canal city of Nan Madol contains over 250 million tons of basalt columns over an 11 square-mile area of artificial islands. Much of the huge city is submerged, and underwater structures can be found to an estimated 80 feet. Islanders' legends claim that the basalt rocks, weighing up to 50 tons, were magically levitated into place by the powerful forefathers. Other ruins in Micronesia that are profiled include the Latte Stones of the Marianas, the menhirs of Palau, the megalithic canal city on Kosrae Island, megaliths on Guam, and more.

256 PAGES. 6x9 PAPERBACK. HEAVILY ILLUSTRATED. INCLUDES A COLOR PHOTO SECTION. BIBLIOGRAPHY & INDEX. $16.95. CODE: AMIC

24 HOUR CREDIT CARD ORDERS—CALL: 815-253-6390 FAX: 815-253-6300
email: auphq@frontiernet.net   http://www.adventuresunlimited.co.nz

# NEW BOOKS

## HAARP
### The Ultimate Weapon of the Conspiracy
### by Jerry Smith

The HAARP project in Alaska is one of the most controversial projects ever undertaken by the U.S. Government. Jerry Smith gives us the history of the HAARP project and explains how it can be used as an awesome weapon of destruction. Smith exposes a covert military project and the web of conspiracies behind it. HAARP has many possible scientific and military applications, from raising a planetary defense shield to peering deep into the earth. Smith leads the reader down a trail of solid evidence into ever deeper and scarier conspiracy theories in an attempt to discover the "whos" and "whys" behind HAARP, and uncovers a possible plan to rule the world. At best, HAARP is science out-of-control; at worst, HAARP could be the most dangerous device ever created, a futuristic technology that is everything from super-beam weapon to world-wide mind control device. The Star Wars future is now. Topics include Over-the-Horizon Radar and HAARP, Mind Control, ELF and HAARP, The Telsa Connection, The Russian Woodpecker, GWEN & HAARP, Earth Penetrating Tomography, Weather Modification, Secret Science of the Conspiracy, more. Includes the complete 1987 Bernard Eastlund patent for his pulsed super-weapon that he claims was stolen by the HAARP Project.
**256 PAGES. 6x9 PAPERBACK. ILLUSTRATED. BIBLIOGRAPHY & INDEX. $14.95. CODE: HARP**

## LOST CONTINENTS & THE HOLLOW EARTH
### I Remember Lemuria and the Shaver Mystery
### by David Hatcher Childress & Richard Shaver

*Lost Continents & the Hollow Earth* is Childress' thorough examination of the early hollow earth books of Richard Shaver and the fascination that fringe fantasy subjects such as lost continents and the hollow earth have had for the American public. Shaver's rare 1948 book *I Remember Lemuria* is reprinted in its entirety, and the book is packed with illustrations from Ray Palmer's *Amazing Stories* issues of the 1940s. Palmer and Shaver told of tunnels running through the earth—tunnels inhabited by the Deros and Teros, humanoids from an ancient spacefaring race that had inhabited the earth, eventually going underground, hundreds of thousands of years ago. Childress discusses the famous hollow earth books and delves deep into whatever reality may be behind the stories of tunnels in the earth, Operation High Jump to Antarctica in 1947 and Admiral Byrd's bizarre statements, tunnel systems in South America and Tibet, the underground world of Agartha, the belief of UFOs coming from the South Pole, more.
**412 PAGES. 6x9 PAPERBACK. ILLUSTRATED. $16.95. CODE: LCHE**

## LIQUID CONSPIRACY
### JFK, LSD, the CIA, Area 51 & UFOs
### by Jim Keith

*Mind Control, World Control* author Keith on the politics of LSD, mind control, Area 51 and UFOs. With JFK's LSD experiences with Mary Pinchot-Meyer the plot thickens the ever expanding web of CIA involvement, underground bases with UFOs seen by JFK and Marilyn Monroe among others to a vaster conspiracy that affects every government agency from NASA to the Justice Department. Focusing on the bizarre side of history, *Liquid Conspiracy* takes the reader on a psychedelic tour-de-force.
**256 PAGES. 6x9 PAPERBACK. ILLUSTRATED. $14.95. CODE: LCON**

## KUNDALINI TALES
### by Richard Sauder, Ph.D.

*Underground Bases and Tunnels* author Richard Sauder's second book on his personal experiences and provocative research into spontaneous spiritual awakening, out-of-body journeys, encounters with secretive governmental powers, daylight sightings of UFOs, and more. Sauder continues his studies of underground bases with new information on the occult underpinnings of the U.S. space program. The book also contains a breakthrough section that examines actual U.S. patents for devices that manipulate mind and thought from a remote distance. Included are chapters on the secret space program and a 130-page appendix of patents and schematic diagrams of secret technology and mind control devices.
**296 PAGES. 7x10 PAPERBACK. ILLUSTRATED. BIBLIOGRAPHY. $14.95. CODE: KTAL**

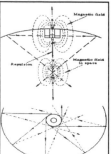

## COSMIC MATRIX
### Piece for a Jig-Saw, Part Two
### by Leonard G. Cramp

Leonard G. Cramp, a British aerospace engineer, wrote his first book *Space Gravity and the Flying Saucer* in 1954. *Cosmic Matrix* is the long awaited, sequel to his 1966 book *UFOs & Anti-Gravity:Piece For A Jig-Saw*. Cramp has had a long history of examining UFO phenomena and has concluded that UFOs use the highest possible aeronautic science to move in the way they do. Cramp examines anti-gravity effects and theorizes that this super-science used by the craft—described in detail in the book—can lift mankind into a new level of technology, transportation and understanding of the universe. The book takes a close look at gravity control, time travel, and the interlocking web of energy between all planets in our solar system with Leonard's unique technical diagrams. *A fantastic voyage into the present and future!*
**364 PAGES. 6x9 PAPERBACK. ILLUSTRATED. BIBLIOGRAPHY. $16.00. CODE: CMX**

---

24 HOUR CREDIT CARD ORDERS—CALL: 815-253-6390 FAX: 815-253-6300

email: auphq@frontiernet.net    http://www.azstarnet.com/~aup

## PATH OF THE POLE
### Cataclysmic Pole Shift Geology
### by Charles Hapgood

*Maps of the Ancient Sea Kings* author Hapgood's classic book *Path of the Pole* is back in print! Hapgood researched Antarctica, ancient maps and the geological record to conclude that the Earth's crust has slipped in the inner core many times in the past, changing the position of the pole. *Path of the Pole* discusses the various "pole shifts" in Earth's past, giving evidence for each one, and moves on to possible future pole shifts. Packed with illustrations, this is the sourcebook for many other books on cataclysms and pole shifts such as *5-5-2000: Ice the Ultimate Disaster* by Richard Noone. A planetary alignment on May 5, 2000 is predicted to cause the next pole shift—a date that is less than a year away! With Millennium Madness in full swing, this is sure to be a popular book.
356 PAGES. 6x9 PAPERBACK. ILLUSTRATED. $16.95. CODE: POP.

## THE TIME TRAVEL HANDBOOK
### A Manual of Practical Teleportation & Time Travel
### edited by David Hatcher Childress

In the tradition of *The Anti-Gravity Handbook* and *The Free-Energy Device Handbook,* science and UFO author David Hatcher Childress takes us into the weird world of time travel and teleportation. Not just a whacked-out look at science fiction, this book is an authoritative chronicling of real-life time travel experiments, teleportation devices and more. *The Time Travel Handbook* takes the reader beyond the government experiments and deep into the uncharted territory of early time travellers such as Nikola Tesla and Guglielmo Marconi and their alleged time travel experiments, as well as the Wilson Brothers of EMI and their connection to The Philadelphia Experiment—the U.S. Navy's forays into invisibility, time travel, and teleportation. Childress looks into the claims of time travelling individuals, and investigates the unusual claim that the pyramids on Mars were built in the future and sent back in time. A highly visual, large format book, with patents, photos and schematics. Be the first on your block to build your own time travel device!
316 PAGES. 7x10 PAPERBACK. ILLUSTRATED. $16.95. CODE: TTH.

## THE CHRIST CONSPIRACY
### The Greatest Story Ever Sold
### by Acharya S.

In this highly controversial and explosive book, archaeologist, historian, mythologist and linguist Acharya S. marshals an enormous amount of startling evidence to demonstrate that Christianity and the story of Jesus Christ were created by members of various secret societies, mystery schools and religions in order to unify the Roman Empire under one state religion. In developing such a fabrication, this multinational cabal drew upon a multitude of myths and rituals that existed long before the Christian era, and reworked them for centuries into the religion passed down to us today. Contrary to popular belief, there was no single man who was at the genesis of Christianity; Jesus was many characters rolled into one. These characters personified the ubiquitous solar myth, and their exploits were well known, as reflected by such popular deities as Mithras, Heracles/Hercules, Dionysos and many others throughout the Roman Empire and beyond. The story of Jesus as portrayed in the Gospels is revealed to be nearly identical in detail to that of the earlier savior-gods Krishna and Horus, who for millennia preceding Christianity held great favor with the people. *The Christ Conspiracy* shows the Jesus character as neither unique nor original, not "divine revelation." Christianity re-interprets the same extremely ancient body of knowledge that revolved around the celestial bodies and natural forces.
256 PAGES. 6x9 PAPERBACK. ILLUSTRATED. $14.95. CODE: CHRC.

## ECCENTRIC LIVES AND PECULIAR NOTIONS
### by John Michell

Michell's fascinating study of the lives and beliefs of over 20 eccentric people: the bizarre and often humorous lives of such people as Lady Blount, who was sure that the earth is flat; Cyrus Teed, who believed that the earth is a hollow shell with us on the inside; Edward Hine, who believed that the British are the lost Tribes of Israel; and Baron de Guldenstubbe, who was sure that statues wrote him letters. British writer and housewife Nesta Webster devoted her life to exposing international conspiracies, and Father O'Callaghan devoted his to opposing interest on loans. The extraordinary characters in this book were—and in some cases still are—wholehearted enthusiasts for the various causes and outrageous notions they adopted, and John Michell describes their adventures with spirit and compassion. Some of them prospered and lived happily with their obsessions, while others failed dismally. We read of the hapless inventor of a giant battleship made of ice who died alone and neglected, and of the London couple who achieved peace and prosperity by drilling holes in their heads. Other chapters on the Last of the Welsh Druids; Congressman Ignatius Donnelly, the Great Heretic and Atlantis; Shakespearean Decoders and the Baconian Treasure Hunt; Early Ufologists; Jerusalem in Scotland; Bibliomaniacs; more.
248 PAGES. 6x9 PAPERBACK. ILLUSTRATED. $14.95. CODE: ELPN.

## THE ARCHCONSPIRATOR
### Essays and Actions
### by Len Bracken

Veteran conspiracy author Len Bracken's witty essays and articles lead us down the dark corridors of conspiracy, politics, murder and mayhem. In 12 chapters Bracken takes us through a maze of interwoven tales from the Russian Conspiracy (and a few "extra notes" on conspiracies) to his interview with Costa Rican novelist Joaquin Gutierrez and his Psychogeographic Map into the Third Millennium. Other chapters in the book are A General Theory of Civil War; A False Report Exposes the Dirty Truth About South African Intelligence Services; The New-Catiline Conspiracy for the Cancellation of Debt; Anti-Labor Day; 1997 with selected Aphorisms Against Work; Solar Economics; and more. Bracken's work has appeared in such pop-conspiracy publications as *Paranoia, Steamshovel Press* and the *Village Voice.* Len Bracken lives in Arlington, Virginia and haunts the back alleys of Washington D.C., keeping an eye on the predators who run our country. With a gun to his head, he cranks out his rants for fringe publications and is the editor of *Extraphile,* described by *New Yorker Magazine* as "fusion conspiracy theory."
256 PAGES. 6x9 PAPERBACK. ILLUSTRATED. BIBLIOGRAPHY. $14.95. CODE: ACON. JUNE PUBLICATION

24 hour credit card orders—call: 815-253-6390 fax: 815-253-6300
email: auphq@frontiernet.net    www.adventuresunlimited.co.nz    www.wexclub.com

## EXTRATERRESTRIAL ARCHAEOLOGY *NEW EDITION!*
### by David Hatcher Childress

With hundreds of photos and illustrations, *Extraterrestrial Archaeology* takes the reader to the strange and fascinating worlds c the Moon, Mars, Mercury, Venus, Saturn and other planets for a look at the alien structures that appear there. Using official NASA and Soviet photos, as well as other photos taken via telescope, this book seeks to prove that many of the planets (and moons) of ou solar system are in some way inhabited by intelligent life. The book includes many blow-ups of NASA photos and detaile diagrams of structures—particularly on the Moon.
•NASA PHOTOS OF PYRAMIDS AND DOMED CITIES ON THE MOON.
•PYRAMIDS AND GIANT STATUES ON MARS.
•HOLLOW MOONS OF MARS AND OTHER PLANETS.
•ROBOT MINING VEHICLES THAT MOVE ABOUT THE MOON PROCESSING VALUABLE METALS.
•NASA & RUSSIAN PHOTOS OF SPACE-BASES ON MARS AND ITS MOONS.
•A BRITISH SCIENTIST WHO DISCOVERED A TUNNEL ON THE MOON, AND OTHER "BOTTOMLESS CRATERS."
•EARLY CLAIMS OF TRIPS TO THE MOON AND MARS.
•STRUCTURAL ANOMALIES ON VENUS, SATURN, JUPITER, MERCURY,URANUS & NEPTUNE.
•NASA, THE MOON AND ANTI-GRAVITY. PLUS MORE. HIGHLY ILLUSTRATED WITH PHOTOS, DIAGRAMS AND MAPS!
•NASA CONFIRMS THAT THERE IS WATER ON THE MOON.
•NEW PHOTOS FROM RUSSIA AND THE LATEST FACE ON MARS PICS.
320 PAGES. 8x11 PAPERBACK. BIBLIOGRAPHY & APPENDIX. $19.95. CODE: ETA

## MAURY ISLAND UFO
### *The Crisman Conspiracy*
### by Kenn Thomas

In 1947 six flying saucers circled above a harbor boat in Puget Sound near Tacoma, Washington, one wobbling and spewin slag. The falling junk killed a dog and burned a boy's arm. His father, Harold Dahl, witnessed it all. The Maury Islan incident became the first UFO event of the modern era. Then came Fred Crisman. Crisman was one of the most curiou characters in the UFO lore and the history of covert intelligence. He fought bizarre underground beings in the caves c Burma, was wounded by a laser before it was invented, and had a background with theOSS. Long dismissed as a fraud an a hoax, the Maury Island case has never been fully examined until now. *Maury Island UFO: The Crisman Conspirac* collects an enormous amount of data from government files, oral history interviews, intelligence agency reports and pr vately held correspondence. Veteran conspiracy and UFO author Thomas at his best.
286 PAGES. 6x9 PAPERBACK. ILLUSTRATED. BIBLIOGRAPHY & APPENDIX. $14.95. CODE: MIL

## CONVERSATIONS WITH THE GODDESS
### by Mark Amaru Pinkham

*Return of the Serpents of Wisdom* author Pinkham tells us that "The Goddess is returning!" Pinkham gives us an alternativ history of Lucifer, the ancient King of the World, and the Matriarchal Tradition he founded thousands of years ago. The name Lucifer means "Light Bringer" and he is the same as the Greek god Prometheus, and is different from Satan, who wa based on the Egyptian god Set. Find out how the branches of the Matriarchy—the Secret Societies and Mystery Schools— were formed, and how they have been receiving assistance from the Brotherhoods on Sirius and Venus to evolve the worl and overthrow the Patriarchy. Learn about the revival of the Goddess Tradition in the New Age and why the Goddess want us all to reunite with Her now! An unusual book from an unusual writer!
296 PAGES. 7x10 PAPERBACK. ILLUSTRATED. BIBLIOGRAPHY. $14.95. CODE: CWTG. NOVEM BER Publication

## EXPLORING THE PHYSICS OF THE UNKNOWN UNIVERSE
### *An Adventurer's Guide*
### by Milo Wolff

Physicist Wolff's easy to read guide to the wonders of quantum reality introduces his ground-breaking "Space Resonance Theory," which explains many of the enigmas that have confounded scientists over the years. It presents a unified picture of Einstein's spe- cial relativity and quantum theory. Wolff tackles classical physics enigmas and para- doxes; a particle model using pairs of resonant spherical waves existing in the fabric of space; explains particles and electricity; more.
251 PAGES. 7x10 PAPERBACK. ILLUSTRATED. $15.95. CODE: EPUU

## JOURNEY OF THE SYMBOLS OF NEW ZEALAND
### by Grace Rawson

*Journey of the Symbols* is about the spiritual essence of New Zealand. It is about the vibration or song of the symbols laid down by the ancients as they attuned to the special places of the power of this land. The messages that Grace received led her to embark on a journey to locate these special places of power and tune in to the legends that linked them.
96 PAGES. 6x9 PAPERBACK. HIGHLY ILLUSTRATED. $12.95. CODE: JSNZ

# NEW BOOKS

## TECHNOLOGY OF THE GODS
### The Incredible Sciences of the Ancients
### by David Hatcher Childress

Popular *Lost Cities* author David Hatcher Childress takes us into the amazing world of ancient technology, from computers in antiquity to the "flying machines of the gods." Childress looks at the technology that was allegedly used in Atlantis and the theory that the Great Pyramid of Egypt was originally a gigantic power station. He examines tales of ancient flight and the technology that it involved; how the ancients used electricity; megalithic building techniques; the use of crystal lenses and the fire from the gods; evidence of various high tech weapons in the past, including atomic weapons; ancient metallurgy and heavy machinery; the role of modern inventors such as Nikola Tesla in bringing ancient technology back into modern use; impossible artifacts; and more.
320 PAGES. 6X9 PAPERBACK. ILLUSTRATED. BIBLIOGRAPHY. $16.95. CODE: TGOD. NOVEMBER PUBLICATION

## LOST SCIENCE   *NEW EDITION*
### by Gerry Vassilatos

Rediscover the legendary names of suppressed scientific revolution—remarkable lives, astounding discoveries, and incredible inventions which would have produced a world of wonder. How did the aura research of Baron Karl von Reichenbach prove the vitalistic theory and frighten the greatest minds of Germany? How did the physiophone and wireless of Antonio Meucci predate both Bell and Marconi by decades? How does the earth battery technology of Nathan Stubblefield portend an unsuspected energy revolution? How did the geoaetheric engines of Dr. Royal Rife provided the solution for every world-threatening disease. Why did the FDA and AMA together condemn this great man to Federal Prison? The static crashes on telephone lines enabled Dr. T. Henry Moray to discover the reality of radiant space energy. Was the mysterious "Swedish stone," the powerful mineral which Dr. Moray discovered, the very first historical instance in which stellar power was recognized and secured on earth? Why did the Air Force initially fund the gravitational warp research and warp-cloaking devices of T. Townsend Brown and then reject it? When the controlled fusion devices of Philo Farnsworth achieved the "break-even" point in 1967 the FUSOR project was abruptly cancelled by ITT. What were the twisted intrigues which surrounded these deliberate convolutions of history? Each chapter is a biographic treasure. Ours is a world living hundreds of years behind its intended stage of development. Complete knowledge of this loss is the key to recapturing this wonder technology.
304 PAGES. 6X9 PAPERBACK. ILLUSTRATED. BIBLIOGRAPHY. $16.95. CODE: LOS

## MYSTERY IN ACAMBARO
### Did Dinosaurs Survive Until Recently?
### by Charles Hapgood, introduction by David Hatcher Childress

*Maps of the Ancient Sea Kings* author Hapgood's rare book *Mystery in Acambaro* is back in print! Hapgood researched the Acambaro collection of clay figurines with Earl Stanley Gardner (author of the Perry Mason mysteries) in the mid-1960s. The Acambaro collection comprises hundreds of clay figurines that are apparently thousands of years old; however, they depict such bizarre animals and scenes that most archaeologists dismiss them as an elaborate hoax. The collection shows humans interacting with dinosaurs and various other "monsters" such as horned men. Both Hapgood and Earl Stanley Gardner were convinced that the figurines from Acambaro were authentic ancient artifacts that indicated that men and dinosaurs had cohabited together in the recent past, and that dinosaurs had not become extinct many millions of years ago as commonly thought. David Hatcher Childress writes a lengthy introduction concerning Acambaro, the latest testing, and other evidence of "living" dinosaurs.
256 PAGES. 6X9 PAPERBACK. ILLUSTRATED. BIBLIOGRAPHY. $14.95. CODE: MIA. NOVEMBER PUBLICATION

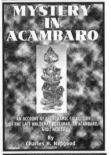

## EXTRATERRESTRIAL ARCHAEOLOGY   *NEW EDITION!*
### by David Hatcher Childress

With hundreds of photos and illustrations, *Extraterrestrial Archaeology* takes the reader to the strange and fascinating worlds of the Moon, Mars, Mercury, Venus, Saturn and other planets for a look at the alien structures that appear there. Using official NASA and Soviet photos, as well as other photos taken via telescope, this book seeks to prove that many of the planets (and moons) of our solar system are in some way inhabited by intelligent life. The book includes many blow-ups of NASA photos and detailed diagrams of structures—particularly on the Moon.
•NASA PHOTOS OF PYRAMIDS AND DOMED CITIES ON THE MOON.
•PYRAMIDS AND GIANT STATUES ON MARS.
•HOLLOW MOONS OF MARS AND OTHER PLANETS.
•ROBOT MINING VEHICLES THAT MOVE ABOUT THE MOON PROCESSING VALUABLE METALS.
•NASA & RUSSIAN PHOTOS OF SPACE-BASES ON MARS AND ITS MOONS.
•A BRITISH SCIENTIST WHO DISCOVERED A TUNNEL ON THE MOON, AND OTHER "BOTTOMLESS CRATERS."
•EARLY CLAIMS OF TRIPS TO THE MOON AND MARS.
•STRUCTURAL ANOMALIES ON VENUS, SATURN, JUPITER, MERCURY, URANUS & NEPTUNE.
•NASA, THE MOON AND ANTI-GRAVITY. PLUS MORE. HIGHLY ILLUSTRATED WITH PHOTOS, DIAGRAMS AND MAPS!
•NASA CONFIRMS THAT THERE IS WATER ON THE MOON.
•NEW PHOTOS FROM RUSSIA AND THE LATEST FACE ON MARS PICS.
320 PAGES. 8X11 PAPERBACK. BIBLIOGRAPHY & APPENDIX. $19.95. CODE: ETA

# CONSPIRACY & HISTORY

## LIQUID CONSPIRACY
### JFK, LSD, the CIA, Area 51 & UFOs
### by George Piccard
Underground author George Piccard on the politics of LSD, mind control, and Kennedy's involvement with Area 51 and UFOs. Reveals JFK's LSD experiences with Mary Pinchot-Meyer. The plot thickens with an ever expanding web of CIA involvement, from underground bases with UFOs seen by JFK and Marilyn Monroe (among others) to a vaster conspiracy that affects every government agency from NASA to the Justice Department. This may have been the reason that Marilyn Monroe and actress-columnist Dorothy Killgallen were both murdered. Focusing on the bizarre side of history, *Liquid Conspiracy* takes the reader on a psychedelic tour de force. This is your government on drugs!
**264 PAGES. 6x9 PAPERBACK. ILLUSTRATED. $14.95. CODE: LIQC**

## INSIDE THE GEMSTONE FILE
### Howard Hughes, Onassis & JFK
### by Kenn Thomas & David Hatcher Childress
*Steamshovel Press* editor Thomas takes on the Gemstone File in this run-up and run-down of the most famous underground document ever circulated. Photocopied and distributed for over 20 years, the Gemstone File is the story of Bruce Roberts, the inventor of the synthetic ruby widely used in laser technology today, and his relationship with the Howard Hughes Company and ultimately with Aristotle Onassis, the Mafia, and the CIA. Hughes kidnapped and held a drugged-up prisoner for 10 years; Onassis and his role in the Kennedy Assassination; how the Mafia ran corporate America in the 1960s; the death of Onassis' son in the crash of a small private plane in Greece; Onassis as Ian Fleming's archvillain Ernst Stavro Blofeld; more.
**320 PAGES. 6x9 PAPERBACK. ILLUSTRATED. $16.00. CODE: IGF**

## HAARP
### The Ultimate Weapon of the Conspiracy
### by Jerry Smith
The HAARP project in Alaska is one of the most controversial projects ever undertaken by the U.S. Government. Jerry Smith gives us the history of the HAARP project and explains how it can be used as an awesome weapon of destruction. Smith exposes a covert military project and the web of conspiracies behind it. HAARP has many possible scientific and military applications, from raising a planetary defense shield to peering deep into the earth. At best, HAARP is science out-of-control; at worst, HAARP could be the most dangerous device ever created, a futuristic technology that is everything from super-beam weapon to world-wide mind control device. Topics include Over-the-Horizon Radar and HAARP, Mind Control, ELF and HAARP, The Telsa Connection, The Russian Woodpecker, GWEN & HAARP, Earth Penetrating Tomography, Weather Modification, Secret Science of the Conspiracy, more. Includes the complete 1987 Eastlund patent for his pulsed super-weapon that he claims was stolen by the HAARP Project.
**256 PAGES. 6x9 PAPERBACK. ILLUSTRATED. $14.95. CODE: HARP**

## MIND CONTROL, WORLD CONTROL
### by Jim Keith
Veteran author and investigator Jim Keith uncovers a surprising amount of information on the technology, experimentation and implementation of mind control. Various chapters in this shocking book are on early CIA experiments such as Project Artichoke and Project R.H.I.C.-EDOM, the methodology and technology of implants, mind control assassins and couriers, various famous Mind Control victims such as Sirhan Sirhan and Candy Jones. Also featured in this book are chapters on how mind control technology may be linked to some UFO activity and "UFO abductions."
**256 PAGES. 6x9 PAPERBACK. ILLUSTRATED. FOOTNOTES. $14.95. CODE: MCWC**

## NASA, NAZIS & JFK:
### The Torbitt Document & the JFK Assassination
### introduction by Kenn Thomas
This book emphasizes the links between "Operation Paper Clip" Nazi scientists working for NASA, the assassination of JFK, and the secret Nevada air base Area 51. The Torbitt Document also talks about the roles played in the assassination by Division Five of the FBI, the Defense Industrial Security Command (DISC), the Las Vegas mob, and the shadow corporate entities Permindex and Centro-Mondiale Commerciale. The Torbitt Document claims that the same players planned the 1962 assassination attempt on Charles de Gaul, who ultimately pulled out of NATO because he traced the "Assassination Cabal" to Permindex in Switzerland and to NATO headquarters in Brussels. The Torbitt Document paints a dark picture of NASA, the military industrial complex, and the connections to Mercury, Nevada which headquarters the "secret space program."
**258 PAGES. 5x8. PAPERBACK. ILLUSTRATED. $16.00. CODE: NNJ**

## MIND CONTROL, OSWALD & JFK:
### Were We Controlled?
### introduction by Kenn Thomas
*Steamshovel Press* editor Kenn Thomas examines the little-known book *Were We Controlled?*, first published in 1968. The book's author, the mysterious Lincoln Lawrence, maintained that Lee Harvey Oswald was a special agent who was a mind control subject, having received an implant in 1960 at a Russian hospital. Thomas examines the evidence for implant technology and the role it could have played in the Kennedy Assassination. Thomas also looks at the mind control aspects of the RFK assassination and details the history of implant technology. A growing number of people are interested in CIA experiments and its "Silent Weapons for Quiet Wars." Looks at the case that the reporter Damon Runyon, Jr. was murdered because of this book.
**256 PAGES. 6x9 PAPERBACK. ILLUSTRATED. NOTES. $16.00. CODE: MCOJ**

**24 hour credit card orders—call: 815-253-6390 fax: 815-253-6300**
email: auphq@frontiernet.net    www.adventuresunlimited.co.nz    www.wexclub.com

# THE SHADOW OF ATLANTIS

**ALEXANDER BRAGHINE**

THIS 1940 CLASSIC ON ATLANTIS, MEXICO AND ANCIENT EGYPT IS BACK IN PRINT

**ATLANTIS REPRINT SERIES**

code: **MASK**

LOST CITIES OF ATLANTIS, ANCIENT EUROPE & THE MEDITERRANEAN

David Hatcher Childress

ANCIENT TONGA
& THE LOST CITY OF MU'A
by David Hatcher Childress

INCLUDING SAMOA, FIJI AND RAROTONGA

THE HISTORY OF THE KNIGHTS TEMPLARS
by
Charles G. Addison

Introduction by David Hatcher Childress

MYSTERY CITIES OF THE MAYA
by Thomas Gann

Archaeology and Adventure in Central America!
Mystic Travellers Series

## The Shadow of Atlantis

The Echoes of Atlantean Civilization Tracked through Space & Time
by Colonel Alexander Braghine
First published in 1940, The Shadow of Atlantis is one of the great classics of Atlantis research. The Shadow of Atlantis amasses a great deal of archaeological, anthropological, historical and scientific evidence in support of a lost continent in the Atlantic Ocean. Braghine covers such diverse topics as Egyptians in Central America, the myth of Quetzalcoatl, the Basque language and its connection with Atlantis, the connections with the ancient pyramids of Mexico, Egypt and Atlantis, the sudden demise of mammoths, legends of giants and much more. Braghine was linguist and spends part of the book tracing ancient languages to Atlantis and studying little-known inscriptions in Brazil, deluge myths and the connections between ancient languages.
288 pages, 6x9 paperback. Illustrated. $16.95.
code: **SOA**

## Maps of the Ancient Sea Kings

Evidence of Advanced Civilization in the Ice Age
by Charles H. Hapgood
Charles Hapgood's classic 1966 book on ancient maps is back in print after 20 years. Hapgood produces concrete evidence of an advanced world-wide civilization existing many thousands of years before ancient Egypt. He has found the evidence in many beautiful maps long known to scholars, the Piri Reis Map that shows Antarctica, the Hadji Ahmed map, the Oronteus Finaeus and other amazing maps. Hapgood concluded that these maps were made from more ancient maps from the various ancient archives around the world, now lost. Hapgood also concluded that the ancient mapmakers were in some ways much more advanced scientifically than Europe in the 16th century, or than the ancient civilizations of Greece, Egypt, and Babylonian. Not only were these unknown people more advanced in mapmaking than any people prior to the 18th century, it appears they mapped all the continents.
316 pages, 7x10 paperback. Heavily illustrated. Bibliography & Index. $19.95.
code: **MASK**

## The History of the Knights Templar

The Temple Church and the Temple by Charles G. Addison. Introduction by David Hatcher Childress
The history of the mysterious Knights Templars as told in 1842 by "a member of the Inner Temple." Includes chapters on the Origin of the Templars, their popularity in Europe and their rivalry with the Knights of St. John, later to be known as the Knights of Malta. Detailed information on the activities of the Templars in the Holy Land, the 1312 A.D. suppression of the Templars in France and other countries of Europe, culminating in the execution of Jacques de Molay. Also includes information on the continuation of the Knights Templars in England and Scotland and the formation of the society of Knights Templars in London and the rebuilding of the Temple in 1816, plenty more. Includes a lengthy introduction on the Templars, the lost Templar Fleet and their connections to the ancient North American searoutes by Lost Cities author David Hatcher Childress.
395 pages, 6x9 paperback. Illustrated. $16.95.
code: **HKT**

## ANCIENT TONGA & the Lost City of Mu'a

by David Hatcher Childress
In this new paperback series, with color photo inserts, Childress takes into the fascinating world of the ancient seafarers that Pacific. Chapters in this book are on the Lost City of Mu'A and its many megalithic pyramids, the Ha'amonga Trilithon and ancient Polynesian astronomy, Samoa and the search for the lost land of Havaiiki, Fiji and its wars with Tonga, Rarotonga's megalithic road, Polynesian cosmology, and a chapter on the predicted reemergence of the ancient land of Mu. May publication.
218 pages, 6x9 paperback. Heavily illustrated. $15.95.
code: **TONG**

## Lost Cities of Atlantis, Ancient Europe & the Mediterranean

by David Hatcher Childress
Atlantis! The legendary lost continent comes under the close scrutiny of maverick archaeologist David Hatcher Childress in this sixth book in the internationally popular Lost Cities series ta it takes him on his quest the lost continent of Atlantis. Childress takes the reader in search of sunken cities in the Mediterranean; across the Atlas Mountains in search of Atlantean ruins; to remote islands in search of megalithic ruins; living legends and secret societies. From Ireland to Turkey, Morocco to Eastern Europe, or remote islands of the Mediterranean and Atlantic Childress takes the reader on an astonishing quest for mankind's past. Ancient technology, cataclysms, megalithic construction, lost civilizations and devastating wars of the past are all explored in this astonishing book. Childress challenges the skeptics and proves that great civilizations not only existed in the past, but the modern world and its problems are reflections of the ancient world of Atlantis. Join David on an unforgettable tale in search of the solutions to the astonishing past.
524 pages, 6x9 paperback. Illustrated. $16.95.
code: **MED**

## Mystery Cities of the Maya

Exploration and Adventure in Lubaantun & Belize
by Thomas Gann
First published in 1925, Gann battles pirates along Belize's coast and goes upriver with Mitchell-Hedges to the lost city of Lubaantun where they excavate a strange lost city where the crystal skull was discovered. Lubaantun is a unique city in the Mayan world as it is built out of precisely carved blocks of stone. Gann shared Michell-Hedges belief in Atlantis and lost civilizations, pre-Mayan, in Central America and the Caribbean. Lots of good photos, maps and diagrams from the 20s.
252 pages, 6x9 paperback. Illustrated. $16.95.
code: **MCOM**

One Adventure Place
P.O. Box 74
Kempton, Illinois 60946
United States of America
Tel.: 815-253-6390 • Fax: 815-253-6300
Email: auphq@frontiernet.net
http://www.adventuresunlimited.co.nz

## ORDERING INSTRUCTIONS

Remit by USD$ Check, Money Order or Credit Card

Visa, Master Card, Discover & AmEx Accepted

Prices May Change Without Notice

10% Discount for 3 or more Items

## SHIPPING CHARGES

### United States

Postal Book Rate { $2.50 First Item
50¢ Each Additional Item

Priority Mail { $3.50 First Item
$2.00 Each Additional Item

UPS { $5.00 First Item
$1.50 Each Additional Item

NOTE: UPS Delivery Available to Mainland USA Only

### Canada

Postal Book Rate { $3.00 First Item
$1.00 Each Additional Item

Postal Air Mail { $5.00 First Item
$2.00 Each Additional Item

Personal Checks or Bank Drafts MUST BE

USD$ and Drawn on a US Bank

Canadian Postal Money Orders OK

Payment MUST BE USD$

### All Other Countries

Surface Delivery { $6.00 First Item
$2.00 Each Additional Item

Postal Air Mail { $12.00 First Item
$8.00 Each Additional Item

Payment MUST BE USD$

Checks and Money Orders MUST BE USD$
and Drawn on a US Bank or branch.

Add $5.00 for Air Mail Subscription to
Future *Adventures Unlimited* Catalogs

## SPECIAL NOTES

RETAILERS: Standard Discounts Available

BACKORDERS: We Backorder all Out-of-
Stock Items Unless Otherwise Requested

PRO FORMA INVOICES: Available on Request

VIDEOS: NTSC Mode Only. Replacement only.

For PAL mode videos contact our other offices:

**European Office:**
Adventures Unlimited, PO Box 372,
Dronten, 8250 AJ, The Netherlands
**South Pacific Office**
Adventures Unlimited Pacifica
221 Symonds Street, Box 8199
Auckland, New Zealand

---

*Please check:* ☑

☐ This is my first order   ☐ I have ordered before   ☐ This is a new address

| | |
|---|---|
| Name | |
| Address | |
| City | |
| State/Province | Postal Code |
| Country | |
| Phone day | Evening |
| Fax | |

| Item Code | Item Description | Price | Qty | Total |
|---|---|---|---|---|
| | | | | |
| | | | | |
| | | | | |
| | | | | |
| | | | | |
| | | | | |
| | | | | |
| | | | | |
| | | | | |
| | | | | |
| | | | | |
| | | | | |

*Please check:* ☑

☐ Postal-Surface

☐ Postal-Air Mail
(Priority in USA)

☐ UPS
(Mainland USA only)

☐ Visa/MasterCard/Discover/Amex

| | |
|---|---|
| Subtotal ⟶ | |
| Less Discount-10% for 3 or more items ⟶ | |
| Balance ⟶ | |
| Illinois Residents 6.25% Sales Tax ⟶ | |
| Previous Credit ⟶ | |
| Shipping ⟶ | |
| Total (check/MO in USD$ only) ⟶ | |

Card Number

Expiration Date

## 10% Discount When You Order 3 or More Items!

| Comments & Suggestions | Share Our Catalog with a Friend |
|---|---|
| | |